Lecture Notes in Computer Science 9672

Commenced Publication in 1973
Founding and Former Series Editors:
Gerhard Goos, Juris Hartmanis, and Jan van Leeuwen

Editorial Board

More information about this series at http://www.springer.com/series/7409

Marta Mattoso · Boris Glavic (Eds.)

Provenance and Annotation of Data and Processes

6th International Provenance
and Annotation Workshop, IPAW 2016
McLean, VA, USA, June 7–8, 2016
Proceedings

Editors
Marta Mattoso
COPPE/UFRJ
Rio de Janeiro
Brazil

Boris Glavic
Illinois Institute of Technology
Chicago, IL
USA

ISSN 0302-9743 ISSN 1611-3349 (electronic)
Lecture Notes in Computer Science
ISBN 978-3-319-40592-6 ISBN 978-3-319-40593-3 (eBook)
DOI 10.1007/978-3-319-40593-3

Library of Congress Control Number: 2016941294

LNCS Sublibrary: SL3 – Information Systems and Applications, incl. Internet/Web, and HCI

Printed on acid-free paper

This Springer imprint is published by Springer Nature
The registered company is Springer International Publishing AG Switzerland

Preface

This volume contains the proceedings of the 6th International Provenance and Annotation Workshop (IPAW), held June 7–8, 2016, at The MITRE Corporation in McLean, Virginia, USA. Following the successful inception of ProvenanceWeek in 2014, this year's installment again co-located the biennial IPAW workshop and the annual Workshop on the Theory and Practice of Provenance (TaPP). Together the two leading provenance workshops anchored ProvenanceWeek 2016, a full week of provenance-related activities that included a shared poster and demonstration session, and the PROV: Three Years Later and Provenance-based Security and Transparent Computing workshops.

This year's installment of IPAW was able to honor the extraordinary achievements of IPAW's authors through a best paper award sponsored by Springer. We would like to use this forum to again congratulate Wellington Moreira de Oliveira, Paolo Missier, Kary Ocaña, Daniel de Oliveira and Vanessa Braganholo, the authors of the paper titled "Analyzing Provenance Across Heterogeneous Provenance Graphs" for receiving this award.

This collection constitutes the peer-reviewed papers of IPAW 2016. These include 12 long papers that report in depth on the results of research around provenance and two short papers that discuss tools and services that were presented in the form of a system demonstration. Finally, we have included 14 short papers that were also presented as part of the joint IPAW/TaPP poster session. The final papers, demos, and short papers accompanied by poster presentations were selected from a total of 54 submissions. All full-length research papers received a minimum of three reviews.

The papers of IPAW 2016 provide a glimpse into state-of-the-art research and practice around the automatic capture, representation, and use of provenance. The papers discussing provenance capture exemplify the diversity of applications with provenance needs including operating systems, scripting environments, and distributed environments. While automated provenance capture is necessary for wide-spread provenance collection, analysis and visualization of provenance enable users to understand and make sense of the collected provenance. Several papers focus on this aspect describing tools for visualizing large provenance graphs, for creating understandable natural language descriptions from provenance graphs, and for analyzing provenance across multiple provenance graphs. Provenance itself is meaningless if not used for a concrete purpose. The proceedings also cover papers reporting on real-world use cases of provenance as well as how to model provenance for specific domains.

In closing, we would like to thank the members of the Program Committee for their thoughtful reviews, Dr. Adriane Chapman (local chair) and her team for their excellent organization of IPAW and ProvenanceWeek 2016 at MITRE, and—last not least—the authors and participants for making IPAW the stimulating and successful event that it was.

June 2016

Boris Glavic
Marta Mattoso

Organization

ProvenanceWeek Senior PC Chair

Marta Mattoso   Federal University of Rio de Janeiro, Brazil

IPAW PC Chair

Boris Glavic   Illinois Institute of Technology, USA

TaPP PC Chair

Sarah Cohen-Boulakia   Université Paris-Sud, France

Local Chair

Adriane P. Chapman   The MITRE Corporation, USA

Program Committee

Khalid Belhajjame	Université Paris-Dauphine, France
Shawn Bowers	Gonzaga University, USA
Vanessa Braganholo	Universidade Federal Fluminense, Brazil
Kevin Butler	University of Florida, USA
James Cheney	University of Edinburgh, UK
Susan Davidson	University of Pennsylvania, USA
Daniel de Oliveira	Fluminense Federal University, Brazil
Anton Dignös	Free University of Bozen-Bolzano, Italy
Mohamed Eltabakh	WPI, USA
Ian Foster	University of Chicago, USA
Daniel Garijo	Universidad Politécnica de Madrid, Spain
Ashish Gehani	SRI International, USA
Paul Groth	Elsevier Labs, The Netherlands
Torsten Grust	Universität Tübingen, Germany
Olaf Hartig	Hasso Plattner Institute, Germany
Melanie Herschel	Universität Stuttgart, Germany
Trung Dong Huynh	University of Southampton, UK
Grigoris Karvounarakis	LogicBlox, USA
Oliver Kennedy	SUNY Buffalo, USA
David Koop	University of Massachusetts at Dartmouth, USA
Bertram Ludäscher	University of Illinois at Urbana-Champaign, USA
Tanu Malik	University of Chicago, USA

Deborah McGuinness	Rensselaer Polytechnic Institute, USA
Paolo Missier	Newcastle University, UK
Beth Plale	Indiana University, USA
Ravi Ramamurthy	Microsoft Research, USA
Dan Suciu	University of Washington, USA
Justin Wozniak	Argonne National Laboratory, USA
Jun Zhao	Oxford e-Research Centre, UK

Contents

System Demonstrations

Joint IPAW/TaPP Poster Session

Provenance Capture

RecProv: Towards Provenance-Aware
User Space Record and Replay

Yang Ji$^{(\boxtimes)}$, Sangho Lee, and Wenke Lee

Georgia Institute of Technology, Atlanta, USA
{yang.ji,sangho}@gatech.edu, wenke@cc.gatech.edu

Abstract. Deterministic record and replay systems have widely been used in software debugging, failure diagnosis, and intrusion detection. In order to detect the Advanced Persistent Threat (APT), online execution needs to be recorded with acceptable runtime overhead; then, investigators can analyze the replayed execution with heavy dynamic instrumentation. While most record and replay systems rely on kernel module or OS virtualization, those running at user space are favoured for being lighter weight and more portable without any of the changes needed for OS/Kernel virtualization. On the other hand, higher level provenance data at a higher level provides dynamic analysis with system causalities and hugely increases its efficiency. Considering both benefits, we propose a provenance-aware user space record and replay system, called RecProv. RecProv is designed to provide high provenance fidelity; specifically, with versioning files from the recorded trace logs and integrity protection to provenance data through real-time trace isolation. The collected provenance provides the high-level system dependency that helps pinpoint suspicious activities where further analysis can be applied. We show that RecProv is able to output accurate provenance in both visualized graph and W3C standardized PROV-JSON formats.

Keywords: Provenance capturing · Record and replay · User space · PROV

1 Introduction

As exploits and intrusions evolve to behave more silently (e.g., Advanced Persistent Threat (APT) [18]), they can rarely be detected by classic intrusion detection and anti-virus solutions. As the best-effort countermeasure to defeat APT, dynamic instrumentation and analysis is able to detect APT's behavior by monitoring execution of instructions and memory operations (e.g., [25]). However, the high overhead induced by dynamic analysis disqualifies it from running on the online production system. The overhead is acceptable for its original intended tasks: debugging, performance profiling, memory leak detection [16,24], and malware analysis [30,36], but is too high for online execution.

To mitigate the high overhead for online execution, researchers propose to record the execution and replay it deterministically with heavy instrumentation

© Springer International Publishing Switzerland 2016
M. Mattoso and B. Glavic (Eds.): IPAW 2016, LNCS 9672, pp. 3–15, 2016.
DOI: 10.1007/978-3-319-40593-3_1

for detecting the APT [6,14,15]. Many record and replay systems rely on kernel module or the OS virtualization to capture non-determinism during recording, and feed back during replaying (e.g., [1,6,14,32]); however, these systems raise concerns over system stability and portability. The user space record and replay systems [10,20,29] do not require any of these changes. They are usually supported on multiple platforms without need for customization. But, they lack of whole system provenance.

On the other hand, provenance is growing to be a key feature in security-sensitive applications and systems. The provenance information inside the system and application is a widely researched topic. Provenance-aware systems are proposed for various application scenarios such as databases, distributed systems, E-science areas [5,9,12,19,31]. The provenance in the system reveals the steps of intrusions and further identifies the source of the attack (e.g., a malicious executable file downloaded from a remote host or a USB drive). Though provenance data alone cannot defeat APT, it can help the dynamic analysis pinpoint suspicious activities. Prior works [14,15,17] rely on the generated provenance graph to pinpoint the exact execution trace in order to further perform finer-grained analysis.

In this paper, we focus on enabling provenance for the user space record and replay system. Specifically, we propose RECPROV, a user space record and replay system that captures the runtime provenance from the recorded trace file. The collected provenance data offer high fidelity, particularly with fine grained versioning files. For security-sensitive scenarios, the untampered provenance data plays a key role in the post-analysis of attacks. Hence, our design also protects the provenance data itself. At a minimum, we guarantee the integrity of provenance until an attacker gains the privilege to arbitrarily delete files. This means the provenance before the compromise can be used to analyze the intrusion procedure for forensic purpose.

RECPROV relies on Mozilla rr [20] running in the user space with minimal operating system changes, with the runtime overhead as low as 20 %. Currently, RECPROV supports the Linux operating system with Intel x86 or x64 architectures. The host can be a bare-metal machine, as long as the CPU supports performance counter, or a virtual machine with a virtual performance counter enabled. In terms of security, RECPROV guarantees backward integrity of trace logs up until the compromise of the system, providing an untampered source for analyzing the exploit and the take-down of the system. The trace logs can be used to replay the execution deterministically, opening doors to heavier and more fine-grained offline analyses that do not burden the online performance.

Beyond the benefits from rr, we summarize the contribution of RECPROV to be the following:

1. RECPROV generates operating-system-level provenance from the runtime trace, considering causalities between processes, files, and socket connections.
2. RECPROV considers the versions of file objects which yield higher fidelity and lower false positives in generating the provenance data.
3. RECPROV has a trace isolation design that largely protects the integrity of the trace, particularly for security-sensitive target hosts.

2 Related Work

In this section we explain previous studies on provenance analysis. We categorize them in terms of how they collect the following provenance information: software instrumentation, whole system monitoring, system emulator, and hardware assistance.

Software Instrumentation. A software-instrumentation-based provenance analysis technique modifies the target software itself in order to record all of its important behavior during execution. Tariq et al. [35] modify an LLVM compiler to statically instrument a program according to the annotation in its source code. This approach allows them to generate finer-grained intra-process provenance, e.g., how frequently a specific function is called. However, one cannot assume that every target software will provide its source code for provenance analysis. DataTracker [33] obtains a program's provenance information without any modification by using libdft [13], a dynamic taint analysis tool based on the Intel Pin [11]. Although the dynamic taint analysis provides highly precise provenance information, its execution overhead (up to 104 %) is significant [13].

Whole System Monitoring. Provenance information mainly consists of interactions between processes or between a process and resources (e.g., file, socket, and peripheral). Such interactions are usually performed via system calls, e.g., open, socket, read, write, and ioctl. Therefore, by monitoring system calls, we can collect almost every high-level provenance information. The easiest way to record all the system calls of a process is using a well-known tool, strace, but its coverage is restricted to an individual process. Thus, to efficiently obtain the whole system provenance information, many studies modify the OS kernel or use a kernel module [3,4,6,14,17,21,22,27]. These approaches ensure low overhead and high coverage, but customizing an OS kernel can lead to stability and portability problems.

System Emulation/Virtualization. Another approach to collect the whole system provenance information while not modifying the OS kernel is using a system emulator. This emulator-based provenance analysis allows us to inspect instruction-level causality. Panorama [36] is a hardware-level system to capture system-wide information flow, implemented on the QEMU. Also, Stamatogiannakis et al. [34] use PANDA [7], a QEMU-based system record and replay platform, to capture low-level provenance information. However, the QEMU is slow, which makes it difficult to collect real provenance information. Unlike the QEMU-based approaches, a virtualization-based intrusion tracking system, BackTracker [15], shows low overhead. But, we need to narrow down the semantic gap between the QEMU/hypervisor and the emulated OS [8] for precise analysis.

Hardware Assistance. The last approach is using a hardware feature to record execution trace. For example, the latest Intel CPU supports the Process Tracing (PT) feature [28] to trace the execution path of a process for precise debugging. Such a hardware feature allows us to record the whole system provenance information without any system modification while incurring negligible overhead [2].

However, currently the Intel PT only provides control-flow information, which is insufficient to construct the complete provenance information without runtime memory snapshot or data. Further, many hardware do not support such features yet, so it cannot yet be widely adopted.

3 System

RECPROV leverages the Mozilla-RR [20] (rr) to perform deterministic record and replay by speculatively executing system calls and feeding back non-deterministic inputs (e.g., RDTSC). RECPROV records the execution of an application in the runtime with low overhead, and simultaneously dumps the trace files off to the host for provenance generating computations. RECPROV interfaces to the Neo4j graph database [23] for data storage and visualization, and also supports data export in W3C standard PROV-JSON formats. Figure 1 illustrates the architecture of RECPROV.

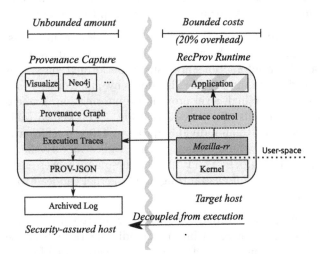

Fig. 1. System architecture.

The recording operation of RECPROV resides at the user space, without kernel module and OS virtualization/emulation assistance. This design choice has two benefits: (1) The recording is portable. RECPROV does not require kernel changes, which makes it directly available in many platforms. While a kernel module has efficient provenance capturing capabilities, the changes to the kernel raise stability and compatibility concerns. (2) Recording performance incurs around 20 % overhead, while the syscall level capturing suffices for building of file/process level provenance. RECPROV also considers the finer-grained versions of files by monitoring the sequence of system calls (i.e., write, mmap, munmap). In addition, the off-host design enables deployment of RECPROV suitable for security-sensitive environments. In the case that the host is compromised, the integrity of the trace log up until the compromise is preserved, as the traces are transferred off of the host in real time.

3.1   Deterministic Record and Replay

Mozilla developed rr to perform deterministic recording and replaying for the purpose of testing and debugging firefox in Linux on both x86 and x64 architectures. rr relies on ptrace to control the execution of programs, and to monitor the CPU state of each user-kernel context switch (i.e., entering and exiting a system call). Moreover, other non-determinism such as RDTSC and signal delivery/receiving are recorded accordingly in the trace. Based on the trace, the execution can be replayed deterministically. The system call arguments and return values are fed back, while the non-determinisms are inserted into the execution sequence at known time points. rr supports multi-threading by performing the scheduling in the user space. It first honors the priority of each task, then does the scheduling in the round-robin way.

During replay, rr can opt to attach the execution to gdb for step by step debugging or complete the replayed execution in a independent "autopilot" way.

Changes to rr. The rr trace log includes the register values at every system call entry and exit. In order to also access the data referenced by the address from the register, we customize rr to dereference the relevant monitored addresses either during record or replay of the execution. Since the replay is deterministic and identical to the recorded execution, the captured data from online and offline methods are equivalent. To access the address space of the traced process, RECPROV uses PTRACE_PEEKDATA of ptrace to dereference the address from the registers. For example, in order to track the causal relation between file and process, RECPROV monitors the file path argument in the open system call. Specifically, at entering the open system call, we access register %RDI and dereference its value to retrieve the file path string buffer. RECPROV monitors the arguments of open, openat, connect and accept.

Second, RECPROV changes the trace I/O part of rr to divert the dump of syscall events trace from local persistence (i.e., local log files) to a remote security-assured host via socket in real time. The trace is compressed before transmission. Instead of transferring the log after the complete recording, RECPROV enables the receiving agent at the remote host to generate provenance from the received syscall sequence in real time. This design enables real-time detection scenarios.

3.2   Provenance Generation

The provenance is retrieved from the trace files. Specifically, we monitor: file operation syscalls open, read, write, close, dup, mmap, munmap; process related syscalls execve, clone, fork; and socket related syscalls socket, connect, accept, sendto, sendmsg, sendmmsg, recvfrom, recvmsg, recvmmsg. RECPROV scans the trace file syscall by syscall to capture the provenance development.

In the event of open system call, RECPROV first retrieves the process ID from the syscall arguments and the file path (via dereferencing the address in %RDI). Then, the stat syscall is made to retrieve the <inode,device_id> to identify the exact file regardless of the different file paths or symlinks being used. The inode may be recycled for use after the file is removed; thus, we also monitor the unlink(at) syscall to invalidate the current inode. Next, the returned file descriptor fd (from %RAX) at the exit of the system call is bookkept. RECPROV tracks the fd to link the presence of files in future file I/O operations like read and write. Particularly, the write system call adds the version of the file object accordingly. The tracking on a certain fd terminates at the relevant close system call. In the event of read and write system calls, an activity is added from the process to the file (via tracking fd).

Through execve syscall, a process starts to execute the file, i.e., the file affects the process. The executable file path, arguments, and environment variables are also retrieved as meta data for the process. The activity arrow points from the file to the process. In the event of system calls clone and fork between processes, the activity adds an edge from the parent process to the child.

The mmap system call maps the file to a memory region to speed up the file I/O operation. Since the rr trace does not have instruction level transparency, RECPROV is unable to tell whether it is a read or a write. Having zero false negatives as a higher priority, we translate mmap to be a special "read/write" activity. Also, we increment the version of the file only at the first mmap, as the exact operations are blind to us and the libc library sometimes calls mmap to enlarge the allocated memory region for memory functions like malloc.

RECPROV also tracks the provenance from networking events. The socket file descriptor sock_fd is first tracked from the socket syscall. Then, the remote host address and port (i.e., sock_addr) are mapped to the sock_fd by tracking the accept and connect syscalls. The recv related syscalls then add the "used" activity from the process to the host. The send syscalls add "wasDerivedFrom" activity from the host to the process.

3.3   Versioning Files

A versioned file offers fine-grained causalities between changed versions of the file over time. This transparency improves the fidelity of causality relation. For example, a binary file A is executed by a process P, and then modified by a process P'. If the version of A is not counted, we have a causality from P' to P. But if different versions of A are considered (i.e., $A(v1)$ at execve, and $A(v2)$ at P' modification), two processes may not be causally related as P' is modifying the later version of A, $A(v2)$, while P only depends on the previous version $A(v1)$.

RECPROV tracks the version variance of files by monitoring write and mmap system calls. Whenever such system calls occur, the file descriptor in register %RDI is used to identify the related file path and inode (see Sect. 3.2). This increments the version of the file. In the case of bulk write operations, a process performs a large number of write system calls with no interference from other processes. We combine consecutive write system calls into a single incrementing of file versions, as long as the combination causes no fidelity loss in the causality representation. To enable access to all versions of files, RECPROV runs on the mainstream versioning file system, nilfs [26]. nilfs makes checkpoints at any file change in the disk partition, and allows one to roll the file system back to any checkpoint. RECPROV maps the file version to the nilfs version by matching the closest timestamps.

3.4 Storage and Visualization

RECPROV interfaces to the Neo4j graph database [23] to store the provenance graph. The boundary of each graph is within the start and end of the execution. A process is represented by its process ID (pid), with the executable file path as the metadata; A file is identified by a uuid with its inode, absolute file path, and version as metadata; A remote host is represented by the IP address it uses to have socket connections with the target host. The process, file, and remote host are modeled as nodes in the database. The system calls that operate upon these nodes are modeled as edges. Additionally, RECPROV outputs the provenance to W3C standardized PROV-JSON formats, ready to be stored and shared at stores like prov-store.

4 Case Study

We perform case studies on baseline programs, a file operation experiment, and the grep command. Also, we test RECPROV on a real phishing attack that installs an extension on a Firefox browser. Note that the metadata of the executable names, arguments, and environments are omitted in the figures but available in the database.

4.1 Use Case 1: File Versioning

We first run an experiment program to demonstrate the effect of differentiating file versions in Fig. 2. The experiment creates two threads, each of which opens a file test.txt, reads from and writes more text to it, and then outputs to stdout. With the versioning data of the file, we can look into causality with processes at every version. In the graph, the cloned thread, 5614, first reads (i.e., "used") the first version of test.txt file, then writes to it yielding its second version. Then, thread 5615 reads the second version, modifies the file again, and generates its third version. Without the versioning, the graph indicates both threads have read and written to the file, but does not reveal the directional dependency that thread 5615 is downstream from 5614 in terms of test.txt.

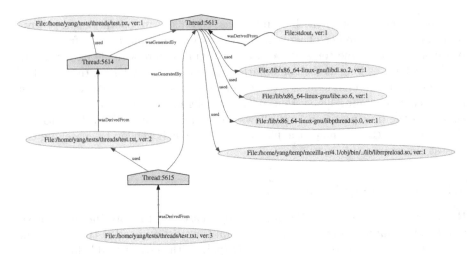

Fig. 2. Use case 1: File versioning.

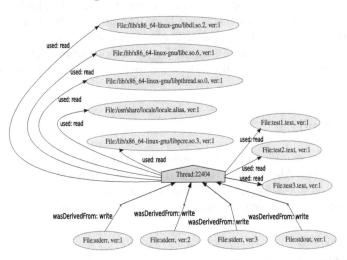

Fig. 3. Use case 2: grep.

4.2   Use Case 2: grep

As a basic utility command for Linux, **grep** searches the given text in the files or directory to match certain pattern. We run **grep** to search a given directory for a specific key word: grep "hello" test/ -rn. The test/ contains three files test1.txt, test2.txt, and test3.txt. The result is displayed at stdout. In addition, the debugging trace of running RECPROV is dumped at stderr. Figure 3 shows the output visualized graph of provenance. The process with a single thread (pid:22404) reads the shared libraries, and the test/{test1.txt,test2.txt,test3.txt} files with "used" activity. The process then writes the result and debugging data to stdout and stderr. In the provenance graph, these files are "wasDerivedFrom". Note that the file objects have the "ver" field indicating the version of the file at the moment of the activity. For example, the debugging data are written to stderr three times, separately yielding file objects with versions 1 to 3. The following snippet gives a simplified version of the PROV-JSON format.

```
{"wasDerivedFrom": {
    [{"prov:usedEntity": "Thread:22404",
      "prov:generatedEntity": "File:stderr, ver:1"},
     {"prov:usedEntity": "Thread:22404",
      "prov:generatedEntity": "File:stderr, ver:2"},
     {"prov:usedEntity": "Thread:22404",
      "prov:generatedEntity": "File:stderr, ver:3"}],
     {"prov:usedEntity": "Thread:22404",
      "prov:generatedEntity": "File:stdout"}}
  "used": {
    {"prov:entity": "File:/lib/x86_64-linux-gnu/libc.so.6, ver:1",
     "prov:activity": "Thread:22404"},
    {"prov:entity": "File:test1.text, ver:1",
     "prov:activity": "Thread:22404"},
    {"prov:entity": "File:test2.text, ver:1",
     "prov:activity": "Thread:22404"},
    {"prov:entity": "File:test3.text, ver:1",
     "prov:activity": "Thread:22404"}},
  "agent": {
    "Thread:22404": {}},
  "entity": {
    "File:test1.text, ver:1": {},
    "File:test2.text, ver:1": {},
    "File:test3.text, ver:1": {},
    "File:/lib/x86_64-linux-gnu/libdl.so.2, ver:1": {},
    "File:stderr, ver:1": {},
    "File:stderr, ver:2": {},
    "File:stderr, ver:3": {}}
}
```

4.3 Use Case 3: Firefox Phishing Attack

We run a phishing attack with RECPROV and generate the provenance graph in Fig. 4 to show the effective provenance extracted by RECPROV. The test runs with the Firefox browser 43.0 on Ubuntu 14.04 LTS on a bare-metal machine with Intel Xeon CPU W3565. In the attack, the user clicks a link from a phishing email and installs a malicious extension on the Firefox browser. We use Gmail as the mailbox; the malicious extension is hosted locally at port 8005. We run

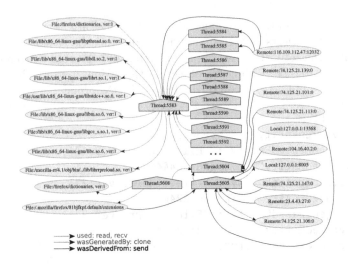

Fig. 4. Use case 3: Firefox phshing. (Color figure online)

RECPROV for the entire procedure from the opening of the browser to the complete installation and the closing of the browser. Figure 4 is a simplified provenance graph drawn from RECPROV. Firefox is a single process, multi-threaded program. The first thread (tid:5583) loads shared libraries by "used" activity; then clones a set of threads establishing "wasGeneratedBy" relations. Moreover, the browser connects external hosts, including multiple Google and Gmail sites and the local host 127.0.0.1:8005, for downloading the extension. The extension is further linked with the .mozilla/firefox/*.default/extension directory.

From the provenance graph, we can trace the installed extension back to the extension directory, to the thread that writes to it, and finally to the remote host from which a recv syscall is made. The installation of the extension can be tagged as a "suspicious" activity for which a further finer-grained analysis can be performed.

5 Discussions

We list the limitations of RECPROV in regards to the width and depth of provenance. First, since RECPROV runs at user space or application level, it does not have whole-system wide transparency. Therefore, the provenance data are only extracted from the traced processes. Also, the provenance can be lost when a certain file is altered by another untraced process. For example, if a file is modified by another untraced process before being read by the traced process, both the causality from the untraced process to the file and the causality extending to the traced process are lost. Second, RECPROV only traces the CPU states at each syscall entry and exit, not the memory data, implying that causalities related to memory operations (e.g., after a file is mmaped) are unknown. In order to obtain such higher fidelity, instruction level trace is desired to unveil the full-depth provenance.

Future work can focus on relieving these limitations. First, we think RECPROV can be customized to trace broader applications while still keeping the performance overhead low. This requires a sophisticated design of the user space scheduling method. Second, in order to perform heavy instrumentation for the higher fidelity of provenance, RECPROV can further conduct the instrumentation during the offline replayed execution. This requires a filtering scheme that can discriminate between executions from the original recording and those from the instrumentation tool (e.g., pin [24]) and track only the original execution.

6 Conclusion

We propose a provenance-aware user space record and replay system. The system is shown to be portable without requiring kernel changes or system virtualization. RECPROV is shown to give accurate provenance data, particularly with versioning files that provide higher fidelity. The generated provenance also complies with the W3C PROV-JSON format, and has interface to the Neo4j graph database. In addition, the integrity of provenance is protected in an off-host environment guaranteeing "until-compromise" integrity. Currently, RECPROV supports step by step debugging during deterministic replay. In the future, we will extend RECPROV to enable various dynamic instrumentation.

Acknowledgment. We would like to thank the anonymous reviewers for their help and feedback. This research was supported by the NSF award CNS-1017265, CNS-0831300, CNS-1149051 and DGE-1500084, by the ONR under grant N000140911042 and N000141512162, by the DHS under contract N66001-12-C-0133, by the United States Air Force under contract FA8650-10-C-7025, by the DARPA Transparent Computing program under contract DARPA-15- 15-TC-FP-006. Any opinions, findings, conclusions or recommendations expressed in this material are those of the authors and do not necessarily reflect the views of the NSF, ONR, DHS, United States Air Force or DARPA.

References

1. Attariyan, M., Chow, M., Flinn, J.: X-ray: automating root-cause diagnosis of performance anomalies in production software. In: Proceedings of the 10th USENIX Symposium on Operating Systems Design and Implementation (OSDI), Hollywood, CA, October 2012
2. Balakrishnan, N., Bytheway, T., Carata, L., Chick, O.R.A., Snee, J., Akoush, S., Sohan, R., Seltzer, M., Hopper, A.: Recent advances in computer architecture: the opportunities and challenges for provenance. In: Proceedings of the 7th USENIX Workshop on the Theory and Practice of Provenance (TaPP) (2015)
3. Bates, A., Tian, D.J., Butler, K.R., Moyer, T.: Trustworthy whole-system provenance for the Linux kernel. In: Proceedings of the 24th USENIX Security Symposium (Security), Washington, DC, August 2015

4. Cantrill, B., Shapiro, M., Leventhal, A.: Dynamic instrumentation of production systems. In: Proceedings of the 2004 USENIX Annual Technical Conference (ATC), Boston, MA, June–July 2004

5. Davidson, S., Freire, J.: Provenance and scientic workflows: challenges and opportunities. In: Proceedings of the 2008 ACM SIGMOD/PODS Conference, Vancouver, Canada, June 2008

6. Devecsery, D., Chow, M., Dou, X., Flinn, J., Chen, P.: Eidetic systems. In: Proceedings of the 11th USENIX Symposium on Operating Systems Design and Implementation (OSDI), Broomfield, Colorado, October 2014

7. Dolan-Gavitt, B., Leek, T., Hodosh, J., Lee, W.: Tappan zee (north) bridge: mining memory accesses for introspection. In: Proceedings of the 20th ACM Conference on Computer and Communications Security (CCS), Berlin, Germany, October 2013

8. Dolan-Gavitt, B., Leek, T., Zhivich, M., Giffin, J., Lee, W.: Virtuoso: narrowing the semantic gap in virtual machine introspection. In: Proceedings of the 32nd IEEE Symposium on Security and Privacy (Oakland), Oakland, CA, May 2011

9. Gehani, A., Tariq, D.: SPADE: support for provenance auditing in distributed environments. In: Proceedings of the 13th USENIX Workshop on the Theory and Practice of Provenance (TaPP) (2012)

10. Guo, Z., Wang, X., Tang, J., Liu, X., Xu, Z., Wu, M., Kaashoek, M.F., Zhang, Z.: R2: an application-level kernel for record and replay. In: Proceedings of the 8th USENIX Symposium on Operating Systems Design and Implementation (OSDI), San Diego, CA, December 2008

11. Intel: Pin - a dynamic binary instrumentation tool. https://software.intel.com/en-us/articles/pin-a-dynamic-binary-instrumentation-tool

12. James, C., Laura, C., Wang-Chiew, T.: Provenance in databases: why, how, and where. Found. Trends Databases 1(4), 379–474 (2009)

13. Kemerlis, V.P., Portokalidis, G., Jee, K., Keromytis, A.D.: libdft: practical dynamic data flow tracking for commodity systems. In: Proceedings of the 8th ACM SIGPLAN/SIGOPS International Conference on Virtual Execution Environments (VEE) (2012)

14. Kim, T., Wang, X., Zeldovich, N., Kaashoek, M.: Intrusion recovery using selective re-execution. In: Proceedings of the 9th USENIX Symposium on Operating Systems Design and Implementation (OSDI), Vancouver, Canada, October 2010

15. King, S.T., Chen, P.M.: Backtracking intrusions. In: Proceedings of the 19th ACM Symposium on Operating Systems Principles (SOSP). Bolton Landing, NY, October 2003

16. Luk, C.K., Cohn, R., Muth, R., Patil, H., Klauser, A., Lowney, G., Wallace, S., Reddi, V.J., Hazelwood, K.: Pin: building customized program analysis tools with dynamic instrumentation. In: Proceedings of the 2005 ACM SIGPLAN Conference on Programming Language Design and Implementation (PLDI), Chicago, IL, June 2005

17. Ma, S., Zhang, X., Xu, D.: ProTracer: towards practical provenance tracing by alternating between logging and tainting. In: Proceedings of the 2016 Annual Network and Distributed System Security Symposium (NDSS), San Diego, CA, February 2016

18. McAfee: White paper: Combating advanced persistent threats, how to prevent, detect and remediate apts. http://www.mcafee.com/us/resources/white-papers/wp-combat-advanced-persist-threats.pdf

19. Moreau, L.: The foundations for provenance on the web. Found. Trends Web Sci. 2(2–3), 99–241 (2010)

20. Mozilla: rr: lightweight recording & deterministic debugging. http://rr-project.org
21. Muniswamy-Reddy, K.K., Braun, U., Holland, D.A., Macko, P., MacLean, D.L., Margo, D.W., Seltzer, M.I., Smogor, R.: Layering in provenance systems. In: Proceedings of the 2009 USENIX Annual Technical Conference (ATC), San Diego, CA, June 2009
22. Muniswamy-Reddy, K.K., Holland, D.A., Braun, U., Seltzer, M.I.: Provenance-aware storage systems. In: Proceedings of the 2006 USENIX Annual Technical Conference (ATC), Boston, MA, May–June 2006
23. Neo Technology: Neo4j: The world's leading graph database. http://www.neo4j.com
24. Nethercote, N., Seward, J.: Valgrind: a framework for heavyweight dynamic binary instrumentation. In: Proceedings of the 2007 ACM SIGPLAN Conference on Programming Language Design and Implementation (PLDI), San Diego, CA, June 2007
25. Newsome, J., Song, D.: Dynamic taint analysis for automatic detection, analysis, and signature generation of exploits on commodity software. In: Proceedings of the 12th Annual Network and Distributed System Security Symposium (NDSS), San Diego, CA, February 2005
26. NTT Laboratories: NILFS - continuous snapshotting filesystem for Linux. http://www.nilfs.org
27. Pohly, D.J., McLaughlin, S., McDaniel, P., Butler, K.: Hi-Fi: collecting high-fidelity whole-system provenance. In: Proceedings of the Annual Computer Security Applications Conference (ACSAC) (2012)
28. Reinders, J.: Processor Trace. https://software.intel.com/en-us/blogs/2013/09/18/processor-tracing
29. Saito, Y.: Jockey: a user-space library for record-replay debugging. In: Proceedings of the 6th International Symposium on Automated Analysis-driven Debugging (2005)
30. Seward, J., Nethercote, N.: Using valgrind to detect undefined value errors with bit-precision. In: Proceedings of the 2005 USENIX Annual Technical Conference (ATC), Anaheim, CA, June–July 2005
31. Simmhan, Y.L., Plale, B., Gannon, D.: Karma2: provenance management for data-driven workflows. In: Web Services Research for Emerging Applications: Discoveries and Trends: Discoveries and Trends, p. 317 (2010)
32. Srinivasan, S.M., Kandula, S., Andrews, C.R., Zhou, Y.: Flashback: a lightweight extension for rollback and deterministic replay for software debugging. In: Proceedings of the 2004 USENIX Annual Technical Conference (ATC), Boston, MA June–July 2004
33. Stamatogiannakis, M., Groth, P., Bos, H.: Looking inside the black-box: capturing data provenance using dynamic instrumentation. In: Ludaescher, B., Plale, B. (eds.) IPAW 2014. LNCS, vol. 8628, pp. 155–167. Springer, Heidelberg (2015)
34. Stamatogiannakis, M., Groth, P., Bos, H.: Decoupling provenance capture and analysis from execution. In: Proceedings of the 7th USENIX Workshop on the Theory and Practice of Provenance (TaPP) (2015)
35. Tariq, D., Ali, M., Gehani, A.: Towards automated collection of application-level data provenance. In: Proceedings of the 4th USENIX Workshop on the Theory and Practice of Provenance (TaPP) (2015)
36. Yin, H., Song, D., Egele, M., Kruegel, C., Kirda, E.: Panorama: capturing system-wide information flow for malware detection and analysis. In: Proceedings of the 14th ACM Conference on Computer and Communications Security (CCS), Alexandria, VA, October–November 2007

Tracking and Analyzing the Evolution
of Provenance from Scripts

João Felipe Pimentel[1(✉)], Juliana Freire[2], Vanessa Braganholo[1],
and Leonardo Murta[1]

[1] Universidade Federal Fluminense, Niterói, Brazil
{jpimentel,vanessa,leomurta}@ic.uff.br
[2] New York University, New York, USA
juliana.freire@nyu.edu

Abstract. Script languages are powerful tools for scientists. Scientists use them
to process data, invoke programs, and link program outputs/inputs. During the
life cycle of scientific experiments, scientists compose scripts, execute them, and
perform analysis on the results. Depending on the results, they modify their
script to get more data to confirm the original hypothesis or to test a new
hypothesis, evolving the experiment. While some tools capture provenance from
the execution of scripts, most approaches focus on a single execution, leaving
out the possibility to analyze the provenance evolution of the experiment as a
whole. This work enables tracking and analyzing the provenance evolution
gathered from scripts. Tracking the provenance evolution also helps to reconstruct the environment of previous executions for reproduction. Provenance
evolution analysis allows comparison of executions to understand what has
changed and supports the decision of which execution provides better results.

1 Introduction

The life cycle of script-based experiments is usually composed of three main phases
[12]: establishing hypotheses and coding scripts that enact the programs involved in the
experiment; running the script over input data, which represent a specific context or
population for the experiment; and analyzing the produced results through visualizations or queries to confirm the research hypotheses. However, the results of the latter
phase may motivate the repetition of the cycle. For instance, when a trial (i.e., one
execution of the experiment) is inconclusive, scientists repeat the cycle after adapting
the script or changing the programs. When a hypothesis is confirmed for a restrict
population, scientists repeat the experiment for a broader population by changing the
input data. Similarly, when a hypothesis is refuted for a broad population, scientists
restrict the population and repeat the cycle also by changing the input data. Moreover,
some scientists design experiments considering multiple inputs or variable programs
and the experiment execution entails many trials at once via parameter sweeping. Thus,
script, programs, data, and the execution environment evolve over time as a natural
consequence of the experimental process.

In the last decade some approaches emerged for capturing provenance from
experiments encoded in scripts [2, 3, 11, 14, 19]. The captured provenance usually

M. Mattoso and B. Glavic (Eds.): IPAW 2016, LNCS 9672, pp. 16–28, 2016.
DOI: 10.1007/978-3-319-40593-3_2

includes the script structure with its functions and variables, all input data, intermediate data, output data, the required libraries, the environment characteristics (computer architecture, operating system, etc.), and the execution flow of the trial (function activations, variable assignments, etc.). However, these approaches either do not track the evolution of the experiment between trials or rely on external tools for such tracking. In both cases, the scientists are limited to intra-trial queries, not being able to contrast the provenance of two trials or to visualize the difference among trials' provenance.

Understanding and visualizing a single trial through intra-trial queries is not enough for the analysis of the whole experiment. To support this claim, we refer to a set of questions related to experiment evolution analysis, which were obtained and adapted from the first Provenance Challenge[1] and ProvBench workshops[2]: Q1 (see footnote 1): if a scientist has executed an experiment twice, but has replaced some procedures in the second trial, what are the trial differences? Q2[3]: comparing multiple executions according to their parameters, what are the differences on execution behavior? Q3[4]: how differences in the input data relate to differences in the output values? Q4 (see footnote 4): using historical provenance, which parts of the execution fail frequently? Q5[5]: which trials are related to a given trial? Q6 (see footnote 5): a given trial was derived from which trial? Q7[6]: what are the available trials, and what are their durations? Q8 (see footnote 6): how many trials are associated to a given source code? Q9 (see footnote 6): how many trials present failures?

To be able to answer these questions, in this work we propose a version model that supports tracking and analyzing the experiment provenance as a whole, considering its multiple trials. This model also allows us to restore any past trial, thus enabling reproducibility. Moreover, our version model supports comparison of different trials for analysis. As a proof of concept, we implemented our version model on top of noWorkflow [14, 16, 17]. noWorkflow is an approach that automatically collects provenance from Python scripts without requiring any modifications on the source code of the experiment. For every trial, noWorkflow generates an identifier and all provenance collected during the execution is stored in a database related to that identifier. Provenance collected by noWorkflow contains function activations (calls) with parameters, variable values, returned values, duration, and caller; imported modules with their versions; environment variables; and all the files accessed during the trial, including source files, module files, and input files, intermediate files, and output files.

This paper is organized in six sections, besides this introduction. Section 2 discusses related work. Section 3 presents our approach to track evolution, analyze provenance, and compare trials. Section 4 presents the implementation details on top of noWorkflow. Section 5 shows the evaluation of our work using the aforementioned

---

[1] http://twiki.ipaw.info/bin/view/Challenge/FirstProvenanceChallenge.

[2] https://sites.google.com/site/provbench/home/provbench-provenance-week-2014.

[3] https://github.com/provbench/Swift-PROV.

[4] https://github.com/provbench/CSIRO-PROV.

[5] https://github.com/provbench/VisTrails-PROV.

[6] https://github.com/provbench/Wf4Ever-PROV.

questions. Finally, Sect. 6 concludes the paper summarizing the contributions and discussing future work.

2 Related Work

Work related to our approach can be grouped into three main categories: (i) configuration management tools, (ii) script-based provenance tools, and (iii) workflow-based provenance tools. Many configuration management tools, such as Git, track the evolution of software through versioning [6]. These tools allow developers to inform the files they want to track and provide different mechanisms for querying the history, such as *bisect*, *blame*, and even some simple *lookups* on previous versions. Developers can also use external visualization tools to have a broader view of source code evolution [5]. Although generic and fast, these tools capture only prospective provenance [8] at coarse grain, when used to version experiment scripts. Thus, they do not track the inner structures of files, the evolution of computations that indicate which input files and parameters actually influence each output files, nor the multiple intermediate states of files. In other words, they do not capture fine-grained prospective provenance [8] nor retrospective provenance [8].

Some approaches can be used to capture provenance from scripts. YesWorkflow [13] captures prospective provenance from scripts through annotations. StarFlow [2] and RDataTracker [11] collect provenance from scripts through dynamic analysis and annotations. Bochner et al. [3] collect provenance from scripts using a library to connect to a remote server and send annotated provenance data. Tariq et al. [19] collect provenance from code compiled with a LLVM compiler. Stamatogiannakis et al. [18] perform dynamic taint analysis on binary files to capture provenance. noWorkflow [14] collects provenance from scripts without requiring any modifications on the script. Most of these approaches capture execution provenance (i.e., retrospective provenance) [14] with intermediate data, and support querying and visualizing provenance during analysis. However, they do not provide mechanisms to compare and contrast different trials. An outstanding exception in this category is Sumatra [7]. It stores each trial in a configuration management tool (either Git or Mercurial) and allows users to tag them and to compare the collected information. However, it does not record the intermediate states of files during execution and is subject to the problems of using configuration management tools for tracking the evolution of experiments.

Finally, workflow-based provenance tools [1, 4] track provenance from scientific experiments. Some tools, such as Vistrails [4] and Kepler [1], not only track the provenance, but also track the workflow evolution and offers all the data for users to analyze it. They also allow users to restore past versions of workflows and re-execute them. Although attractive in terms of features, these tools require converting script-based experiments into workflows, which is not an option for many scientists for different reasons. This motivates the creation of a version model for script-based experiments, detailed in the next section.

3   Script-Based Provenance Evolution

Supporting evolution analysis of experiments requires the provenance-capturing tool to be evolution-aware. This can be achieved through versioning. Versioning enables tracking the evolution of the experiment and also navigating on the evolution history, allowing the user to restore previous versions, if needed. Additionally, such an evolution-aware provenance capture system should provide a way to compare different trials on the history. In Sect. 3.1, we propose a version model for provenance collected from scripts. In Sect. 3.2, we propose techniques to compare provenance from different trials.

3.1   Version Model

Conradi and Westfechtel [6] state that a version model should define the organization of the *version space* (i.e., how a product is versioned) and the interrelation of the *product space* (i.e., how a product is structured) and the version space. We define our *product space* as an experiment, containing its scripts, data, execution traces, etc. The entry point of our product space is the main script of the experiment. From this script, we recursively capture imported modules, accessed files during execution, and the execution provenance. Thus, we have scripts (including imports), input files, inter-mediate files, and output files as *file objects*. We identify file objects solely by their path within the experiment directory.

File objects describe the structure of the experiment: that is, all files needed by the experiment, which includes the script itself (definition provenance [14]), imported modules (deployment provenance [14]), and accessed (read/write) files (execution provenance [14]). On the other hand, we also have logical provenance information that is not stored in files: functions called during execution, parameters values, variable values, etc. In our product space, we have a special object called *logical object* that contains all the aforementioned logical provenance information. This way, we can say that our product space is composed of multiple file objects and one logical object.

Our *version space* [6] has two levels of versioning: *trial version* (i.e., the trial *id*) and *file object version*. Trial versions represent the state of the experiment in terms of file object versions read or written within each trial, together with the logical object version produced by the trial. On the other hand, file object versions represent the state of file objects at each file access during the whole experiment execution (throughout all trials). File object versions may contain extra attributes (metadata) besides the state of file objects: modules may have their semantic versions declared by developers (e.g., 3.5.1), files may have their moment of opening and opening mode (read/write), etc.

We apply this distinction between trial versions and file object versions because scripts can write to some file objects more than once, generating more than one version of the file object within a single trial. Due to this distinction, our version space supports restoring trial versions as a whole, with all input file objects, or specific file object versions (e.g., an intermediate version of a file object). However, to restore a specific file object version, users should inform which object they want to restore individually and in which moment (i.e., by indicating a timestamp, the file content hash code, or its access position in a sequential list by timestamp).

While we associate file objects to both version concepts (trial version and file object version), we associate logical objects only to trial versions, because they are unique for each trial and already contain all execution steps (i.e., each function activations, each variable state, etc.) within a trial. Nonetheless, restoring a trial version does not restore the logical object of that trial, as it is not a tangible object, even though it is still useful for auditing or reproducing a trial.

Figure 1 presents an example of this version model with two trial versions for an experiment, where the user only edited "experiment.py" and added "converter.py" before executing the second trial. Circles represent object versions and dotted squares represent trial versions. Note that the file "warp.warp" has four file object versions in Trial 1, and those versions were written four times, and read four times. Note also that Trial 1 does not have file object versions for "converter.py", "atlas-x.ppm", and "atlas-x.jpg" because file object versions refer to the state of files at their access and Trial 1 did not access these files. Equivalently, there is no file object version for "atlas-x.gif" at Trial 2, since Trial 2 did not access it. Moreover, we can observe that both trials accessed the same file object version of "external.py" and "anatomy1.img" and that the user edited "experiment.py" after Trial 1. The logical object, on the other hand, has a single and unique version on each trial, since it contains runtime data such as function activations, start and finish times, variable values, etc. This kind of data is already time-sensitive, not demanding an extra layer of versioning.

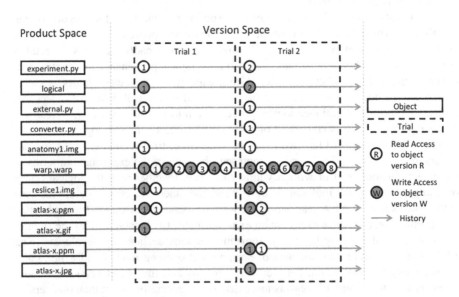

Fig. 1. Version model example

As mentioned before, users can use trial versions to restore states of the experiment. The main goal when restoring a trial is for reproducing it. For this reason, restoring Trial 1 would only restore the files "experiment.py", "external.py", and "anatomy1.img" (all at version 1). In addition, it would remove "warp.warp", "reslice1.img", "atlas-x. pgm", and "atlas-x.gif", because these files did not exist prior to Trial 1. However, restoring Trial 2 would restore "experiment.py" (at version 2), "external.py" (at version 1), "converter.py" (at version 1), "anatomy1.img" (at version 1), "warp.warp" (at version 4), "reslice1.img" (at version 1), and "atlas-x.pgm" (at version 1); and it would remove "atlas-x.ppm" and "atlas-x.jpg". Note that it would not touch "atlas-x.gif", since Trial 2 has not accessed it. Note also that it would restore "warp.warp", "reslice1.img", "atlas-x. pgm" because the state of these files before Trial 2 is equal to the state after Trial 1.

Trial versions not only identify the state of an experiment, but also track its evolution. In the example of Fig. 1 we can see that Trial 2 is an evolution of Trial 1, because it was an execution of "experiment.py" after Trial 1. If the user executes a new script, "experiment2.py" (that is in the same directory as "experiment.py"), she would have a new trial, with version 3, but it would not be an evolution of Trial 2. However, if she executes again "experiment.py", she would have Trial 4 based on Trial 2.

We also provide a special type of trial version to avoid losses on the restore operation. If a user changes the content of "experiment.py" but instead of running a new trial using the modified script, she restores Trial 2, she would lose all changes. To avoid these losses, we create a special "backup" trial with the current content of all file objects in the last version (i.e., file objects edited after Trial 4). In this case, we would have Trial 5 as a backup trial, with contents of "experiment.py", "external.py", "converter.py", "anatomy1.img", "warp.warp", "reslice1.img", "atlas-x.pgm", "atras-x. ppm", and "atlas-x.jpg". At least one of these files should be different from the ones of Trial 4 for the backup trial to be created.

After restoring Trial 2, if a user runs Trial 6, it would be based on Trial 2. We keep track of this information by storing the base version of each trial. Before Trial 6, we had the base version restored to 2. After running Trial 6, we update the base version to 6. This allows our version model to track the evolution in a non-linear way. In fact, by considering the evolution of "experiment.py", as presented in Fig. 2, it is possible to see two *branches* of Trial 2: one that goes from Trial 2 to Trial 4, and another that goes from Trial 2 to Trial 6. A branch is a sequence of trials that were executed in parallel to other sequences of trials. Branches can have either a common ancestor to other branch or no ancestor at all. In this case, Trial 2 is the common ancestor of both branches, and Trial 4 and 5 belong to the same branch.

Figure 2 presents an evolution history bigger than what we described so far. In the figure, Trials 1, 2, 4, 5, 6, and 7 are related to "experiment.py" and Trials 3, 8, 9, and 10

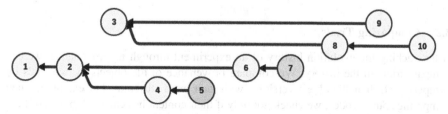

Fig. 2. Evolution history. Nodes represent trial versions (Color figure online)

are related to "experiment2.py". We represent trials that did not finish (i.e., halted due to an error) as red nodes and backup trials as yellow nodes. According to the Figure, Trial 7 did not finish and Trial 5 is a backup trial. In addition, after getting an error on "experiment.py" execution (i.e., Trial 7), the user executed "experiment2.py" (Trial 8). Then she restored Trial 3 and executed "experiment2.py" again, creating a new branch. Finally, she restored Trial 8 and executed "experiment2.py", generating Trial 10.

Note that we have two branches of "experiment.py" and two branches of "experiment2.py" in the end. Users can use branches to try different processes for their experiments and to execute their experiment on the same code base, but with different input files or parameters.

Figure 3 presents an UML representation of our version model. The gray classes, *FileObject* and *LogicalObject*, belong to the product space. The white classes, *FileObjectVersion, LogicalObjectVersion, TrialVersion, RestoreVersion, SourceCode Version,* and *FileAccessVersion*, belong to the version space. Note that a *TrialVersion* has one or more *FileObjectVersion*. This composition represents all file object versions accessed (read or written) in a trial. However, when restoring a trial version, only a subset of them is actually overwritten. We identify these by the RestoreVersion association class. Note also that a trial version always has at least one file object version (and corresponding file object): its main script.

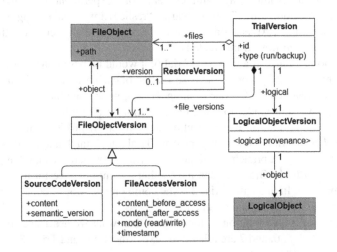

Fig. 3. UML representation of the version model

3.2   Comparing Trials

After tracking the evolution history of an experiment through its provenance, we can compare trials in the history. We compare provenance of file objects in two trials by comparing all their file object versions, with their extra attributes. For example, when comparing source codes, we check not only if their content has changed, but also if the declared version has changed. This way, we can identify that a module content has changed because the user upgraded it from version "1.0.1" to "1.0.2". During the comparison of changes, we ignore attributes that are always different, such as the moment of opening input and output files.

In addition to reporting changes on file object versions that exist in both trials, we also report file objects that exist in the first trial but do not exist in the second one as *removals* and file objects that exist in the second trial but do not exist in the first one as *additions*. Hence, when we compare Trial 1 and Trial 2 of Fig. 1, we have "atlas-x.gif" as a removal, because Trial 2 did not access it. We also have "converter.py", "atlas-x.jpg", and "atlas-x.ppm" as additions because only Trial 2 accessed these files. Finally, we have "experiment.py" as a change, because it has changed to import "converter.py".

In the previous example, we also have the former versions of "warp.warp", "reslice1.img", and "atlas-x.pgm" (the ones on Trial 1) as removals; and the later versions of the same files (the ones on Trial 2) as additions. This occurs because input and output files can have more than one state (file object version) during a trial and it is not possible to identify them only by their path. Thus, we identify them considering also their content before and after the access. Since these files did not exist before Trial 1, we identify them as different file objects versions than before Trial 2, as at that moment their content is the last version written on Trial 1 (e.g., content just before version 5 of "warp.warp" is its content at version 4).

As our version model groups the entire logical provenance in a special object (the logical object), comparing it is specific for each implementation. Thus, we describe our logical provenance comparison in Sect. 4.

4   Implementation in noWorkflow

We implemented the proposed approach on top of noWorkflow [14]. noWorkflow transparently captures provenance from Python scripts by running `now run <script>`. After running the script, it creates a unique *trial id* to identify the collected provenance and stores the provenance in two databases: a content database for storing file objects and a relational database for storing logical objects and metadata of file objects. noWorkflow uses hash codes to associate metadata of file objects in the relational database to their actual content in the content database.

noWorkflow captures the main script, imported modules, and file accesses as *file object provenance*. As *logical provenance*, noWorkflow captures trial start time, finish time, command line, success status (i.e., indication if the trial finished successfully), environment variables, function activations (calls) with parameters, returned values, duration, caller, variables, and variable dependencies.

We support restoring previous trial versions through the command `now restore <trial_id>`. This command restores the trial version as described in Sect. 3.1. Even though noWorkflow captures source code of external modules, this command only restores local modules to avoid breaking the Python installation. It is possible to filter the restore command to restore only the main experiment script, input files, or local modules.

For visualizing the evolution history, we offer the command `now history`. It supports filtering by experiment script or trial status (e.g., finished, unfinished, or backup).

Trials can be compared by the command now diff <trial_id1> <trial_id2>. This command has options to specify what should be compared. For instance, -f compares file access to input and output files. We use the techniques described in Sect. 3.2 to compare file objects. For comparing equality of contents, we use only hash codes, instead of looking for all differences within files. To understand differences between file object versions, users can run external diff tools over the file versions. The diff command also compares logical provenance. Since most trials have at least start time, finish time, command line, and success status as logical provenance, we always compare these attributes when running this command. With the option -e, we support comparison of environment attributes (i.e., part of logical provenance) through a similar process that identifies changes, additions, and removals. Figure 4 presents an excerpt of a brief diff between file accesses from Trial 1 and 2. Note that before presenting file access diff, it presents the diff of these attributes.

```
$ now diff 1 2 -f --brief
[now] trial diff:
  Start changed from 2016-02-11 04:49:09.008354
                  to 2016-02-11 04:49:09.898675
  Finish changed from 2016-02-11 04:49:09.536409
                  to 2016-02-11 04:49:10.276422
  Duration text changed from 0:00:00.528055 to 0:00:00.377747
  Code hash changed from cd1be11a2308ab217327a7d361138cb7f6c25106
                    to 2f637ec102961a7677e3f629ab88612d8875f04f
  Parent id changed from <None> to 1

[now] Brief file access diff
[Additions]              | [Removals]                | [Changes]
(rb) atlax-x.ppm         | (w) atlax-x.gif (new)     |
(w) atlax-x.jpg (new)    | (w) atlax-x.pgm (new)     |
(w) atlax-x.pgm          | (w) reslice1.img (new)    |
(w) atlax-x.ppm (new)    | (wb) warp.warp (new)      |
(w) reslice1.hdr         | ...                       |
(wb) warp.warp           |                           |
...                      |                           |
```

Fig. 4. Brief diff between file access from Trial 1 and 2

The process of comparing function activations is a bit more complex. First, noWorkflow exports function activations of both trials to a graph format. Next, it transforms both graphs into lists of nodes. Then, it applies the longest common subsequence (LCS) algorithm [9] over the lists. Finally, it recombines nodes into a graph that displays common nodes, additions, and removals. The idea behind using LCS is that activations are in sequence and the generated graph keeps the activation order at some degree. Thus, it is possible to use the LCS and match common nodes.

Currently, we do not compare function activations with the diff command. For comparing them, we provide a visualization tool that can be accessed by running the command now vis. The visualization tool also presents the history graphically (shown in Fig. 2). It is also possible to use Jupyter Notebook to visualize the diff and history [17].

Figure 5 presents activation graphs of Trial 1 and Trial 2 and their comparison. Nodes represent function activations and their colors represent their duration in a traffic light scale, where red fills represent the slowest activations and green fills represent the fastest ones. The trial script is an activation itself and it is pointed out by a straight arrow. In this case, "experiment.py" is the trial script. In the graph, black arrows represent the start of activations; blue arrows represent sequence of calls within activations; and dashed arrows represent returns. In the graph comparison, nodes and arrows with black borders exist in both trials; nodes and arrows with red borders exist only on Trial 1; and nodes and arrows with green borders exist only on Trial 2. Note that "convert" activations exist only on Trial 1, while "pgmtoppm" and "pnmtojpeg" activations exist only on Trial 2. Trial 2 has also an activation representing the import "convert.py". Moreover, nodes that exist in both trials show colors side-by-side to easy comparison. For instance, one can easily notice that slice_convert was slightly faster in Trial 1 than in Trial 2.

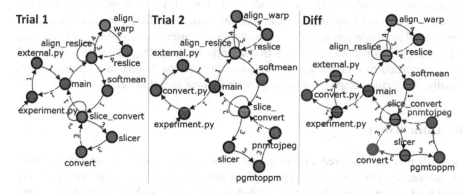

Fig. 5. Activation graphs of Trial 1 and 2, and their comparison (Color figure online)

5   Evaluation

We evaluate our approach by presenting how noWorkflow answers the questions related to provenance evolution listed in Sect. 1. We answered those questions using the example described in Sect. 3.1. This example is in fact the workflow of the first Provenance Challenge implemented in Python with procedures implemented as "dummies". The full history of this experiment can be obtained on noWorkflow by running now demo 3.

Q1: if a scientist has executed an experiment twice, but has replaced some procedures in the second trial, what are the trial differences? Q2: comparing multiple executions according to their parameters, what are the differences on execution behavior? Figure 5 presents the comparison of Trial 1 and Trial 2 activation graphs. It is possible to see that "convert" was replaced by "pgmtoppm" and "pnmtojpeg". To compare execution behaviors according to parameters, we can compare trials that share the same code base, but have different parameters.

Q3: how differences in the input data relate to differences in the values? We can use the now diff -f command to compare file accesses of trials (as shown in Fig. 4). This command compares input data, output data, and arguments. Thus, it is possible to get the differences on inputs, and compare them to output values by restoring them.

Q4: using historical provenance, which parts of the execution fail frequently? A SQL query can look for failures on all trials. If we specify that the return value "−1" of a function activation represents a failure, the following query would return the most frequent failures on all trials combined:

```
SELECT name, count(name) AS c FROM function_activation
WHERE return_value = "-1" GROUP BY name ORDER BY c DESC;
```

Q5: which trials are related to a given trial? Q6. a given trial was derived from which trial? Q7. what are the available trials, and what are their durations? Q8. how many trials are associated to a given source code? Q9. how many trials present failures? Looking at the Evolution History (as shown in Fig. 2), it is possible to see both the ancestor of a given trial and all trials that derive from it. The evolution history also presents all available graphs. To get their duration, a user can activate tooltips on now vis or Jupyter Notebook and access trial information, including its duration. To get all trials associated to a given source code, we can filter the history to a specific script. Finally, the history graph presents trials with failures as red nodes.

6 Conclusion

In this paper, we presented a novel approach for tracking and analyzing the evolution of provenance collected from scripts. With our approach, a scientist can precisely record all provenance information related to each trial, switch between trials and adapt/reproduce specific trials, and compare trials. We implemented our approach as an extension to *noWorkflow*, which is available as open source software at https://github.com/gems-uff/noworkflow.

While the proposed version model is suitable for any tool that collect multiple versions of files during the execution of a trial, it may impact the execution time of experiments. This occurs because our version model requires the collection to be performed at runtime, reading file contents multiple times during a trial. Additionally, our current implementation captures and stores provenance versions at fine-grain. On the one hand, this provides a powerful support for further analysis. On the other hand, this is known to compromise scalability in terms of execution time and storage space [15]. In particular, storing many different versions of fine-grained data can be wasteful in some cases. This motivates the need for optimization techniques that attempt to balance storage and re-computation costs. We plan to address this issue in the future. Another limitation of the implementation is that we restore only local modules during the restore operation. If the user updates an external module, the experiment reproduction may produce different results. We intend to use virtual environments to avoid this issue.

We also intend to explore alternatives on detecting file object changes, and to work on better algorithms to compare activation graphs. We already started looking for existing graph matching techniques [10]. Additionally, we plan to work on a semantic versioning for trials that encodes the intention of evolution, and to improve *logical provenance* comparison on noWorkflow to compare not only activation graphs and environment variables, but also variables, variable dependencies, parameters, and return values on activations. Finally, we foresee the elaboration of different formats for provenance visualization that would help on comparing trials.

References

1. Altintas, I., et al.: Kepler: an extensible system for design and execution of scientific workflows. In: International Conference on Scientific and Statistical Database Management (SSDBM), Santorini, Greece, pp. 423–424 (2004)
2. Angelino, E., Yamins, D., Seltzer, M.: StarFlow: a script-centric data analysis environment. In: McGuinness, D.L., Michaelis, J.R., Moreau, L. (eds.) IPAW 2010. LNCS, vol. 6378, pp. 236–250. Springer, Heidelberg (2010)
3. Bochner, C., Gude, R., Schreiber, A.T.: A python library for provenance recording and querying. In: Freire, J., Koop, D., Moreau, L. (eds.) IPAW 2008. LNCS, vol. 5272, pp. 229–240. Springer, Heidelberg (2008)
4. Callahan, S.P., et al.: VisTrails: visualization meets data management. In: ACM SIGMOD, Chicago, USA, pp. 745–747 (2006)
5. Collberg, C., et al.: A system for graph-based visualization of the evolution of software. In: ACM Symposium on Software Visualization (SoftVis), New York, NY, USA, p. 77–ff (2003)
6. Conradi, R., Westfechtel, B.: Version models for software configuration management. ACM Comput. Surv. **30**(2), 232–282 (1998)
7. Davison, A.P.: Automated capture of experiment context for easier reproducibility in computational research. Comput. Sci. Eng. **14**(4), 48–56 (2012)
8. Freire, J., et al.: Provenance for computational tasks: a survey. Comput. Sci. Eng. **10**(3), 11–21 (2008)
9. Hunt, J.W., Szymanski, T.G.: A fast algorithm for computing longest common subsequences. Commun. ACM **20**(5), 350–353 (1977)
10. Koop, D., et al.: Visual summaries for graph collections. In: IEEE Pacific Visualization Symposium (PacificVis), pp. 57–64 (2013)
11. Lerner, B.S., Boose, E.R.: Collecting provenance in an interactive scripting environment. In: Workshop on the Theory and Practice of Provenance (TaPP), Cologne, Germany (2014)
12. Mattoso, M., et al.: Towards supporting the life cycle of large scale scientific experiments. Int. J. Bus. Process Integr. Manag. **5**(1), 79–92 (2010)
13. McPhillips, T., et al.: YesWorkflow: a user-oriented, language-independent tool for recovering workflow information from scripts. Int. J. Digit. Curation **10**, 1 (2015)
14. Murta, L., Braganholo, V., Chirigati, F., Koop, D., Freire, J.: noWorkflow: capturing and analyzing provenance of scripts. In: Ludaescher, B., Plale, B. (eds.) IPAW 2014. LNCS, vol. 8628, pp. 71–83. Springer, Heidelberg (2015)
15. Murta, L.G.P., et al.: Odyssey-SCM: an integrated software configuration management infrastructure for UML models. Sci. Comput. Program. **65**(3), 249–274 (2007)
16. Pimentel, J.F., et al.: Fine-grained provenance collection over scripts through program slicing. In: Mattoso, M., Glavic, B. (eds.) IPAW 2016. LNCS, vol. 9672, pp. 199–203. Springer, Heidelberg (2016)

17. Pimentel, J.F.N., et al.: Collecting and analyzing provenance on interactive notebooks: when IPython meets noWorkflow. In: Workshop on the Theory and Practice of Provenance (TaPP), Edinburgh, Scotland (2015)
18. Stamatogiannakis, M., Groth, P., Bos, H.: Looking inside the black-box: capturing data provenance using dynamic instrumentation. In: Ludaescher, B., Plale, B. (eds.) IPAW 2014. LNCS, vol. 8628, pp. 155–167. Springer, Heidelberg (2015)
19. Tariq, D., et al.: Towards automated collection of application-level data provenance. In: Workshop on the Theory and Practice of Provenance (TaPP), Boston, MA, USA (2012)

Trade-Offs in Automatic Provenance Capture

Manolis Stamatogiannakis[1(✉)], Hasanat Kazmi[2], Hashim Sharif[2],
Remco Vermeulen[1], Ashish Gehani[2], Herbert Bos[1], and Paul Groth[3]

[1] Computer Science Institute, Vrije Universiteit Amsterdam,
Amsterdam, The Netherlands
{manolis.stamatogiannakis,r.vermeulen,h.j.bos}@vu.nl
[2] SRI International, Menlo Park, USA
{hasanat.kazmi,hashim.sharif,ashish.gehani}@sri.com
[3] Elsevier Labs, Amsterdam, The Netherlands
p.groth@elsevier.com

Abstract. Automatic provenance capture from arbitrary applications is
a challenging problem. Different approaches to tackle this problem have
evolved, most notably *a. system-event trace analysis*, *b. compile-time
static instrumentation*, and *c.* taint flow analysis using *dynamic binary
instrumentation*. Each of these approaches offers different trade-offs in
terms of the granularity of captured provenance, integration requirements, and runtime overhead. While these aspects have been discussed
separately, a systematic and detailed study, quantifying and elucidating
them, is still lacking. To fill this gap, we begin to explore these trade-offs
for representative examples of these approaches for automatic provenance capture by means of evaluation and measurement. We base our
evaluation on UnixBench—a widely used benchmark suite within systems research. We believe this approach will make our results easier to
compare with future studies.

Keywords: Provenance · SPADE · Taint tracking · LLVM · Strace

1 Introduction

Automated provenance capture systems[1] which collect provenance information
with minimal or no modification to a given application are important solutions
for tracking and exposing provenance [4]. Mainly, they reduce the need for software to be re-engineered specifically for provenance. Additionally, they can capture more complete provenance as instrumentation can be done both broadly
(e.g., across every application) and deeply (e.g., within the application itself).
Automated provenance capture is complementary to disclosed provenance systems such as workflow management systems, version control systems, or databases, which require active engineering of the software to enable them to capture
provenance [4].

The original version of this chapter was revised.

An erratum to this chapter can be found at 10.1007/978-3-319-40593-3_29

[1] These are sometimes termed OS level provenance systems.

© Springer International Publishing Switzerland 2016
M. Mattoso and B. Glavic (Eds.): IPAW 2016, LNCS 9672, pp. 29–41, 2016.
DOI: 10.1007/978-3-319-40593-3_3

There are number of different methods for automated provenance collection with varying trade-offs in requirements (e.g., the availability of source code), impact on application performance, granularity of provenance collected, and level of instrumentation required. The aim of this paper is to investigate these trade-offs. In particular, we compare three representative methods—system-event trace analysis, compile-time static instrumentation, and dynamic binary instrumentation—using their implementations for SRI's open source SPADEv2 [9] provenance middleware.

Our analysis is based on UnixBench [20], a widely used benchmark suite. We are aware that UnixBench emphasizes on performance of system calls and is not meant as a comprehensive performance benchmark. However, we believe that the results produced by it are still relevant for the evaluation of automatic provenance collection: Most such systems [3,8,12,18] tap (one way or another) into information derived from system calls. This is also true for the three systems we study (see Sect. 3). For this, supplemented with knowledge of specific features and requirements of a workload, the results produced by UnixBench can be used as input to decide on the suitability of a particular provenance collection method or system.

To the best of our knowledge, this is the first paper to comparatively benchmark provenance systems using a common systems benchmark. The need for exactly such benchmarks in provenance systems has been highlighted by the ProvBench series of workshops[2]. We discuss further steps towards the standardization of provenance benchmarks in Sect. 6. Standardized benchmarks are essential to provide a baseline for comparing iterations of the The contributions of this paper are as follows:

- A systematic comparison of three automated provenance capture systems using the UnixBench benchmark suite.
- An examination of the trade-offs when using these three methods.

The rest of this paper is organized as follows, we begin with a description of the evaluation platform and the three systems used. Experimental results are then presented. This is followed with a discussion of those results and their implications. Finally, we present future work and conclude.

2 Evaluation Platform

In this section, we discuss the framework we use for the evaluation, as well as some implementation details for the three fundamentally different methods of automated provenance capture we study.

2.1 SPADE

The SPADEv2 [9] provenance middleware aims to track the provenance of data that arises from multiple sources, possibly distributed over the wide area, and at

---

[2] https://sites.google.com/site/provbench/.

varied levels of abstraction. Our choice of the SPADEv2 middleware was motivated by a number of factors. First, SPADEv2 has a modular design, allowing most of its provenance filtering, storage, and query infrastructure to be used regardless of the instrumentation approach. Second, the distribution includes a number of *reporter* modules, each of which can be used to collect provenance using a different methodology. As a result, we can easily plug the different methods of instrumentation for our comparison while benefiting from SPADEv2's infrastructures. Third, the system supports storage of provenance in a number of data formats, including queryable ones such as the Neo4j graph database and the H2 (or any JDBC-compliant) SQL database. Fourth, the SPADEv2 platform can be configured and managed with a control utility. This allows an analysis to be repeatably executed (in order to measure behavior over multiple runs).

It is worth noting that the results of collecting provenance from the same program on different operating systems may differ substantially in runtime and storage overhead. Our comparisons have all been performed on Linux (see also Sect. 2.3).

2.2 Provenance Collection Methods and Reporters

In our experiments, we used implementations of three representative methods for automatic (i.e., non-disclosed) provenance capture: *a.* system-event trace analysis, *b.* compile-time static instrumentation, and *c.* instruction-level dynamic instrumentation An overview of the properties of these methods is presented in Table 1. We now present the details of the specific SPADEv2 reporters we used that implement these methods. It is important to emphasize that the implementations of the three methods used in this evaluation are not necessarily the best or the fastest, but they serve as representative examples. For instance, it may be that a highly optimized taint analysis solution improves the performance of instruction-level dynamic instrumentation significantly, but the performance gap with compile-time solutions would most likely remain.

Table 1. Overview of provenance collection methods properties.

	System call analysis	Static, compile-time instrumentation	Dynamic, instruction-level instrumentation
Integration effort	Easy	Medium	Easy
Prov. granularity[a]	File-level	Function-level	Byte-level
Analysis scope	Process and children	Process, no dyn. lib	Process and children
False positives	Many	Depends on configured scope	Negligible, tracks use of individual bytes
Execution overhead	Depends on the size of program I/O	Depends on the number of function calls	High, depends on the taint tag type used
Reporter	strace reporter	LLVMTrace	DataTracker

[a] We use concrete rather than relative terms to describe the granularity of provenance. This is because in different application domains, a relative term (e.g. "fine-grained") may refer to different granularities.

System-Event Trace: Strace Reporter. This first method for collecting data provenance treats the monitored program as a black box. By watching its interaction with the operating system, the method infers the set of artifacts that the program uses and generates.

The implementation we use monitors such interaction with the strace tool, which is available for Linux and Android. strace uses the *ptrace* facility available in Unix-like operating systems to learn which system calls (along with their arguments) are made by the program being monitored for provenance collection.

While tapping on strace simplifies the implementation of the reporter, it comes at a high cost because strace pauses the process twice for each system call. In order to avoid unnecessary overhead, strace reporter configures strace so that only the subset of system calls related to data flow are traced. Even after that performance may still be degraded for system-call heavy workloads.

The output of strace is parsed to generate the appropriate Open Provenance Model (OPM) [17] provenance elements.[3] Doing so imposes an additional overhead, compared to an implementation building directly upon the *ptrace* facility. The particular OPM elements generated are: *a. Process* elements for the operating system analog, *b. Artifact* elements for the files read or written, *c. Used* or *WasGeneratedBy* edges (depending on the use of the files), and *d. WasTriggeredBy* edges when one process creates another.

Compile-Time Solutions: LLVMTrace. The second approach for provenance capture is to instrument programs at compile time. Since a compilation of the application is required to enable provenance collection, compile-time solutions come closest to disclosed provenance capture techniques. However, no manual adaptation of the software is required.

Here, we use LLVMTrace as our representative implementation. It tracks intra-program data flows, providing a more precise dependency analysis. LLVM-Trace utilizes the LLVM framework [14] to automatically add provenance instrumentation to applications at compile-time, using a custom compiler optimization pass [22]. The instrumentation is added at the entry and exit of each function call and logs its name, arguments, return value, and the thread that invoked it. Thus, LLVMTrace enables us to record the trace of function calls that occur during program execution. While this analysis obviously does not extend to dynamic libraries (see analysis scope in Table 1), compile-time library interposition is used to intercept and log calls to libc functions.

The produced logs are parsed in order to produce OPM provenance elements: *a. Process* elements are generated for each function call, *b. Artifact* elements are used to represent the function call arguments and return value, *c. Used* edges are used to associate a function with its argument, and *d. WasGeneratedBy* edges are used for return values.

Thread-specific attributes are added to each provenance element, in order to to separate recorded activity from different threads into individual paths in the resulting provenance graph. The transformation from the function call trace to

---

[3] OPM can then be easily converted to the W3C PROV recommendation [11].

the provenance representation only captures *direct* data flows. Other types of information flow (e.g. use of shared buffers) are not captured.

Dynamic Instruction-Level Solution: DataTracker. DataTracker [21] is a tool that captures provenance using *Dynamic Taint Analysis* (DTA). The analysis is applied as *Dynamic Binary Instrumentation* (DBI) using the Intel Pin [15] and libdft [13] frameworks. DataTracker adds instrumentation which determines how the application uses the data as it executes. This allows the tool to strongly reduce the number of false positives in the captured provenance compared to methods based on heuristics—albeit at a high cost. Like system-events based solutions, DBI has the benefit that provenance can be collected directly from unmodified binaries, without requiring development effort to make applications provenance-aware.

The type of taint metadata used by DataTracker is configurable. In [21], sets of $<file\,descriptor,\,offset>$ pairs are used for tracking the provenance of each memory location. In this work, we instead opted to use *bitsets*—where each bit represents a file descriptor. We made this change because the implementation of `std::set` in `libstdc++` proved very inefficient in practice. The research of data structures that will enable DTA to track each input byte individually, while offering reasonable performance, is an open problem.

We used SPADEv2's *Domain-Specific Language Reporter* [9] (DSL reporter) to integrate DataTracker with SPADEv2. DSL reporter is middleware to allow the quick integration of new provenance sources with the SPADEv2 kernel. A converter transforms DataTracker's intermediate provenance representation to the OPM-based [17] language of DSL-reporter. The following OPM provenance elements are produced: *a. Process* elements are generated for each tracked OS process, *b. Artifact* are used to represent files and byte ranges[4], *c. Used* edges are used to associate input artifacts with processes, and *d. WasGeneratedBy, WasDerivedFrom* edges are used to associate output byte ranges with processes and input artifacts.

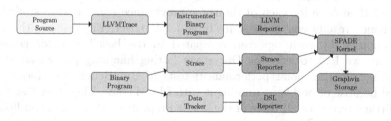

Fig. 1. Provenance collection workflow for the three SPADEv2 reporters.

The integration of the three reporters results in the provenance collection workflow illustrated in Fig. 1. As we are not interested in querying the capture

---

[4] Byte ranges have a `memberof:` field pointing back to the file they come from.

provenance, we used the Graphviz storage backend of SPADEv2. An advantage of this choice is that it makes it easy to extend this work by adding results for the volume of collected provenance. Such information is readily available directly from Graphviz.

2.3 Hardware and OS

We ran our experiments on a machine featuring Intel Xeon E5-2630 CPU, with 6 cores clocked at 2.30 GHz. The machine was configured with 1 GB DDR3 memory module and a SSD storage module with 40 GB capacity. We used 32 bit Ubuntu Linux 14.04.3 LTS to run our experiments. We used GCC 4.8.4 and LLVM 3.6.0 to compile UnixBench. GCC was used for `strace` reporter and DataTracker. LLVM was used for LLVMTrace.

3 Experimental Results

For our experiments, we use the UnixBench [20] benchmark suite. UnixBench was originally developed in 1983 at Monash University. It was adopted and popularized by Byte magazine in the 1990's and updated and revised by many people over the years. It still remains a popular general-purpose benchmark suite for the evaluation of the overall performance of Unix-like systems.

UnixBench is comprised of multiple parts that measure different aspects of a system's performance. Its main focus is to test how a system performs in basic operations such as file I/O, IPC, process creation, and system call invocation. Such operations are often tapped to extract provenance information [3,8,12,18], and thus are relevant to capturing provenance. This is also the case for the three SPADEv2 provenance reporters we study: *a.* `strace` reporter produces provenance solely by analyzing system calls, *b.* LLVMTrace traces the wrapper functions of the system calls, and finally *c.* DataTracker introduces taint when data are read, and logs provenance on writes.

We ran UnixBench first without any provenance reporter running (*baseline*) and then once for each of the three provenance collectors we study. The performance results can be seen in Table 2. Moreover, Fig. 2 shows the slow-down imposed by each reporter, compared to the baseline performance. In our study, we had to skip the Dhrystone (string handling performance) and Whetstone (floating point performance) tests of UnixBench. The former was skipped because of problems running it with LLVMTrace. The latter test would be of little interest, as all three of the studied reporters do not focus on floating point computation. The list of the performed UnixBench tests and a description of what they measure are as follows:

1. **execl-xput:** How fast the current process image can be replaced with a new one, as a result of an `execve` system call.
2. **fcopy-256, fcopy-1024, fcopy-4096:** Speed of a file-to-file copy using different buffer sizes.

3. **pipe-xput, pipe-cs:** Speed of communication over pipes. In the first test, the read and writes on the pipe happen from a single process. In the second test a second process is spawned, so the communication also includes a context switch between the two.
4. **spawn-xput:** A simple `fork-wait` loop to measure how much time is needed to create and then destroy a process.
5. **shell-1, shell-8:** Execution speed for the processing of a data file. The processing is implemented using common unix utilities, wrapped in a shell script. The two tests differ in the number of concurrently executing scripts.
6. **syscall:** System call overhead. The test uses `getpid` to measure this. The specific system call is chosen because it requires minimal in-kernel processing, so its main overhead comes from the switch between kernel and user mode.

Table 2. Performance and index scores for UnixBench tests. Units for ops are as following: *a.* KBps for the fcopy-* tests *b.* loops per minute for the shell-* tests *c.* loops per second for the rest of the tests.

Test	Baseline		Strace		LLVMTrace		DataTracker	
	ops	index	ops	index	ops	index	ops	index
execl-xput	2285.5	531.5	668	155.4	1816.8	422.5	0.8	0.2
fcopy-256	120115.1	725.8	3303.5	20	91354.1	552	3624.7	21.9
fcopy-1024	352158.3	889.3	13133.3	33.2	397054.4	1002.7	7737.1	19.5
fcopy-4096	885101	1526	50492	87.1	954774	1646.2	11025.7	19
pipe-xput	813880.7	654.2	13745.5	11	711530.6	572	27658.9	22.2
pipe-cs	132217.1	330.5	6537.8	16.3	105752.7	264.4	11083.3	27.7
spawn-xput	7525.9	597.3	3229.9	256.3	1.4	0.1	12.2	1
shell-1	3816.4	900.1	1219.8	287.7	2291.3	540.4	2.6	0.6
shell-8	491.1	818.5	166.2	277.1	480.6	801	0.3	0.6
syscall	1140408.8	760.3	8388.9	5.6	695653	463.8	17921.7	11.6
Index Score		**720.8**		**53.3**		**257.8**		**4.6**

4 Discussion of Experimental Results

In Table 1, we presented the overall features of three representative provenance collection methods. After evaluating their performance with UnixBench, we can draw conclusions with regard to the performance trade-offs involved when choosing which provenance method to use.

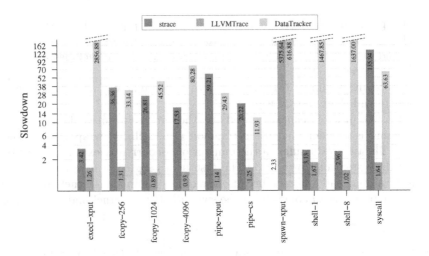

Fig. 2. Slowdown for the individual UnixBench tests.

Integration Effort. The integration effort for using each reporter is associated with the changes required: *a.* for the tracked programs themselves *b.* the platform where the programs run on. There seems to be a correlation between the integration effort required and the runtime overhead of provenance collection. From the studied reports, LLVMTrace requires the most integration effort because each tracked program has to be recompiled from its source. However, it also presents the lowest runtime overhead during provenance collection. On the other hand, strace reporter and DataTracker are the easiest to deploy, requiring no modification to the underlying platform (Linux) and working on unmodified binaries. However, their runtime overhead would be ranked from high to prohibitive. Specifically for system-event tracing, the overhead can easily be reduced if some integration effort is invested to modify the underlying platform. This is the approach taken in [3,18] which impose a very low runtime overhead (<4 %). It should be noted however that these works either exclude the store runtime overhead from performance measurements [18], or use in-memory databases [3] to reduce it.

Provenance Granularity. The UnixBench results appear to be counterintuitive when correlated with the granularity at which each method works. One would expect that system call tracing, which only tracks file-level provenance, would be the method with the lowest overhead. However, this doesn't appear to be the case for the implementations we study. The reason for this are two-fold: *a.* UnixBench focuses on system-call stress-testing, so a method relying on system-call analysis will suffer. *b.* The strace tool was not designed with efficiency in mind. It has to stop the program execution two times for each system call, in order to inspect its arguments and return value. In x86 this translates to trapping the SYSENTER, SYSEXIT instructions, a particularly expensive operation.

Another important observation related to provenance granularity, is that tracking such fine-grained provenance may nullify benefits from batching I/O. This is attested by the fcopy-* tests for DataTracker, where we can see that there is no benefit from using a larger buffer size. This can be explained by the fact that irrespective of the buffer size, DataTracker has to individually update/log the metadata from all the memory locations.

False Positives. False positives are highly undesirable when collecting any type of data. Their presence degrades the value of a dataset. Provenance is no exception to this. However, as our measurements showed, in the case of provenance reducing false positives to very low levels comes at a significant runtime cost. Thus, in cases where false positives can be tolerated or easily filtered-out later, faster methods should be preferred.

In principle, provenance-based false positives originate from the fact that we treat software components as black-boxes and try to "guess" the provenance relations they produce. When a bad guess is made, a false positive is generated. DTA (as implemented by DataTracker), on the other hand, is a "track everything" attempt to see how those software black-boxes use the data, thus eliminating the need for guessing. In cases where the functionality of a software module is well known, this approach is clearly overkill. Recent efforts [16] attempt to eliminate this trade-off by switching between DTA and lightweight logging.

Analysis Scope. Not extending the scope of analysis to dynamic libraries, as LLVMTrace does, may appear as a limitation at first blush. However, it turns out that usually, this is a reasonable trade-off. This is because dynamic libraries usually have well-known behavior, which makes it possible to keep runtime overhead low by not tracking the internals of the library while still producing accurate provenance. This could be problematic however in programs that have pushed functionality into dynamic libraries. This is a quite common design strategy for many web-browsers. In that case, specific dynamic libraries have to also be recompiled to include provenance instrumentation. This choice represents a potential trade-off between the analysis scope and the ease of integration.

Overall, we see that when selecting a provenance system, there are key trade-offs between the extent of instrumentation both from a breadth and depth perspective and the resulting performance. We suggest that, when quick deployment is of importance, system event tracing is a good choice. Depending on whether the deployment will be permanent or not, one may choose to invest on deploying tools like Hi-Fi [18] or LPM [3] instead of using the tool used in our study. On the other hand, compile-time instrumentation can combine good performance with potentially less false positives for applications where the source code is available. The reduced false positives is a result of tracking provenance at a finer granularity than system events analysis. However, the effort required to properly apply compile-time instrumentation may become substantial for programs that use multiple dynamic libraries. Finally, the overhead added by DataTracker is prohibitive for time-critical applications. For this, it is best reserved for special cases. E.g. if one is interested in understanding the provenance produced by legacy applications (no source code, little/no documentation), tools like Data-Tracker may help identify properties that are masked by tools operating on a higher level.

5   Related Work

Performance and overhead of provenance capture systems has been identified as an important topic for the adoption of provenance systems. In their provenance primer [5], Carata et al. identify two dimensions of overhead: *a.* temporal overhead, which is the focus of this work, and *b.* spatial overhead, which is associated with the cost of storing the captured provenance. An important observation they make, is that the available data about performance of provenance capture systems are *not directly comparable*. This calls for the standardization of some benchmarks which can be used to have comparable results for future systems.

In general, it seems there is more interest in the spatial aspect of provenance overhead. Simmhan et al. [19] include only spatial overhead as a dimension in their provenance taxonomy. The ProvBench [1] effort focuses on collecting reference traces to help assess provenance storage and query processing time. Firth and Missier [7] have proposed to synthetically create provenance graphs. Similar efforts would help to also get better understanding of provenance collection runtime overheads.

This focus on spatial overhead could be partially explained by the fact that for many disclosed provenance systems, the runtime overhead is already low [5]. Glavic [10] observes that provenance can be intensive both in terms of computation and required storage. Moreover, he notes that by using DTA to capture fine-grained provenance (similar to DataTracker), one can generate a very large volume of provenance data from a small set of input files. So, provenance collection can be used as a benchmark workload for Big Data.

Finally, we note that we use only three implementations of automatic provenance capture methods. There are many other implementations such as PASS [12], ES3 [8], OPUS [2], Hi-Fi [18], Linux Provenance Modules [3] and PLUS [6]. Each of these systems has there own optimizations and capabilities for provenance. However, we believe the methods described here are broadly representative of these approaches.

6   Future Work and Conclusion

6.1   Future Work

In this work, we focus on exploring trade-offs related to the performance of provenance capture. There are many opportunities for future work. Here, we focus on those opportunities to do with further benchmarking.

Non-performance Trade-Offs. The community has shown interest in issues related to the storage and querying of captured provenance (see Sect. 5). So we believe that it would be interesting to include measurements about the storage required by each provenance capture method. Another systems-related aspect that would be of interest is the memory requirements of each approach. Having low-memory requirements becomes important in shared environments (e.g. virtualized servers or multi-purpose server boxes).

Comprehensive Benchmarking. As we have already mentioned, UnixBench puts emphasis on the system call performance. However, in many real-life workloads system calls account only for a fraction of the execution time. To achieve a more comprehensive evaluation, more types of benchmarks should be used. We initially had planned to use selected Coreutils[5] as micro-benchmarks to complement the results of UnixBench in this work. Coreutils include small data manipulation programs with well-understood behavior, which may also include substantial computation in the user-space. However, due to time constraints, we had to defer their publication. Another option would be to use a set of more complex programs as the basis for comparing provenance tools and methods. E.g. [18] uses the compilation of the Linux kernel as a benchmark and the Postmark mail server benchmark. In addition to that, [3] uses the BLAST benchmark which is based on biological sequencing. Using larger benchmark suites should also be investigated. However, it is not necessary that all tests in a benchmark suite will be suitable for benchmarking provenance capture. E.g. the SPEC benchmark makes heavy use of interpreted programs.

Qualitative Benchmarks. Another aspect of provenance capture is the quality of the produced provenance. In order to assess a method or tool with regard to its quality, we need an established ground truth against which we compare. If we know the ground truth for a given set of tasks, then we can calculate the precision/recall of each compared method and rank them accordingly. Disclosed provenance systems could be used to establish a ground truth for qualitative benchmarks of non-disclosed tools and methods. Another option would be to use tools like DataTracker which are not prone to false positives and can produce fine-grained provenance.

6.2   Conclusion

In this paper, we studied the performance of three methods for automated provenance capture, as implemented for the SPADEv2 provenance middleware. We used UnixBench, a widely used benchmark, focusing mostly on performance of system calls. As UnixBench does not include adequate variety of workloads, our presented results are clearly not enough to fully evaluate the performance of the

---

[5] GNU Coreutils: http://www.gnu.org/software/coreutils/.

studied methods. However, we believe that the trade-offs we present can still provide some insights on the suitability of the methods for capturing provenance of specific workloads. More importantly, we consider this work as a first step for the systematic and multi-faceted performance evaluation of provenance capture systems. Having such information will provide a baseline for the concrete assessment of improvements in future provenance capture methods and systems.

Acknowledgments. This material is based upon work supported by the National Science Foundation under Grant IIS-1116414. Any opinions, findings, and conclusions or recommendations expressed in this material are those of the authors and do not necessarily reflect the views of the National Science Foundation.

References

1. ProvBench: A Provenance Repository for Benchmarking (2013). https://github.com/provbench. Accessed Feb 2016
2. Balakrishnan, N., Bytheway, T., Sohan, R., Hopper, A.: OPUS: a lightweight system for observational provenance in user space. In: Proceedings of USENIX TaPP 2013, Lombard, IL, USA, April 2013
3. Bates, A., Tian, D., Butler, K.R.B., Moyer, T.: Trustworthy whole-system provenance for the Linux Kernel. In: Proceedings of USENIX SEC 2015, Washington, DC, USA, August 2015
4. Braun, U., Garfinkel, S.L., Holland, D.A., Muniswamy-Reddy, K.-K., Seltzer, M.I.: Issues in automatic provenance collection. In: Moreau, L., Foster, I. (eds.) IPAW 2006. LNCS, vol. 4145, pp. 171–183. Springer, Heidelberg (2006)
5. Carata, L., Akoush, S., Balakrishnan, N., Bytheway, T., Sohan, R., Seltzer, M., Hopper, A.: A primer on provenance. ACM Queue **12**(3), 10:10–10:23 (2014)
6. Chapman, A., Blaustein, B.T., Seligman, L., Allen, M.D.: PLUS: a provenance manager for integrated information. In: Proceedings of IEEE IRI 2011, Las Vegas, NV, USA, August 2011
7. Firth, H., Missier, P.: ProvGen: generating synthetic PROV graphs with predictable structure. In: Ludaescher, B., Plale, B. (eds.) IPAW 2014. LNCS, vol. 8628, pp. 16–27. Springer, Heidelberg (2015)
8. Frew, J., Metzger, D., Slaughter, P.: Automatic capture and reconstruction of computational provenance. Concurr. Comput.: Pract. Exp. **20**(5), 485–496 (2008)
9. Gehani, A., Tariq, D.: SPADE: Support for Provenance Auditing in Distributed Environments. In: Narasimhan, P., Triantafillou, P. (eds.) Middleware 2012. LNCS, vol. 7662, pp. 101–120. Springer, Heidelberg (2012)
10. Glavic, B.: Big data provenance: challenges and implications for benchmarking. In: Rabl, T., Poess, M., Baru, C., Jacobsen, H.-A. (eds.) WBDB 2012. LNCS, vol. 8163, pp. 72–80. Springer, Heidelberg (2014)
11. Groth, P., Moreau, L.: PROV-Overview. An Overview of the PROV Family of Documents. W3C Working Group Note NOTE-prov-overview-20130430, W3C. http://www.w3.org/TR/2013/NOTE-prov-overview-20130430/
12. Holland, D.A., Seltzer, M.I., Braun, U., Muniswamy-Reddy, K.K.: PASSing the provenance challenge. Concurr. Comput.: Pract. Exp. **20**(5), 531–540 (2008)
13. Kemerlis, V.P., Portokalidis, G., Jee, K., Keromytis, A.D.: libdft: practical dynamic data flow tracking for commodity systems. In: Proceedings of VEE 2012, London, UK, March 2012

14. Lattner, C., Adve, V.: LLVM: a compilation framework for lifelong program analysis & transformation. In: Proceedings of CGO 2004, Palo Alto, CA, USA (2004)
15. Luk, C.K., et al.: Pin: building customized program analysis tools with dynamic instrumentation. In: Proceedings of PLDI 2005, Chicago, IL, USA, June 2005
16. Ma, S., Zhang, X., Xu, D.: ProTracer: towards practical provenance tracing by alternating between logging and tainting. In: Proceedings of NDSS 2016, San Diego, CA, USA, February 2016
17. Moreau, L., et al.: The open provenance model core specification (v1.1). Future Gener. Comput. Syst. **27**(6), 743–756 (2011)
18. Pohly, D.J., McLaughlin, S., McDaniel, P., Butler, K.: Hi-Fi: collecting high-fidelity whole-system provenance. In: Proceedings of ACSAC 2012, Orlando, FL, USA, December 2012
19. Simmhan, Y.L., Plale, B., Gannon, D.: A survey of data provenance in e-Science. SIGMOD Rec. **34**(3), 31–36 (2005)
20. Smith, B., Lucas, K., et al.: UnixBench: The original BYTE UNIX benchmark suite (2011). https://github.com/kdlucas/byte-unixbench. Accessed Feb 2016
21. Stamatogiannakis, M., Groth, P., Bos, H.: Looking inside the black-box: capturing data provenance using dynamic instrumentation. In: Ludaescher, B., Plale, B. (eds.) IPAW 2014. LNCS, vol. 8628, pp. 155–167. Springer, Heidelberg (2015)
22. Tariq, D., Ali, M., Gehani, A.: Towards automated collection of application-level data provenance. In: Proceedings of USENIX TaPP 2012, Boston, MA, USA (2012)

Analysis of Memory Constrained
Live Provenance

Peng Chen[1]([⊠]), Tom Evans[2], and Beth Plale[1]

[1] School of Informatics and Computing,
Indiana University, Bloomington, USA
{chenpeng,plale}@indiana.edu
[2] Department of Geography, Indiana University,
Bloomington, USA
evans@indiana.edu

Abstract. We conjecture that meaningful analysis of large-scale provenance can be preserved by analyzing provenance data in limited memory
while the data is still in motion; that the provenance needs not be fully
resident before analysis can occur. As a proof of concept, this paper
defines a stream model for reasoning about provenance data in motion
for Big Data provenance. We propose a novel streaming algorithm for the
backward provenance query, and apply it to the live provenance captured
from agent-based simulations. The performance test demonstrates high
throughput, low latency and good scalability, in a distributed stream
processing framework built on Apache Kafka and Spark Streaming.

Keywords: Live data provenance · Stream processing · Agent-Based
model

1   Introduction

The traditional persistent approach that operates on static provenance is not
suitable for continuously generating provenance data. Our earlier work [6] showed
that data provenance enables deeper analysis of the internal dynamics of agent
based models (ABMs), by exposing dynamics that were previously hidden inside
what is effectively a black box. However, [6] further shows that vast and unwieldy
amounts of provenance can be captured continuously from running simulations
with even a modest tens of thousands of interacting components (agents). In this
case it quickly becomes infeasible to store all of the provenance data, requiring
reassessment and reinterpretation of analysis techniques to operate over *live
provenance data*, that is, before it gets written to disk.

Tasks such as debugging and model calibration are refinement processes,
requiring repeated runs. When a refinement process requires an experiment to
either fail or finish, it can be very time consuming. Our earlier work demonstrated
that provenance data is useful for both debugging [7] and model analysis [6],
and since provenance captures the dependencies between input parameters and

© Springer International Publishing Switzerland 2016
M. Mattoso and B. Glavic (Eds.): IPAW 2016, LNCS 9672, pp. 42–54, 2016.
DOI: 10.1007/978-3-319-40593-3_4

simulated results that do not match real data, it is suitable for model calibration as well. The challenge, however, is to overcome storing and wading through vast volumes of information to quickly isolate behavior of interest.

An approach to faster and more targeted intervention is to process provenance continuously as a stream of data. Algorithms under this model are constrained to processing a potentially unbounded stream in the order it arrives while using limited memory [3]. Earlier work on data streams [1,3,21] often modeled the stream as a sequence of timestamped events and generally assumed homogeneous streams that could be centrally processed. Provenance data lends itself to being modeled as a graph, and a general graph stream consists of undirected edges arriving in random-order [17]. Recent work on graph-based streams focuses on the semi-streaming model [12], in which the data stream algorithm is permitted $O(npolylogn)$ space, where n is the number of nodes in the graph. This space use is not well suited to voluminous provenance, nor does it meet the constraints of continuous processing for exclusive in-memory use.

In this paper, we distinguish a provenance stream from a general graph stream by emphasizing the temporal order in a provenance graph. From that we develop an algorithm for the backward provenance query on streaming data that has a space complexity limited by the maximum number of data values that the program can access at any given time during its execution. In an agent-based model this number is proportional to the number of declared variables. We extend our earlier tool [6] to automatically capture provenance streams from running NetLogo [28] simulations and store them into Apache Kafka [15]. We then implement our proposed algorithm on Apache Spark Streaming [30] to support the parameter readjustment and online debugging for agent-based model. The performance evaluation shows high throughput, low latency and good scalability.

The remainder of the paper is organized as follows: Sect. 2 discusses related work. Section 3 defines the stream model of dependency provenance. Section 4 introduces our framework that supports the capture and query of provenance streams. Section 5 presents the evaluation on a real-world environmental agent-based model. Section 6 concludes the paper and discusses future work.

2   Related Work

Research on stream provenance focuses on the provenance about data streams. It can be categorized with coarse-grained provenance methods that identify dependencies between streams or sets of streams [26,27], and fine-grained methods that identify dependencies among individual stream elements [10,18,22,23]. Sansrimahachai et al. [23] propose the Stream Ancestor Function – a reverse mapping function to express precise dependencies between input and output stream elements (fine-grained). Our study focuses on the continuous processing of large provenance data streams, a problem that has received less attention. The most closely related work is Sansrimahachai et al. [22] who track fine-grained provenance in stream processing systems through an on-the-fly provenance tracking service that performs provenance queries dynamically over streams of provenance assertions without requiring the assertions to be stored persistently. However, their focus is on provenance tracking by essentially pre-computing the query results at each stream operation and storing results into provenance assertions as the provenance-related property.

There is research on provenance collection that treats provenance data as continuously generating events. For example, Komadu [24] receives provenance events and attributes as XML messages in a separate standalone system and can infer relationships between events after their arrival; SPADEv2 [13] has reporters that transparently transform computational activity into provenance events. However, neither system models provenance events as a stream. In contrast, we present our early work on a stream model for provenance events. Our preliminary model only covers the dependencies between data products (analogous to the "Derivation and Revision" in W3C PROV [20]) and their temporal ordering. We demonstrate that this model is sufficient for the continuous backward provenance query.

Provenance can be represented as a DAG, and there is work on querying provenance graph databases [19,25]. Our study focuses on the continuous querying of massive provenance data streams. McGregor [17] surveys algorithms for processing massive graphs as streams, which focus on the semi-streaming model of $O(n\text{polylog}n)$ space. There has been little research on the stream processing of graph queries, and the most closely related work is the stream processing of XPath queries [14] and SPARQL queries [2,4]. XPath queries need to consider the relationships between XML messages (similar to graph edges), and SPARQL queries are performed on RDF graphs. However, these extended SPARQL languages are developed for specific goals such as to support semantic-based event processing and reasoning on abstractions, not to support typical graph analysis based on the node/path patterns. The same holds true for XPath queries.

3   Stream Model of Provenance Graph

An agent-based model (ABM) is a simulation of distributed decision-makers (agents) who interact through prescribed rules. We demonstrate in [6] that the dependency provenance in an ABM can explain certain results tracked to input data, and can yield insight into cause-effect relations among system behaviors. The concept of dependency provenance [8,9] is based on the dependency analysis techniques used in program slicing, which is different from "where-provenance" and "data lineage", but similar to "how-provenance" or "why-provenance" [5] in that it identifies a data slice showing the input data relevant to the output data. In this paper, we focus on the dependency provenance that consists of the data products and their dependencies, which can be considered as analogous to the "Derivation and Revision" in W3C PROV [20].

We use the same mapping to W3C PROV as in [6] to express the dependency provenance in ABM. PROV models provenance as a static graph, but the provenance capture can be viewed as a process of appending node/edge to the graph in their generation order. While a general graph can be streamed into a sequence

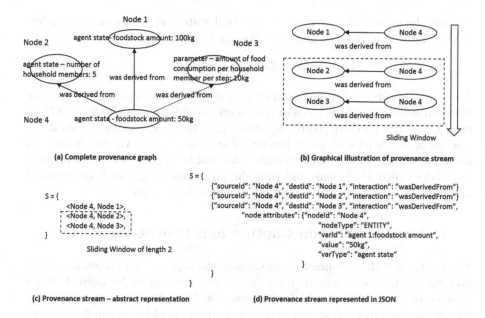

Fig. 1. Illustration of the provenance stream model.

of undirected edges in random-order, a provenance graph could be represented as a sequence of directed edges following the order of node/edge generation (see Fig. 1 for an example).

We propose a limited stream model of provenance that captures just a subset of provenance relationships and their ordering. We denote a dependency provenance graph as $G = (V, E, A)$, where $V = \{v_1, v_2, ..., v_n\}$ is the set of data products (nodes); $E = \{e_1, e_2, ..., e_m\}$ is the set of dependency relationships (edges), in which an edge $e = \langle v_i, v_j \rangle$ specifies that v_i depends on v_j; $A(v) = \{a_1, a_2, ...\}$ represents an arbitrary number of attributes of v.

Definition 1. *A stream of dependency provenance consists of a sequence of time ordered pairs* $e = \langle v_i, v_j \rangle$:

$$S = \{e_1, e_2, ..., e_n, e_{n+1}\} \tag{1}$$

where $e = \langle v_i, v_j \rangle$ *is a dependency relationship from* v_i *to* v_j *in* V, *and* $timestamp(e_n) < timestamp(e_{n+1})$.

If the temporal order of node/edge generation is properly preserved during capture, the provenance stream will follow a partial order specified below:

Property 1. For any two edges $e_l = \langle v_i, v_j \rangle$ and $e_m = \langle v_k, v_i \rangle$ that share a common node v_i, $timestamp(e_l) < timestamp(e_m)$

The provenance stream is append only and is potentially unbounded in size. Once an element of the stream has been processed it is discarded, and a query can only be evaluated over a limited internal state and/or the sliding window (with length w) of recently processed elements (at time t):

$$W = \{e_{t-w+1}, ..., e_t\} \tag{2}$$

There are two processing models in current distributed processing systems: the *record-at-a-time* processing model that receives and processes each individual record; and the batched processing model that treats streaming workloads as a series of batch jobs on small batches of streaming data. We implement our streaming algorithm in Spark Streaming [30] that is based on a batched processing model called *D-Streams*, and thus the provenance edges in S are received and processed during each batch interval (denoted by *bInterval*).

4   Provenance Stream Capture and Processing

We develop a scalable framework to support the capture and processing of live provenance streams generated from simulations running in NetLogo. Figure 2 gives an overview of its two major components. The *provenance stream capture* component captures live provenance streams from agent-based simulations and stores them into a Kafka messaging cluster. The *provenance stream processing* component is built on a Spark Streaming cluster to support query and other analytical operations. The details are illustrated in the rest of the section.

4.1   Provenance Stream Capture

In [6] we capture the provenance traces of a NetLogo simulation through probes added to the model's source code, and develop a NetLogo extension that collects and saves the provenance traces to be processed offline. In this paper, we modify the NetLogo extension to send the provenance traces directly to a converter that converts provenance traces into a live stream of provenance edges (in JSON format), which are then forwarded to the Kafka messaging system and processed in real-time. This provenance capture mechanism is illustrated in Fig. 3.

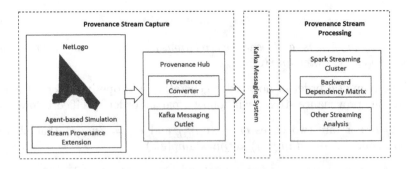

Fig. 2. Architecture of the provenance stream capture and processing framework.

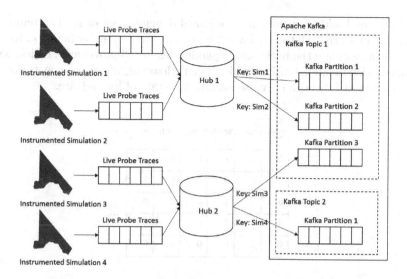

Fig. 3. Provenance capture from multiple running NetLogo simulations.

Note that each provenance hub uses multi-threading to receive probe traces from multiple simulations and send them to Apache Kafka [15], which is a distributed publish-subscribe messaging system that is designed to be fast, scalable, and durable. The provenance streams from different simulations can be separated by keys (uniquely formed by combining the hub ID with the stream ID). Each provenance hub can be configured either to send its streams into different partitions within one Kafka topic or into separate Kafka topics. This flexibility in organizing streams by topics and partitions can be used to improve the throughput and the level of parallelism of stream processing in Spark Streaming (see Sect. 5). For agent-based simulations distributed across multiple machines, we can deploy one or more provenance hubs on each machine.

4.2 Stream Processing Algorithm

Now we present our Backward Dependency Matrix (BDM) algorithm, which uses a dependency matrix to answer the backward provenance query for the most recent provenance nodes (*i.e.*, data products) in the stream. Given the temporal order defined in Sect. 3, we use a dynamic matrix to store and calculate the dependencies between all provenance nodes and the input/global parameters. For a newly arriving provenance node, the matrix is consulted to find the input/global parameters on which it depends. Figure 4 illustrates the dynamic matrix, with rows and columns added and removed on demand. The rows in the matrix correspond to provenance nodes (data products), and the columns correspond to input/global parameters. A cell of value 1in the matrix means a backward dependency from its row to its column. Each time a new provenance edge $e = \langle v_i, v_j \rangle$ arrives, we extract the backward dependencies of v_j (value 1 s in its row), and add them into the backward dependencies of v_i. The temporal order guarantees that all the backward dependencies of v_j arrive before e. In this way, we can calculate the backward dependencies for all provenance nodes, with the matrix size being potentially unbounded. However, under the constraints of our stream model, we can only use an internal state of limited size.

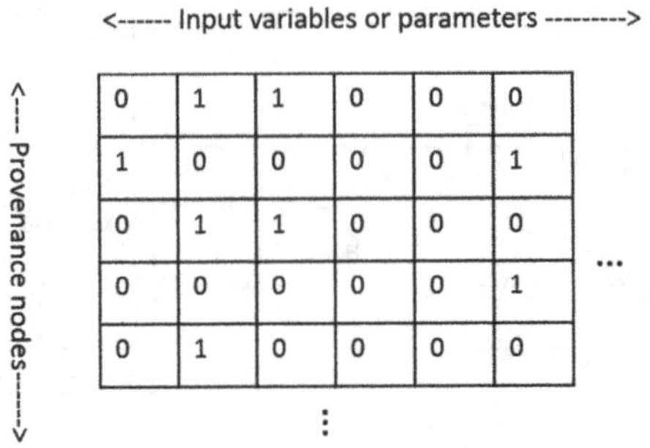

<------ Input variables or parameters ---------->

0	1	1	0	0	0
1	0	0	0	0	1
0	1	1	0	0	0
0	0	0	0	0	1
0	1	0	0	0	0

<----- Provenance nodes ------->

Fig. 4. Dynamic dependency matrix (0: dependent; 1: independent).

One observation on the agent based model in NetLogo, and in many other applications too, is that there exists only one instance (or value) of any variable at any moment – a universal value of a global variable, one copy of an agent variable within each agent, and one value of a local variable inside a function invocation – and we only need to query the backward dependencies for the current value of a variable. Thus the matrix only needs to keep the dependencies of the current variable instances, and those that could be used in future calculations.

In our stream model of provenance graph, each node is assigned with a node ID (unique within the stream) and a variable ID during the provenance capture (see Fig. 1(d)). The variable ID is formed by concatenating the context information and the declared name of that variable. For example, "global:variable 1", "agent 1:variable 2", and "procedure 1, level 1:variable 3" ("level" specifies the depth of recursion). Two provenance nodes with different node ID but same variable ID represent different values of the same variable. We keep dependencies of the most recent provenance node for each variable ID, except in the case that the most recent value of a variable depends on its earlier value – we use a cache matrix to temporarily store the dependencies of its earlier value. The algorithm is shown in Fig. 5. It has a space complexity of $O(N)$, where N is the number of variables declared in the model that is independent of the unbounded stream length. The matrix *state.current* stores the dependencies of current nodes to input data that can be queried using the function **getBackwardProvenance**.

4.3 Stream Processing Implementation

We implement the proposed algorithm inside a stream processing platform called Apache Spark Streaming [30]. Apache Spark [29] is a batch processing framework

1: **function** UPDATESTATE(*element, state*)   ▷ *element*: a newly arrived element (dependency edge) in the stream; *state*: the internal state with two dynamic matrices *current* and *purge*, and one HashMap *varIdToNodeId*

2:     *sourceNode* ← *element.source*

· 3:   *destNode* ← *element.dest*

4:     **if**   *state.varIdToNodeId*.containsKey(*sourceNode.varId*)   and *state.varIdToNodeId*.get(*sourceNode.varId*) != *sourceNode.nodeId* **then**

5:         remove all *dependencies* from *state.current* whose sources match *sourceNode.varId*

6:         cache removed *dependencies* in *state.purge*   ▷ older dependencies in *state.purge* whose sources match *sourceNode.varId* are also purged

7:     **end if**

8:     *state.varIdToNodeId*.put(*sourceNode.varId, sourceNode.nodeId*)

9:     **if** *destNode.varId* is an input/global variable **then**

10:        add new dependency *sourceNode.varId* ⇒ *destNode.varId* into *state.current*

11:    **end if**

12:    **if** *destNode.varId* == *sourceNode.varId* **then**

13:        *inputVars* ← **getBackwardProvenance**(*destNode.varId, state.purge*)

14:    **else**

15:        *inputVars* ← **getBackwardProvenance**(*destNode.varId, state.current*)

16:    **end if**

17:    **for** *var* in *inputVars* **do**

18:        add new dependency *sourceNode.varId* ⇒ *var* into *state.current*

19:    **end for**

20: **end function**

21: **function** GETBACKWARDPROVENANCE(*varId, matrix*)   ▷ *varId*: ID of the variable that we want to find its related input/global parameters; *matrix*: a dependency matrix.

22:     *dependencies* ← all dependencies in *matrix* whose sources match *varId*

23:     **return** destinations of *dependencies*

24: **end function**

Fig. 5. The BDM algorithm that maintains a dependency matrix to support the backward query on provenance stream.

with the Spark Streaming extension to support continuous stream processing. We choose Spark Streaming because the provenance stream usually has a very high speed (thousands of events per second) and Spark Streaming achieves higher throughput compared with other streaming platforms like Storm [16].

Spark Streaming uses a resilient distributed dataset (RDD) as the basic processing unit, which is a distributed collection of elements that can be operated on in parallel. There are two approaches to fetching messages from Kafka: the first is the traditional approach using Receivers and Kafka's high-level API to communicate with ZooKeeper; the second is a direct mode, introduced with Spark 1.3, which directly links and fetches data from Kafka brokers. We integrate Spark Streaming with Kafka using the latter approach for its better efficiency and simplified parallelism – it creates one RDD partition for each Kafka partition (*i.e.*, each provenance stream). Since Kafka implements the per-partition ordering and each RDD partition is processed by one task (thread) in Spark Streaming, the temporal order of node/edge generation we defined in Sect. 3 is preserved in both provenance capture and processing. Finally, the Kryo serialization is enabled for the BDM algorithm to reduce both the CPU and memory overhead caused by its internal state (*i.e.*, two dynamic matrices and one HashMap).

5   Experimental Evaluation

In evaluating the performance of our framework, we use a food security agent-based model we built for Monze District in Zambia, Africa [11]. In that model, 53,000 household agents make labor sharing and planting decisions biweekly based on a utility maximization approach within the context of local institutional regimes (*i.e.*, ward). The goal of the model is to understand the impact of climate change on adaptive change capacity among households. We use the source code analyzer [6] to add probes into the NetLogo code and the extended provenance extension to capture the live provenance stream while the simulation is running. The amount of raw provenance traces generated by running the model on one ward in the Monze District for one year is around 66 MB, which is 357 MB of provenance nodes/edges in JSON format. In our experiments, we run the model continuously for five growing seasons that generates about 1.7 GB of provenance stream data to be processed in real-time. *Throughput* of our streaming framework is measured as below:

$$throughput = pSize * nSim/(nBatch * bInterval) \qquad (3)$$

where *pSize* is total amount of provenance data generated by one simulation (1.7 GB in our evaluation), *nSim* is number of simulations, *nBatch* is number of batches taken to finish processing all data, and *bInterval* is batch interval. *Latency* is measured as average total time to handle a batch (*i.e.*, sum of scheduling delay and processing time).

We run the experiments using the "Big Red II" supercomputer at Indiana University where each CPU-only compute node contains two 2.5 GHz AMD Opteron 16-core CPUs and 64 GB of RAM, and is connected to a 40-Gb Infiniband network. In each experiment run, we use one node to run NetLogo (v5.2.0) simulations and our provenance hub, one to run the Kafka server and broker (v0.8.2), and up to nine nodes of Spark Streaming (v1.5.1) standalone clusters – one master and eight slaves. The Kafka log directory and the Spark Streaming checkpoint directory are both placed in Big Red II's shared Data Capacitor II (DC2) Lustre file system, which is connected via a 56-Gb FDR InfiniBand network. By default, the Spark standalone cluster (v1.5.1) supports only a simple FIFO scheduler across applications. To allow multiple concurrent applications, we divide the resources by setting the maximum number of resources each application can use (*i.e.*, parameter "spark.cores.max"). Since the actual number of non-idle tasks is determined by the number of RDD partitions (a.k.a. the number of provenance streams), we also set "spark.default.parallelism" (the number of parallel tasks) equal to the number of provenance streams.

For a Spark Streaming application to be stable, the batch interval must be set so that the system can process data at the arrival rate. If the provenance arrival rate is consistently higher than the maximum processing speed, we can throttle it by slowing down the ABM simulation speed. However, in our evaluation, we do not throttle the arrival rate, instead we measure the maximum processing speed at different batch intervals, by enabling the "backpressure" feature in Spark Streaming – it automatically figures out the receiving rate so that the batch processing time is lower than the batch interval (see Fig. 6(a)).

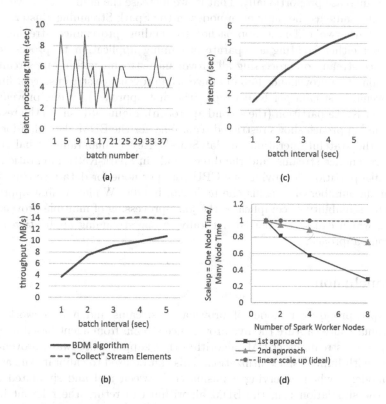

Fig. 6. (a) a BDM algorithm run with batch interval 5 s and data receiving rate automatically controlled by Spark Streaming "backpressure" feature. Note that the trial and error at the beginning to find the right receiving rate; (b) throughput of running BDM algorithm at different batch intervals compared with maximum throughput when receiving provenance in Spark Streaming; (c) latency of running BDM algorithm at different batch intervals; (d) scalability test of BDM algorithm at 5 s batch interval.

We first measure the throughput and latency of the BDM algorithm running on a single-node Spark Streaming cluster, and the size of its internal state serialized in memory. To determine the maximum throughput under the condition of simply receiving stream elements, we also measure the Spark "collect" operation running alone. As can be seen from Fig. 6(b) and (c), our proposed BDM algorithm can achieve throughput as high as 10.8 MB/s per stream (77 % of the maximum throughput of 14M B/s), and latency as low as 1.5 s; when increasing the batch interval, the BDM algorithm will have higher throughput but also longer latency. In all scenarios, the maximum size of the internal state (an RDD cached in memory) is the same – 10.2 MB.

Since our algorithm does not parallelize the processing within a provenance stream, we evaluate its scalability by measuring *Scaleup* – the ability to keep the same performance levels (response time) when both workload and compute resources increase proportionally. That is, we increase the number of provenance streams the same as the number of nodes in the Spark Streaming cluster.

There are two different approaches to sending provenance streams into processing: either creating a separate streaming application to process each provenance stream, or processing all provenance streams within one streaming application. The provenance hub organizes the provenance streams accordingly: one provenance stream per Kafka topic (the first approach), or one provenance stream per Kafka partition (the second approach). Figure 6(d) shows the results. The second approach shows restricted scalability for the BDM algorithm for two reasons: the stateful operation "updateStateByKey()" maintains global states for all provenance streams; and the direct mode in Spark-Kafka integration has each Kafka partition occupying one CPU core per node for data receiving, thus limiting the number of streams one node can handle. While the first approach has better scalability, it complicates the joint-processing of multiple provenance streams, which can be supported naturally in one streaming application using the second approach.

6 Conclusion

This paper proposes a model of provenance streams and a framework that can automatically capture the live provenance stream from agent-based models. We propose a streaming (BDM) algorithm that supports backward provenance querying with limited space utilization. This can be used to calibrate the agent-based model – when observing a mismatch between real and simulated data during the simulation run, the BDM algorithm can return the relevant input parameters to be readjusted on-the-fly. The framework and the BDM algorithm have been tested with a real-world environmental agent-based model that has thousands of household agents. The performance results show good throughput, latency and scalability.

Future work is to refine our definition of the stream model to include other types of provenance entities and relationships. In addition, how to handle out-of-order arrivals and how to parallelize the processing of one provenance stream remain open questions.

Acknowledgment. This work is funded in part by the National Science Foundation under award number 1360463.

References

1. Abadi, D.J., Ahmad, Y., Balazinska et al.: The design of the Borealis stream processing engine. In: CIDR, vol. 5, pp. 277–289 (2005)
2. Anicic, D., Fodor, P., Rudolph, S., Stojanovic, N.: EP-SPARQL: a unified language for event processing and stream reasoning. In: WWW, pp. 635–644. ACM (2011)
3. Babcock, B., Babu, S., Datar, M., Motwani, R., Widom, J.: Models and issues in data stream systems. In: PODS, pp. 1–16. ACM (2002)
4. Barbieri, D.F., Braga, D., Ceri, S., Della Valle, E., Grossniklaus, M.: C-SPARQL: SPARQL for continuous querying. In: WWW, pp. 1061–1062. ACM (2009)
5. Buneman, P., Khanna, S., Tan, W.-C.: Why and where: a characterization of data provenance. In: Van den Bussche, J., Vianu, V. (eds.) ICDT 2001. LNCS, vol. 1973, p. 316. Springer, Heidelberg (2000)
6. Chen, P., Plale, B., Evans, T.: Dependency provenance in agent based modeling. In: eScience, pp. 180–187. IEEE (2013)
7. Chen, P., Plale, B.A.: Proverr: system level statistical fault diagnosis using dependency model. In: CCGrid, pp. 525–534. IEEE (2015)
8. Cheney, J.: Program slicing and data provenance. IEEE Data Eng. Bull. **30**(4), 22–28 (2007)
9. Cheney, J., Ahmed, A., Acar, U.A.: Provenance as dependency analysis. In: Arenas, M. (ed.) DBPL 2007. LNCS, vol. 4797, pp. 138–152. Springer, Heidelberg (2007)
10. De Pauw, W., Leţia, M., Gedik, B., Andrade, H., Frenkiel, A., Pfeifer, M., Sow, D.: Visual debugging for stream processing applications. In: Barringer, H., Falcone, Y., Finkbeiner, B., Havelund, K., Lee, I., Pace, G., Roşu, G., Sokolsky, O., Tillmann, N. (eds.) RV 2010. LNCS, vol. 6418, pp. 18–35. Springer, Heidelberg (2010)
11. Evans, T., Plale, B., Attari, S.: WSC-Category 2 collaborative: Impacts of agricultural decision making and adaptive management on food security in africa, National Science Foundation grant 1360463 (2014)
12. Feigenbaum, J., Kannan, S., McGregor, A., Suri, S., Zhang, J.: On graph problems in a semi-streaming model. Theor. Comput. Sci. **348**(2), 207–216 (2005)
13. Gehani, A., Tariq, D.: SPADE: Support for Provenance Auditing in Distributed Environments. In: Narasimhan, P., Triantafillou, P. (eds.) Middleware 2012. LNCS, vol. 7662, pp. 101–120. Springer, Heidelberg (2012)
14. Gupta, A.K., Suciu, D.: Stream processing of XPath queries with predicates. In: SIGMOD, pp. 419–430. ACM (2003)
15. Kreps, J., Narkhede, N., Rao, J., et al.: Kafka: a distributed messaging system for log processing. In: NetDB, pp. 1–7 (2011)
16. Lu, R., Wu, G., Xie, B., Hu, J.: Stream bench: towards benchmarking modern distributed stream computing frameworks. In: UCC, pp. 69–78. IEEE (2014)
17. McGregor, A.: Graph stream algorithms: a survey. ACM SIGMOD Rec. **43**(1), 9–20 (2014)
18. Misra, A., Blount, M.L., Kementsietsidis, A., Sow, D., Wang, M.: Advances and challenges for scalable provenance in stream processing systems. In: Freire, J., Koop, D., Moreau, L. (eds.) IPAW 2008. LNCS, vol. 5272, pp. 253–265. Springer, Heidelberg (2008)

19. Cuevas-Vicenttín, V., Kianmajd, P., Ludäscher, B., Missier, P., Chirigati, F., Wei, Y., Koop, D., Dey, S.: Provenance storage, querying, and visualization in PBase. In: Ludaescher, B., Plale, B. (eds.) IPAW 2014. LNCS, vol. 8628, pp. 239–241. Springer, Heidelberg (2015)
20. Moreau, L., Missier, P., et al.: PROV-DM: The PROV Data Model. W3C Working Group Note 30, April 2013
21. Plale, B., Schwan, K.: Dynamic querying of streaming data with the dQUOB system. TPDS **14**(4), 422–432 (2003)
22. Sansrimahachai, W., Moreau, L., Weal, M.J.: An on-the-fly provenance tracking mechanism for stream processing systems. In: ICIS, pp. 475–481. IEEE (2013)
23. Sansrimahachai, W., Weal, M.J., Moreau, L.: Stream ancestor function: a mechanism for fine-grained provenance in stream processing systems. In: RCIS, pp. 1–12. IEEE (2012)
24. Suriarachchi, I., Zhou, Q., Plale, B.: Komadu: a capture and visualization system for scientific data provenance. J. Open Res. Softw. **3**(1), e4 (2015). http://doi.org/10.5334/jors.bq
25. Vicknair, C., Macias, M., Zhao, Z., Nan, X., Chen, Y., Wilkins, D.: A comparison of a graph database and a relational database: a data provenance perspective. In: ACMSE, p. 42. ACM (2010)
26. Vijayakumar, N., Plale, B.: Tracking stream provenance in complex event processing systems for workflow-driven computing. In: EDA-PS Workshop (2007)
27. Vijayakumar, N.N., Plale, B.: Towards low overhead provenance tracking in near real-time stream filtering. In: Moreau, L., Foster, I. (eds.) IPAW 2006. LNCS, vol. 4145, pp. 46–54. Springer, Heidelberg (2006)
28. Wilensky, U.: Netlogo (1999). http://ccl.northwestern.edu/netlogo/
29. Zaharia, M., Chowdhury, M., Franklin, M.J., Shenker, S., Stoica, I.: Spark: cluster computing with working sets. In: HotCloud, vol. 10, p. 10. USENIX (2010)
30. Zaharia, M., Das, T., Li, H., Shenker, S., Stoica, I.: Discretized streams: an efficient and fault-tolerant model for stream processing on large clusters. In: HotCloud. p. 10. USENIX (2012)

Provenance Analysis and Visualization

Analyzing Provenance Across Heterogeneous Provenance Graphs

Wellington Oliveira[1,2(✉)], Paolo Missier[3], Kary Ocaña[4],
Daniel de Oliveira[1], and Vanessa Braganholo[1]

[1] Instituto de Computação,
Universidade Federal Fluminense (UFF), Niterói, Brazil
{wellmor,danielcmo,vanessa}@ic.uff.br
[2] DACC, Instituto Federal do Sudeste de Minas Gerais,
Rio Pomba Campus, Rio Pomba, Brazil
[3] School of Computing Science, Newcastle University,
Newcastle upon Tyne, UK
paolo.missier@ncl.ac.uk
[4] Laboratório Nacional de Computação Científica (LNCC),
Petrópolis, Brazil
karyann@lncc.br

Abstract. Provenance generated by different workflow systems is generally expressed using different formats. This is not an issue when scientists analyze provenance graphs in isolation, or when they use the same workflow system. However, when analyzing heterogeneous provenance graphs from multiple systems poses a challenge. To address this problem we adopt ProvONE as an integration model, and show how different provenance databases can be converted to a global ProvONE schema. Scientists can then query this integrated database, exploring and linking provenance across several different workflows that may represent different implementations of the same experiment. To illustrate the feasibility of our approach, we developed conceptual mappings between the provenance databases of two workflow systems (e-Science Central and SciCumulus). We provide *cartridges* that implement these mappings and generate an integrated provenance database expressed as Prolog facts. To demonstrate its usage, we have developed Prolog rules that enable scientists to query the integrated database.

1 Introduction

Workflow Management Systems (WfMS) facilitate the design and implementation of data-driven computational science experiments, through a high-level programming model and a middleware-based runtime environment. A number of WfMS also capture and store *retrospective* provenance [1], and provide query languages and other analytical tools to help scientists use the resulting provenance traces [2–4].

Consider a scenario where two or more collaborative research teams work independently on common scientific goals, adopting slightly different approaches and producing workflows that differ in design, implementation, and execution middleware, but are otherwise similar in terms of intent, using comparable tools and algorithms.

© Springer International Publishing Switzerland 2016
M. Mattoso and B. Glavic (Eds.): IPAW 2016, LNCS 9672, pp. 57–70, 2016.
DOI: 10.1007/978-3-319-40593-3_5

The concrete example we use throughout the paper is that of two research groups, both interested in generating phylogenetic trees. The two groups independently design and implement two workflows, SciPhy [5] and ML[1], using different WfMS, namely SciCumulus [6] and e-Science Central [7]. Each of these has their specificities, but both are capable of collecting retrospective provenance traces from their workflow runs. Since both workflows use either the same or similar input data and produce similar outputs, it seems natural to try and use the provenance of their runs to compare and discuss the results. However, the two WfMS use different proprietary schemas and logical data models to represent their respective provenance (relational and graph-based, respectively) as well as to store it. Furthermore, the different nature of the WfMS middleware leads to different levels of details in the provenance traces.

Thus, while in theory it should be possible for researchers to ask questions on both provenance graphs seamlessly and transparently, the heterogeneity in the design, implementation, and execution of their workflows translates into provenance traces that are themselves heterogeneous, making it difficult to analyze them jointly. Ultimately, this lessens the role of provenance in facilitating scientific discourse.

Promoting provenance interoperability has been the goal of several recent community efforts in provenance modeling, starting with the Open Provenance Model (OPM) [8] and culminating with PROV [9], a W3C recommendation. Further, ProvONE [3] and PROV-Wf [10] independently extended PROV, adding explicit representation of *prospective* provenance [1] to the model.

Contributions. In this paper we build upon these efforts to show how provenance interoperability that includes integration of the traces and their seamless querying, can be achieved in a practical setting where we can assume a degree of similarity amongst the traces, as in the science scenario just outlined.

The paper offers the following specific contributions: (i) Firstly, we argue that, to be useful, an integration model should include both retrospective and prospective provenance (which we henceforth concisely refer to as *r-prov* and *p-prov*). We use a number of example queries to show the benefits of an integrated provenance database that accommodates both r-prov and p-prov traces from two or more heterogeneous workflow runs. In our proposed approach, we use ProvONE as the integration model, as it is fairly comprehensive including both p-prov and r-prov and allows for easy integration of terms from external vocabularies, including Dublin Core or WfMS. ProvONE is also fairly stable, and supported by a large data conservation project, DataONE (dataone.org); (ii) We then map the proprietary provenance models of SciCumulus and e-Science Central to ProvONE, showing that ProvONE is indeed a viable target integration model; (iii) Thirdly, we present an actual mapping of provenance traces, obtained from running the example workflow on the two WfMS, to the ProvONE model. This exercise also shows the limitations of each of the provenance capture systems, as both proprietary traces miss some of the provenance elements (entities, activities, actors, and relationships) that are available in ProvONE; (iv) As an illustration of system-level integration we have implemented provenance components, or *cartridges*, for SciCumulus and e-Science Central, which translate the traces to

---

[1] http://eubrazilcloudconnect.eu/content/leishmaniasis-virtual-laboratory.

ProvONE and write them to an integrated provenance database, and (v) Finally, we implement the example queries mentioned in (i) to show provenance querying on our integrated model.

In our proof-of-concept implementation we have used Prolog as it allows great flexibility both in producing the integrated database, because provenance relationships translate to Prolog facts, and in formulating powerful queries with inference capability, using Prolog rules. We should note that Prolog has been also used to query and analyze provenance generated from scripts in the noWorkflow approach [11], and that it is also a natural choice owing to its syntactic similarity to PROV-N [12].

Running Example: Phylogenetic Analysis Workflows. As anticipated, our running example is a phylogenetic analysis experiment designed by two research groups and executed in two different WfMS. This analysis aims at generating phylogenetic trees along with other statistics, which can then be used to infer the evolutionary ancestry of a set of genes, species, or other taxa. Each of the workflows presents different designs and specifications (*e.g.* number and name of activities), but they have similar goals, which makes useful to compare the achieved results. To clarify the use of specific parameter values in both workflows, domain experts from the two groups defined semantic mappings between pairs of workflow activities in the SciPhy and ML workflows, as shown in Table 1. We use this mapping to compare the provenance of similar activities from distinct and heterogeneous provenance graphs, and later to drive the design of cross-traces queries.

Table 1. Semantic relationships between activities of two scientific workflows

SciPhy	ML	Description
DataSelection	ImportFile and FilterDuplicates	Importing, filtering, and selection of data
Mafft	ClustalW	Sequence alignment
ReadSeq	–	Conversion of alignment format
ModelGenerator	–	Choice of the evolutionary model
RAxML	MEGA-Maximum Likelihood	Generation of the phylogenetic tree
–	CSVExport	Exporting filtered sequences on CSV format
RAxML	ExportFiles	Exporting of the phylogenetic tree

Specifically, the SciPhy workflow consists of five activities: (i) DataSelection; (ii) Mafft; (iii) ReadSeq; (iv) ModelGenerator; and (v) RAxML. The ML workflow is composed of six activities: (i) ImportFile; (ii) FilterDuplicates; (iii) ClustalW; (iv) MEGA-Maximum Likelihood; (v) CSVExport; and (vi) ExportFiles. The two workflows were set up with similar input data and parameters. Although the number of their activities differs, two key activities appear in both, namely *sequence alignment* and *tree generation*. Their mappings: Mafft → ClustalW and RAxML → MEGA help us compare the critical elements of the workflows (the other activities are responsible for format conversions and some optional optimizations in the process).

2 Provenance Analysis Across Heterogeneous Provenance Graphs

2.1 A Reference Classification of the Provenance Space and of Its Queries

We argue that, in the collaborative scenario just outlined, scientists will benefit from provenance graphs that (a) include both p-prov and r-prov, and (b) include traces from both experiments. The case for combining p-prov and r-prov has been made before [10, 13, 14], namely that p-prov enables new types of queries to be made on r-prov, such as *find all data produced by any activity that occurs downstream from block X in the workflow*. Other interesting queries that span r-prov and p-prov are presented later in this section. The case for point (b) is that the ability to perform analysis on combined provenance graphs will help collaborative teams obtaining deeper understanding from related workflows with different levels of details. As we have seen, this is possible because these workflows typically share similarities on their activities, data flows, or input parameters. When detailed provenance graphs from similar workflows are available, scientists can use those sources to clarify their understanding and get more insights about the experiment.

Given two traces *PG1* and *PG2*, each from a different workflow run (from the same or different workflows), and each providing both r-prov and p-prov, we can categorize the set of all possible provenance queries as illustrated in Fig. 1. In this Venn diagram, queries are classified according to the provenance data needed to answer them. For instance, queries in class *C1* operate on p-prov only and on one graph at a time, while *C3* queries require both p-prov and r-prov, on one graph. Class *C6* is perhaps the most challenging, as it operates simultaneously on p-prov and r-prov, and on both graphs. Note that our classification is conceptual, and the actual fragment returned by a query is sensitive to the values of query parameters.

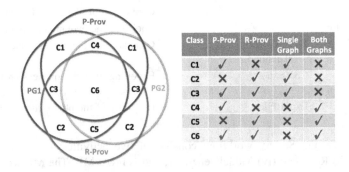

Class	P-Prov	R-Prov	Single Graph	Both Graphs
C1	✓	✗	✓	✗
C2	✗	✓	✓	✗
C3	✓	✓	✓	✗
C4	✓	✗	✗	✓
C5	✗	✓	✗	✓
C6	✓	✓	✗	✓

Fig. 1. Classification of provenance fragments and corresponding queries

Example queries for each of the classes are listed in Table 2. Note that queries from classes C1, C2 and C3 are easily answered using provenance captured by most WfMS. However, queries of classes C4, C5 and C6 require additional mapping information that is not automatically provided by those systems. This mapping encompasses two aspects: (a) a syntactic mapping between heterogeneous schemas of provenance data and (b) a semantic mapping that informs the similarity or equivalence between p-prov elements. The syntactic mapping of local and global provenance schemas using Pro-vONE is described next, while a sample of a semantic mapping of two workflows specifications appears in Table 1. Note that the semantic mapping comes from the researchers/domain experts' mind and is used just as auxiliary information to perform queries by filtering results. Later, we will come back with the queries and classes presented here and we will demonstrate how an integrating architecture enables their implementation.

Table 2. Provenance queries on intersection classes

#	Queries	Class
Q1	Retrieve all programs with their input and output ports for the workflow w' and provenance graph g'	C1
Q2	Retrieve all activity executions with their generated data for the workflow execution w' and provenance graph g'	C2
Q3	Retrieve the time consumed by each activity execution for the workflow execution w' and provenance graph g'	C2
Q4	Retrieve the complete activity execution trace that influenced the generation of the data d'	C2
Q5	Retrieve the complete dataflow trace of the output data d' for the workflow execution w' and provenance graph g'	C2
Q6	Retrieve all programs (plans) of each execution and their input parameters for the workflow execution w' and provenance graph g'	C3
Q7	Retrieve the workflow version, and the time consumed by each workflow execution for the workflow wf' and provenance graph g'	C3
Q8	Retrieve all programs with their input and output ports for each workflow specification	C4
Q9	Retrieve all activity executions with their generated data for each workflow execution	C5
Q10	Retrieve the time consumed by each activity execution for each workflow execution	C5
Q11	Retrieve the ports, workflow executions, provenance graphs, and the complete activity execution trace that influenced the generation of all data	C6
Q12	Retrieve the complete dataflow trace and workflow for each workflow execution	C6
Q13	Retrieve the time consumed by each workflow execution for each workflow and provenance graph	C6
Q14	Retrieve all programs (plans) of each activity execution and their input parameters for each workflow wf'	C6

2.2 Mapping Provenance Models to ProvONE

Executing queries in each of these classes requires converting *PG1* and *PG2* to a common provenance model. We now illustrate the integration process using two

WfMS, SciCumulus and e-Science Central. As mentioned before, SciPhy [5] and ML, which run on each of these WfMS respectively, share the common goal of generating phylogenetic trees. The two WfMS collect provenance data at different levels of detail and heterogeneity is present both in format as well as in content.

SciCumulus captures p-prov and r-prov and stores them in relational tables in a PostgreSQL database, while e-Science Central stores just r-prov as a graph in a Neo4J database. However, it maintains information about the workflow structure in a relational database (PostgreSQL) blended with several additional data related to the workflow viewing (*i.e.*, coordinates of each graph object) and exports it to JSON files.

We use ProvONE (Fig. 2) as the target global schema for integration of the provenance traces produced by the two systems. ProvONE extends the PROV model with an explicit representation of p-prov, thus capturing the most relevant information on scientific workflow processes, and is designed to accommodate extensions for specific scientific workflow systems [3].

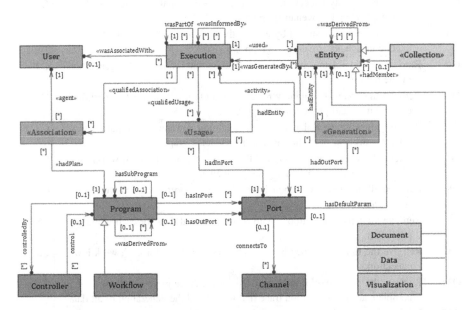

Fig. 2. ProvONE conceptual model, from the DataONE documentation

Table 3 describes the logical mapping between elements of the two source provenance traces, and the corresponding ProvONE elements. Each relational table from SciCumulus and JSON element from e-Science Central, which hold p-prov, were mapped to the corresponding ProvONE entities and relationships. Furthermore, the nodes and edges of e-Science Central database (Neo4J) and also relational tables of

Table 3. Mapping between ProvOne, SciCumulus, and e-Science Central provenance models

#	ProvONE	SciCumulus	e-Science Central
1	provone:workflow	cworkflow	invocation
2	provone:program	cactivity	blocks
3	provone:port	crelation	connections
4	provone:execution	eworkflow, eactivity, eactivation	Service Run, Workflow Run
5	provone:execution (Workflow Execution)	eworkflow, eactivity, eactivation	Service Run, Workfow Run
6	provone:user	emachine	–
7	provone:document	efile	DataVersion
8	provone:data	idataselection, odataselection, omafft, oreadseq, omodelgenerator, oraxml	properties
9	provone:hadPlan	eactivation, eactivity, cactivity, eworkflow, cworkflow	Service Run, blocks
10	prov:wasDerivedFrom (Data)	efile, cmapping	Used, DataVersion
11	prov:wasDerivedFrom (Program)	–	Run_Of, Instance_Of, Service Run, Service Version, Workflow Version
12	prov:used	efile, cmapping	Used, DataVersion, Service Run
13	prov:wasGeneratedBy	eafile	Was_Generated_By, DataVersion, Service Run
14	prov:wasAssociatedWith	eactivation, emachine	–
15	prov:wasInformedBy	cmapping	Used, Was_Generated_By, Service Run
16	provone:hasInPort	crelation, cmapping, cactivity	blocks, connections
17	provone:hasOutPort	crelation, cmapping, cactivity	blocks, connections
18	provone:hasSubProgram	cworkflow, cactivity	invocation, blocks
19	provone:hasDefaultParam	cfield	connections, properties
20	provone:wasPartOf	eworkflow, eactivity, eactivation	Contained, Service Run
21	provone:hadInPort	crelation, cmapping, cactivity, eactivity, eactivation	Service Run, connections
22	provone:hadOutPort	crelation, cmapping, cactivity, eactivity, eactivation	Service Run, connections

SciCumulus that hold r-prov were mapped to ProvONE entities and relationships. The gaps in the SciCumulus and e-Science Central column indicate missing information.

As there is no previous relation between p-prov and r-prov in the e-Science Central database and the exported JSON files, we use some information such as invocations and blocks identifiers to unify them. The relation between p-prov and r-prov is straightforward in SciCumulus, since it first stores p-prov and then collects and stores r-prov during the workflow execution (*i.e.* at runtime).

2.3   ProvONE Assertions as Prolog Facts

We now show examples of how provenance traces from specific workflow executions are represented as Prolog facts. We have chosen Prolog as it allows great flexibility both in producing the integrated database (provenance relationships are translated to facts) and in formulating powerful queries with inference capability (rules).

Two fragments of provenance graphs for e-Science Central and SciCumulus, respectively, are depicted in Figs. 3 and 4, after mapping to ProvONE. Gray boxes represent p-prov, orange boxes correspond to r-prov, and light blue boxes are entities (p-prov and r-prov). Since both provenance graphs are represented using the same model, queries can easily traverse both provenance graphs. Table 4 presents examples of Prolog facts for these workflow fragments (the complete set of facts is available at GitHub at https://github.com/dew-uff/integrated-provenance-analysis). As Prolog facts syntax is similar to the PROV-N notation, each entity and activity was named and labeled in a similar style, using an identifier followed by a set of properties delimitated by brackets. Relationships use the identifiers for each ProvONE element. Furthermore, entity identifiers were modified to make them unique in the global schema and facts were created to identify the provenance graphs and relate them to their workflows.

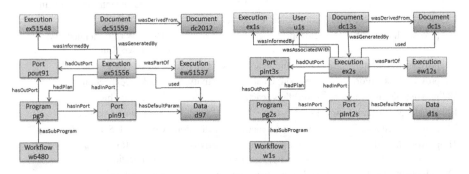

Fig. 3. Part of e-Science Central provenance   **Fig. 4.** Part of SciCumulus provenance

Regarding relative incompleteness, note that the e-Science Central provenance graph (rows 3 and 10 of Table 4) does not hold information about the agent, while the SciCumulus provenance graph does not store the program versions (row 7).

3   Implementation: Adapters and Global Queries

Integration Architecture. Converting from SciCumulus and e-Science Central proprietary provenance to ProvONE requires the implementation of specialized adapters,

Table 4. Prolog instances for each ProvOne construct

#	Prolog Instances for e-Science Central	Prolog Instances for SciCumulus
1	entity(w6480,[prop(prov:type,['prov:plan', 'provone:workflow']),prop(prov:label,'ML Pipeline')]).	entity(w1s,[prop(prov:type,['prov:plan', 'provone:workflow']),prop(prov:label,'sciphy ')]).
2	entity(pg9,[prop(prov:type,['prov:plan','provone: program']),prop(prov:label,'CSVExport')]).	entity(pg2s,[prop(prov:type,['prov:plan', 'provone:program']),prop(prov:label,'mafft')]).
3	-	agent(u1s,[prop(prov:type,['provone:user']),p rop(prov:label,'wellington-VirtualBox')]).
4	entity(dc51559,[prop(prov:type,['provone:docu ment']),prop(prov:label,'sequence-map.csv'), prop(prov:type,'null'),prop(prov:value,'null')]).	entity(dc13s,[prop(prov:type,['provone: document']),prop(prov:label,'FILE13'), prop(prov:value,'ORTHOMCL256.mafft')]).
5	hadPlan(ex51556,pg9).	hadPlan(ex2s,pg2s).
6	wasDerivedFrom(dc51559,dc2012).	wasDerivedFrom(dc13s,dc1s).
7	wasDerivedFrom(pg9, pgV50025).	-
8	used(ex51556,d97).	used(ex2s,dc1s).
9	wasGeneratedBy(dc51559,ex51556).	wasGeneratedBy(dc13s,ex2s).
10	-	wasAssociatedWith(ex2s,u1s).

or *cartridges*, one for each system. Provenance obtained from these cartridges is stored in a unified knowledge base as Prolog facts, as described earlier. The cartridges were implemented in Java using the mapping of ProvONE, SciCumulus, and e-Science Central provenance models presented in Table 3. The implementation is simple and is not time consuming. All code and some data are also available on GitHub.

Using the knowledge base, various teams may access provenance and work collaboratively on provenance analysis. They can use pre-defined logical rules to query provenance, and thus get more information about similar experiments. Figure 5 gives an overview of the provenance gathering, conversion, integration and query processes. The example cartridges are specific to our case study.

Consistent with the mappings presented in Table 3, SciCumulus cartridge gets p-prov and r-prov from the relational database and converts them to Prolog. In turn, e-Science Central cartridge fetches r-prov from the graph database and extracts p-prov from JSON files. Clearly, extending the approach to integrating other provenance sources requires new cartridges to be developed. This effort is similar to database integration efforts that are well known in the literature [15].

Querying the Integrated Traces. Using our integration architecture, we are now able to express queries that span different types of provenance and different types of graphs. Queries over the integrated schema are expressed in Prolog as rules. To illustrate, we have implemented the queries listed in Table 2, which exemplify the intersection classes of Fig. 1. (Due to space restrictions we only present a subset of the queries). Specifically, the *dataTrace* and *dataFlow* rules implement queries *Q5* and *Q12*. Query *Q5* covers class *C2* and retrieves r-prov from either provenance graph *PG1* or

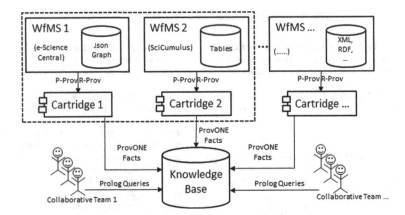

Fig. 5. Provenance integration architecture

provenance graph *PG2*, while *Q12* covers class *C6* and retrieves p-prov and r-prov from both *PG1* and *PG2*. Although these queries are quite similar, *Q12* retrieves the trace of data for all executions, while *Q5* considers only one of the workflow systems. The following rules were designed for retrieving all data that influenced the generation of a particular data product. The query result is a historical data trace that shows which input files influenced the generation of a given output.

```
dataTrace(DstName, WkfName, WExName, OutputId, InputId):-
    dataSet(DsId, DstName), hasDataSet(WkfId, DsId),
    activity(WExId,[prop(prov:type,['provone:execution']),
    prop(prov:label, WExName),_,_,_]),
    entity(WkfId,[prop(prov:type,['prov:plan', 'provone:workflow']),
    prop(prov:label,WkfName)]), hadPlan(WExId,WkfId),
    wasPartOf(ExId, WExId), wasGeneratedBy(OutputId, ExId),
    dataFlow(OutputId, InputId).
dataFlow(Output, Input):- wasDerivedFrom(Output, Input).
dataFlow(Output, Input):- wasDerivedFrom(Output, X), dataFlow(X, Input).
```

Table 5 shows the query calls (and their results) with the parameters used to query the data trace for a specific result generated by SciCumulus and e-Science Central respectively. Query Q5 retrieves the input files that influenced the generation of the *dc19 s* output file on the *scyphy-1* execution of the *sciphy* workflow that was executed in SciCumulus, while Q12 does the same for the *dc51559* output of the *ML Pipeline* workflow run on e-Science Central. These query instances hide the complexity of the Prolog rules and become suitable for non-experts in the Prolog language. Note that the user may bind none, one, or multiple parameter values. For example, if one specifies no parameter values, the query will return the graph name, workflow name, execution name, along with the input and output data for both datasets. This makes Prolog queries a flexible resource to retrieve provenance according to specific requirements.

Table 5. Prolog queries and results on SciCumulus and e-Science Central provenance graphs

SciCumulus	`dataTrace('SciCumulus', 'sciphy', 'sciphy-1', dc19s, InputId).`
	`InputId = dc6s; InputId = dc12s; InputId = dc13s; InputId = dc14s;` `InputId = dc1s; InputId = dc1s;  InputId = dc1s;  InputId = dc1s;`
e-Science Central	`dataTrace('e-Science Central', 'ML Pipeline', 'Testing ML Pipeline',` `dc51559, InputId).`
	`InputId = dc2012;`

4 Related Work

Working on the integration of provenance models, Ellqvist *et al.* [16] propose an architecture based on a generic mediator that blends different provenance data sources. In this approach, a global schema is presented to the user who specifies a generic query that is converted into specific queries for each database. Wrappers access the data from the data source and convert them to the mediator model. Apart from this, it uses a proprietary mediation schema that is not compatible with the OPM or PROV models. Also based on interoperability issues that were exposed by the Third Provenance Challenge (PC3), Ding *et al.* [17] approach provenance reuse using OPM, OWL and Linked Data. They argue that provenance trace reuse requires generic provenance and domain-specific data (*e.g.*, a classification of artifact types). Their OPM ontology (PC3OPM) was extended and modularized to cover interoperability gaps found in the PC3. Such approach allows one to import provenance from OPM/XML, export it to RDF, query, and improve provenance by creating new relations with SPARQL-based rule inferences. Similarly, Braun and Seltzer [18] propose a Common Provenance Framework to provide provenance interoperability. To develop the framework, they analyzed the problems and challenges encountered in importing PASS [19] data into the PLUS system [20]. Their framework includes concepts, constraints, and tools to provide semantics and structure to query provenance across different systems using the OPM model and XML Schema. Both [17, 18] use OPM as mediator model, which does not consider p-prov as ProvONE does.

Missier *et al.* [21] present an approach to solve problems found in the implicit collaboration between different provenance systems that use the result from another workflow execution as part of their input. The local provenance is mapped to a common model and stored in a database with new global identifiers. This allows the tracking of provenance for workflows, systems and user group executions. Differently from our approach, their aim is to provide a data model to track the provenance across different workflows. Similarly, Altintas *et al.* [22] propose a data model based on collaborative views and develop QLP, a query language for provenance. QLP was designed to facilitate querying implicit collaboration in interoperable provenance datasets. In the same direction of the previous authors, they propose the union of several data sources into one single repository to be handled by one single query. On the other hand, they use OPM as the provenance model and cannot represent p-prov.

Aiming to facilitate publication, sharing, exchanging, and reuse of self-contained units of knowledge, Bechhofer *et al.* [23] introduce Research Objects (RO). These are semantic aggregations of resources (eg data, methods, metadata) that are produced and consumed by common services. Similarly, SHIWA [24], a EU project to support workflow sharing, was designed to integrate the execution of different workflows that use different workflow systems, different workflow languages, and different distributed infrastructures. Although these approaches allow storing and sharing provenance from different sources, they do not enable provenance querying across different data sources.

5 Final Remarks

The integration of heterogeneous data sources can be a powerful tool for provenance analytics. In particular, it can provide considerable advantages for research teams that work collaboratively on similar experiments. In this paper, we have presented an approach that enables integrating and querying provenance data from similar workflows designed and implemented in different systems with different specifications. To achieve this, we use an integration model (ProvONE) that includes both p-prov and r-prov and create cartridges that convert different provenance databases to a global ProvONE schema of Prolog facts.

Our approach introduces classes that explore intersection between p-prov, r-prov, and heterogeneous provenance graphs and presents related queries that run across both provenance graphs and retrieve information with different contents and levels of detail. Prolog rules were developed for each pre-defined query, taking advantage of inference and unification facilities catered by Prolog. As a proof-of-concept, Prolog queries were executed and they could retrieve the data traces from both provenance graphs. New Prolog rules can easily be designed to accommodate new requirements., and new cartridges can be developed for other workflow systems using the proposed architecture.

As future work, we plan to develop a benchmark of completeness to evaluate provenance from different WfMSs. We also intend to investigate how to cover gaps in similar provenance graphs by using our intersection classes.

References

1. Freire, J., Koop, D., Santos, E., Silva, C.T.: Provenance for computational tasks: a survey. Comput. Sci. Eng. **10**, 11–21 (2008)
2. Lim, C., Lu, S., Chebotko, A., Fotouhi, F., Kashlev, A.: OPQL: querying scientific workflow provenance at the graph level. Data Knowl. Eng. **88**, 37–59 (2013)
3. Missier, P., Dey, S., Belhajjame, K., Cuevas-Vicenttín, V., Ludäscher, B.: D-PROV: extending the PROV provenance model with workflow structure. In: TaPP (2013)
4. Dey, S., Köhler, S., Bowers, S., Ludäscher, B.: Datalog as a lingua franca for provenance querying and reasoning. In: TaPP (2012)

5. Ocaña, K.A., de Oliveira, D., Ogasawara, E., Dávila, A.M., Lima, A.A., Mattoso, M.: SciPhy: a cloud-based workflow for phylogenetic analysis of drug targets in protozoan genomes. In: Norberto de Souza, O., Telles, G.P., Palakal, M. (eds.) BSB 2011. LNCS, vol. 6832, pp. 66–70. Springer, Heidelberg (2011)
6. Oliveira, D., Ogasawara, E., Baião, F., Mattoso, M.: SciCumulus: a lightweight cloud middleware to explore many task computing paradigm in scientific workflows. In: International Conference on Cloud Computing (2010)
7. Watson, P., Hiden, H., Woodman, S.: e-Science central for CARMEN: science as a service. Concurr. Comput. Pract. Expert. **22**, 2369–2380 (2010)
8. Moreau, L., Freire, J., Futrelle, J., McGrath, R.E., Myers, J., Paulson, P.: The open provenance model: an overview. In: Freire, J., Koop, D., Moreau, L. (eds.) IPAW 2008. LNCS, vol. 5272, pp. 323–326. Springer, Heidelberg (2008)
9. Moreau, L., Missier, P.: PROV-DM: The PROV Data Model. http://www.w3.org/TR/2013/REC-prov-dm-20130430/
10. Costa, F., Silva, V., de Oliveira, D., Ocaña, K., Ogasawara, E., Dias, J., Mattoso, M.: Capturing and querying workflow runtime provenance with PROV: a practical approach. In: EDBT/ICDT Workshops (2013)
11. Murta, L., Braganholo, V., Chirigati, F., Koop, D., Freire, J.: noWorkflow: capturing and analyzing provenance of scripts. In: Ludaescher, B., Plale, B. (eds.) IPAW 2014. LNCS, vol. 8628, pp. 71–83. Springer, Heidelberg (2015)
12. Moreau, L., Missier, P.: PROV-N: The Provenance Notation. http://eprints.soton.ac.uk/356852/
13. Missier, P., Sahoo, S.S., Zhao, J., Goble, C., Sheth, A.: Janus: from workflows to semantic provenance and linked open data. In: IPAW (2010)
14. Belhajjame, K., Zhao, J., Garijo, D., Gamble, M., Hettne, K., Palma, R., Mina, E., Corcho, O., Gómez-Pérez, J.M., Bechhofer, S., Klyne, G., Goble, C.: Using a suite of ontologies for preserving workflow-centric research objects. Web Semant. Sci. Serv. Agents World Wide Web **32**, 16–42 (2015)
15. Batini, C., Lenzerini, M., Navathe, S.B.: A Comparative analysis of methodologies for database schema integration. ACM Comput. Surv. **18**, 323–364 (1986)
16. Ellqvist, T., Koop, D., Freire, J., Silva, C., Strömbäck, L.: Using mediation to achieve provenance interoperability. In: IEEE World Conference on Services (2009)
17. Ding, L., Michaelis, J., McCusker, J., McGuinness, D.L.: Linked provenance data: a semantic Web-based approach to interoperable workflow traces. Future Gener. Comput. Syst. **27**, 797–805 (2011)
18. Braun, U.J., Seltzer, M.I., Chapman, A., Blaustein, B., Allen, M.D., Seligman, L.: Towards query interoperability: PASSing PLUS (2011)
19. Muniswamy-Reddy, K.-K., Holland, D.A., Braun, U., Seltzer, M.I.: Provenance-aware storage systems. Harvard University (2006)
20. Blaustein, B., Seligman, L., Morse, M., Allen, M.D., Rosenthal, A.: PLUS: synthesizing privacy, lineage, uncertainty and security. In: International Conference on Data Engineering Workshops (2008)
21. Missier, P., Ludascher, B., Bowers, S., Dey, S., Sarkar, A., Shrestha, B., Altintas, I., Anand, M.K., Goble, C.: Linking multiple workflow provenance traces for interoperable collaborative science. In: Workshop on Workflows in Support of Large-Scale Science (WORKS) (2010)
22. Altintas, I., Anand, M.K., Crawl, D., Bowers, S., Belloum, A., Missier, P., Ludäscher, B., Goble, C.A., Sloot, P.M.: Understanding collaborative studies through interoperable workflow provenance. In: McGuinness, D.L., Michaelis, J.R., Moreau, L. (eds.) IPAW 2010. LNCS, vol. 6378, pp. 42–58. Springer, Heidelberg (2010)

23. Bechhofer, S., De Roure, D., Gamble, M., Goble, C., Buchan, I.: Research objects: towards exchange and reuse of digital knowledge. Nat. Precedings (2010). doi:10.1038/npre.2010. 4626.1
24. Terstyanszky, G., Kukla, T., Kiss, T., Kacsuk, P., Balasko, A., Farkas, Z.: Enabling scientific workflow sharing through coarse-grained interoperability. Future Gener. Comput. Syst. **37**, 46–59 (2014)

Prov Viewer: A Graph-Based Visualization Tool for Interactive Exploration of Provenance Data

Troy Kohwalter[1(✉)], Thiago Oliveira[1], Juliana Freire[2], Esteban Clua[1], and Leonardo Murta[1]

[1] Instituto de Computação, Universidade Federal Fluminense, Niterói, RJ, Brazil
`tkohwalter@ic.uff.br`
[2] New York University, New York, NY, USA

Abstract. The analysis of provenance data for an experiment is often crucial to understand the achieved results. For long-running experiments or when provenance is captured at a low granularity, this analysis process can be overwhelming to the user due to the large volume of provenance data. In this paper we introduce, *Prov Viewer*, a provenance visualization tool that enables users to interactively explore provenance data. Among the visualization and exploratory features, we can cite zooming, filtering, and coloring. Moreover, we use of other properties such as shape and size to distinguish visual elements. These exploratory features are linked to the provenance semantics to ease the comprehension process. We also introduce collapsing and filtering strategies, allowing different levels of granularity exploration and analysis. We describe case studies that show how *Prov Viewer* has been successfully used to explore provenance in different domains, including games and urban data.

Keywords: Provenance · Visualization · Graph · Analysis · Tool

1 Introduction

Displaying provenance is an issue in present times. While there are many tools that capture data provenance, most of them offers basic visualizations or requires exporting the data to a format compatible with existing visualization tools. Ideally, provenance data are captured and stored for each task of the scientific workflow in terms of basic relationships among individual tasks. More complex relationships are inferred during an analysis process [5] by using visualization techniques to facilitate the understanding of the captured data, especially when dealing with complex workflows.

However, a provenance graph might contain data that did not cause any significant change or provides information that might not be related to the desired analysis. Another problem occurs when analyzing provenance data that is segregated into different trials (workflow executions), which results in analyzing multiple individual graphs to extract meaningful knowledge since each trial is normally represented by a separate graph. Moreover, a common representation of the provenance graph is based on traditional node-link diagrams. These diagrams may impair the analysis process depending on the size and domain peculiarities of the graph. Using simple node-link

© Springer International Publishing Switzerland 2016
M. Mattoso and B. Glavic (Eds.): IPAW 2016, LNCS 9672, pp. 71–82, 2016.
DOI: 10.1007/978-3-319-40593-3_6

diagrams to represent provenance data can also harden the graph understanding when dealing with the wealth of information that can be contained in a single provenance node, even when using the different shapes to distinguish the information.

Although there are some tools in the literature for provenance analysis [2, 8, 18, 19], they are based on these simple node-link diagrams with only basic visualization features, such as labels and colors to distinguish edges and vertices, neighbor detection, and size for different intensities. Moreover, they are not directly compatible with the PROV model [17], requiring additional steps to convert the data.

In this paper, we introduce *Prov Viewer*, a novel graph-based visualization tool for interactive exploration of provenance data that is compatible with the PROV, and consequently, with any other application that exports provenance using the PROV model. *Prov Viewer* processes the collected provenance data to generate an interactive provenance graph to provide advanced visualization features for identifying steps and contributors to a given result.

The PROV model has proved to be useful for other domains besides scientific workflows, such as electronic games or urban data. Thus, in a previous work [13], we introduced the usage of digital provenance in games and proposed a conceptual framework (PinG) for collecting information during a game session, mapping them to provenance terms, and providing the means for a post-game analysis. We experimented with rudimentary ways to visualize provenance in the context of games [12]. We developed an initial prototype for provenance visualization and used it on the SDM [15] game to assess whether provenance data visualization can be helpful in the understanding of game events [14]. This prototype was also used in another application that extracts game provenance through image processing mechanisms [11]. More recently, it is being used to visualize provenance from urban data.

The tool we present in this paper is the result of several extensions and new techniques we developed to address issues encountered in different scenarios. We have designed new visual representations and interaction mechanisms that address many of the aforementioned challenges: (1) collapsing, highlighting the relevant information in the graph; (2) filtering, removing information that is not relevant for a given analysis; (3) graph merge, integrating the analysis of multiple trials; (4) specialized layouts, organizing the graph in a more understandable way; (5) domain configuration, customizing the visualization for specific needs; (6) shapes, sizes, and colors, supporting a clear distinction of information types, and (7) interoperability, supporting PROV-N for importing provenance data.

This paper is organized as follows: Sect. 2 presents some of the related work in the area of provenance visualization. Section 3 details our provenance visualization tool, *Prov Viewer*. Section 4 presents two different case studies using our tool. Section 5 concludes this work by listing some future work.

2 Related Work

Our related work can be grouped into two categories: workflow management systems that have built-in provenance visualizations and standalone provenance visualization tools. The workflow management systems that have build-in provenance visualizations

[1, 4, 10] allow easy integration between provenance collection and analysis. However, they have a shortcoming of not supporting provenance data generated by other workflow management systems or standalone provenance gathering tools, even when they are compatible with well known provenance models. Furthermore, workflow management systems normally lack graph manipulation features for viewing provenance graphs.

On the other hand, there are some standalone provenance visualization tools that resemble our work. Provenance Explorer [5] takes RDF-based provenance outputs from capture systems and dynamically generates customized views of provenance trail. However, it focuses on provenance data and inference rules associated with processing events in a laboratory or manufacturing plant, lacking the support for data processing activities in the digital domain. Furthermore, their provenance model is based on the ABC ontology model. Lastly, their collapse feature only supports one expansion level, instead of multiple levels of detail.

The ZOOM [3] prototype provide users with an interface to query provenance information generated by a workflow system through SQL queries. An interesting aspect is that it allows the user to dynamically modify the graph by hiding irrelevant information, updating the provenance graph for the new view. Another existing tool is the PROV Toolbox, which converts W3C PROV data model representations. However it lacks a built-in visualization and requires the use of a generic graph tool (*Graphviz*) to visualize the provenance data. Another similar tool is PROV Translator, which validates PROV representations and translates them to other representations. It also provides graph visualizations based on their previous work [7], which displays a provenance graph using PROV's vertex shape and color to identity the vertex type. The PROV-O-Viz [9] tool is a web-based visualization tool for provenance based on PROV that uses *Sankey Diagrams* for visualization. *Sankey Diagrams* are used to visualize flow magnitude between nodes in a network and in PROV-O-Viz the activity or entity width is based on the information flow.

Some related work is limited to specific domains (*i.e.*, Provenance Explorer), require additional knowledge (*i.e.*, ZOOM, PROV-O-VIZ), or they are not compatible with provenance data from other tools (*i.e.*, Kepler, VisTrails, Taverna). Furthermore, they individually provide some interesting features, such as interactive graphs, level of detail, summary nodes, merges, and filters. However, these approaches do not provide these features in an integrated way, hindering the analysis due to visualization and manipulation restrictions, which sometimes require additional external procedures to analyze the data. Moreover, they lack any means of overlaying provenance information onto a spatial structure for analysis.

3   Prov Viewer

In this paper we present a provenance visualization tool named *Prov Viewer* (Provenance Viewer[1]). Our tool is compatible with the PROV-N notation, allowing its adoption in different domains and applications. The provenance data, which contains

---

[1] *Prov Viewer* is available at https://github.com/gems-uff/prov-viewer.

the provenance information among entities and their relationships, is processed to generate a provenance graph. This graph is a visual representation of the provenance data and supports user interaction, which is a key feature for understanding how each action influenced in the outcome and how they influenced each other. It is also possible to manipulate the graph by omitting facts and collapsing chains of actions for a better understanding and visualization experience. No information is lost in this process, so that the user can undo any changes made during analysis.

Prov Viewer uses the PROV notation, where square vertices represent activities, circles represent entities, and pentagons represent agents. Furthermore, each vertex is composed of multiple attributes that describe the vertex. Each attribute contains a name and a value that is associated with it (*e.g.*, startTime: 2012-05-25T11:15:00, endTime: 2012-05-25T12:00:00). The edges in the provenance graph represent the relationships between vertices. As such, activity vertex can be positively or negatively influenced by other vertex and have relationships with entities and agents.

Before using *Prov Viewer*, it is necessary to configure it to understand the domain peculiarities and customize the visualization features. This is accomplished by creating a config.xml file based on the configuration schema of *Prov Viewer*. This configuration file allows the user customize the graph visualization. *Prov Viewer* also has a feature for automatic detection and configuration for each edge type and color scheme, which represents most of the configuration effort of the tool, according to the graph being used. Note that the user will need to manually input specific parameters in the configuration xml in order to use some of our tool layouts. However, this task is done only once for a new domain.

Figure 1 shows the high-level architecture of our tool, illustrating some of its features available that allow users to interact with the provenance data to identify relevant actions that impacted in the results. The following sub-sections describe the most relevant features, including shapes and colors to distinguish information, manual collapses, graph merges, layouts, and an automatic collapse feature.

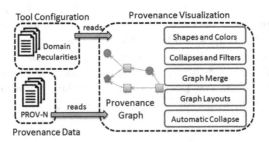

Fig. 1. *Prov Viewer's* high-level architecture (Color figure online)

3.1 Shapes and Colors

Prov Viewer builds its visualization strategy based on shapes and colors, for both vertices and edges. Shapes are used to map semantic concepts from the provenance and colors are used to map scalar values, such as intensity or orientation. The vertex shape is directly related to provenance semantics (*i.e.*, agent, activity, entity), while the vertex color is used for mapping scalar values through the usage of a color scheme. When selecting the desired attribute, all vertices with the specified status have their colors changed according to their respective values. We adopt the traffic light scale [6], which indicates the status of the variable using gradients from three colors: red, yellow, and green. The resulting color is automatically inferred from minimum and maximum values for that attribute or using boundaries manually specified by the user in the configuration xml. Enabling this type of feature allows the user to easily identify situations where the desired attribute value fluctuates throughout the data.

Both the edge shape (*i.e.*, thickness) and its color are used to show the intensity of the relationship. The intensity is the value associated with the edge, if any, and is more common on influences (*i.e.*, *wasInfluencedBy*). A thin edge with a darker color represents a low influence relationship (*i.e.*, the assigned value to the edge is low). On the other hand, thicker and brighter edges represent a strong or intense relationship. Figure 2a shows an example of edges with different colors and thickness and Fig. 2b shows the vertex color based on their time values (also represented by columns). This feature can be used to quickly identify strong influences in the graph just by looking at the edge's thickness and brightness. The edge's color is also used to represent any additional numeric information contained in the relationship (*e.g.*, influences that has numeric data), which can be any of these three types: positive, which is represented as green and indicates an increase in the numeric value (*i.e.*, when the edge has an associated positive value); negative, which is represented as red and indicates a decrease; and neutral, which is represented as blue and indicates no numeric chances.

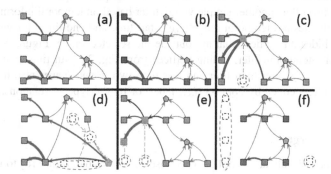

Fig. 2. (*a*) Original graph; (*b*) graph with a color schema; (*c*) collapse of two activities; (*d*) collapsing of the agent's activities; (*e*) graph *c* after another collapse; and (*f*) temporal filter (Color figure online)

3.2   Collapses and Filters

Our tool provides a vertex collapse feature to aid in the analysis of the graph and allows a manual collapse of selected vertices in order to compact the graph size, grouping the selected vertices together in a single summarized vertex. No information is lost in this process and it can be reverted by the user. Figure 2c shows an example of collapsing activity vertices. The grey markings represent vertices before the collapse and the grey arrow represents where they were collapsed to. Another usage of the collapse feature is to group activities related to the same agent, allowing the user to see all the influences and changes that the agent did throughout his tasks. Figure 2d shows such an example. The size of the collapsed vertex is bigger than the rest due to the number of vertices in the collapse group (and is proportional to the number of vertices). Furthermore, the shape is the same as that of an agent vertex because there is an agent vertex in the collapse group.

The summarized information is displayed as follows: For String values, it shows all different values separated by a comma (*e.g.*, *String_Value1*, *String_Value2*, *String_Value3*). For attributes with numeric values in a collapse group composed of two vertices, the tool shows the average value for that attribute followed by the minimum and maximum values. Otherwise (collapse group containing more than two vertices), the tool displays the average value followed by the five-number summary (minimum value, 1st quartile, median, 3rd quartile, maximum value).

Similar edges (*i.e.*, same type) that have the same target and type are also grouped together when collapsing vertices. The collapsed edge's information (*i.e.*, color, thickness, and value) is computed by summing or averaging the values of the participating edges, depending on their type. For example, *Prov Viewer* can use the *sum* function for edges representing expenses and the *average* function for edges representing percentage. However, the user needs to parameterize each edge. Otherwise the tool will always use the default *sum* function. Figure 2e shows an example of collapsing edges that occurred when collapsing another group of vertices after collapsing the vertices in Fig. 2c. Note that the colors for each edge changed after the collapse due to the new maximum value (from the sum of the collapsed edges).

The tool also offers another simple vertex filter based on temporal information. The user defines the desired temporal range (*e.g.*, start time and end time) for visualization and the tool hides all vertices that are outside the selected range. Figure 2f shows an example of the temporal filter, hiding vertices from Fig. 2a with time (which can be seen by the rows) greater than four and less than two. *Prov Viewer* also has an edge filter, which filters edges by context (*i.e.*, label) or by the type of relationship.

3.3   Graph Merge

Our provenance visualization tool also proposes a feature based on [16] to merge two provenance graphs in order to generate a single unified provenance graph. The merge process combines the current displayed graph with another graph (chosen by the user) to generate a single unified graph for visualization. The merge process is composed of four steps: (1) vertex matching, which selects pairs of vertices from the graphs; (2) similarity verification between vertices, which receives two vertices from the first step and informs if they are similar. Vertices are considered similar if they belong to the same vertex type and have the same properties with similar numeric values within a configurable margin of error; (3) merge vertices that were considered similar in the previous step; and (4) creation of the unified graph for visualization, which only occurs after the matching process is over. The resulting graph can be exported using the PROV-N notation for future usage.

Figure 3 illustrates the graph merge of two distinct graphs from the same domain. Red vertices in the merged graph (Fig. 3c) belong exclusively to the first graph (Fig. 3a), while grey vertices represent common vertices (*i.e.*, merged vertices) from both graphs, and green vertices belong exclusively to the second graph (Fig. 3b). This graph merge feature is useful when analyzing multiple sessions or trials by detecting common sections. Merged vertices from this feature also provide similar summarized information using the five-number summary.

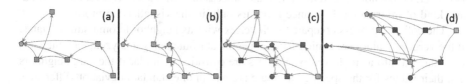

Fig. 3. Two graphs (*a* and *b*) merged into a single graph (*c*) and with a temporal layout (*d*) (Color figure online)

3.4 Graph Layouts

Our visualization tool allows the user to interactively change the graph layout to better visualize the result. We created two provenance graph visualization layouts: temporal and spatial.

The **temporal layout** organizes the graph in a chronological order similar to a timeline (or spreadsheet) for each agent. Thus, each timeline (or line) of the graph groups activities of the same agent and each column in the graph represents the passage of time. This makes easier to know the entity or agent responsible for executing each activity by just looking at the agent responsible for that line. Invalid temporal values are considered as zero for the purpose of positioning them in the graph. Thus, the graph positions the vertices in the *x* axis according to the chosen scale. Figure 3d illustrates an example of our temporal layout, displaying the graph similarly to a spreadsheet and organizing the vertices by their chronological order. Note that now it is much easier to identify the agent responsible for each activity as the leftmost nodes and their chronological order by looking at the activity's placement in the graph. The horizontal position represents the time axis (passage of time) and the vertical position represents the agent axis (the responsible for the activity).

The **spatial layout** organizes the vertices in the graph by their spatial coordinates and can be used for spatial or georeferencing the data. The layout also supports the usage of an orthographic image or maps taken from *Google Maps* and *OpenStreetMaps* as background for the graph. This is particularly useful for corresponding elements with other graphical representations, such as a map of a city or a game scene. When dealing with real world maps, *Prov Viewer* automatically transform the latitude and longitude to pixel coordinates. This automatic process requires only three input values to correctly align the image with the graph and is described in the tool's documentation. When using the spatial layout in conjunction with a background image, the user sees where each event occurred just by looking at the graph's placement in the image.

3.5 Automatic Collapse

Prov Viewer offers an automatic collapse feature to highlight the relevant information in the provenance graph by summarizing the tracked data. This automatic collapse groups sequential information that has similar values or represents the same state, allowing the user to quickly identify relevant information or state transitions. This process is similar to data deduplication, which hides duplicate copies of repeating data. Currently, this form of collapse uses only one vertex attribute to define similarity. However, unlike normal deduplication, the process in *Prov Viewer* is reversible without any kind of information loss since it occurs only in the visualization process.

The collapse process compares each vertex with its neighbor to omit similar states. If the vertices' values are similar for the specific attribute being analyzed, then they can be collapsed into a single vertex. Vertices are considered similar if they are neighbors and their values for the specified attribute are within one standard deviation difference. Since the goal is to combine all similar states, it is necessary to go beyond the vertex direct neighbor. If any of the vertices in the collapse group have an edge to a vertex outside of the collapse group and that vertex has a similar attribute value to those in the group, then it is added to the collapse group. Thus, the collapse group will keep growing until a significant change of state is detected. Figure 4 illustrates an example of our similarity collapse for the gathered provenance data from a racing car doing multiple laps in a racing-track. Sequential vertices that had similar speeds were collapsed into a single vertex. Note that the collapse preserves the notion of different laps (differently from the merge feature) and that the collapsed vertices (with varying sizes according to the number of collapsed vertices) have similar speeds. This allows the analyst to detect behavior patterns and locations where the driver had more difficulties.

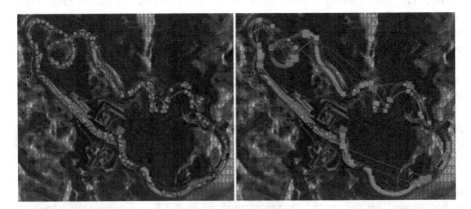

Fig. 4. Similarity collapse (right) according to the speed of the car from the original graph (left) (Color figure online)

4   Case Studies

As discussed in the introduction section, we adopted *Prov Viewer* in two different provenance domains: digital games and urban data. In the game domain, our visualization tool was used for the analysis of game sessions of five different games (*SDM*, *Super Mario World*, *Unity's Tower Defense*, *Unity's Angry Bots*, and *Unity's Car Tutorial*) and for the urban data domain our tool was used to analyze bus traffic data from the city of Rio de Janeiro. More than thirty people, including researchers and students, used *Prov Viewer* to analyze provenance data, where 29 were students analyzing data gathered from a serious game [14]. In the following sub-sections we present two case studies of our visualization tool.

4.1   Game Session Provenance

The first case study is the *Angry Bots* game, an open-source demo from Unity asset store. The provenance graph used in this example contains 1275 vertices and 2976 edges. Figure 5 illustrates one of the possible visualizations of the provenance graph from the game using our visualization tool, which was captured using the PinG approach. The tool was configured to include the background rendering from the scene.

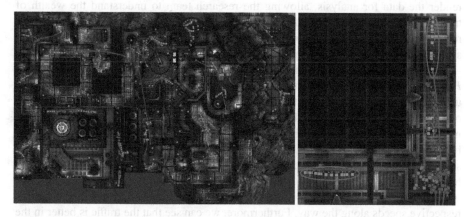

Fig. 5. Provenance graph (left) rendered with *Prov Viewer* from the *Angry Bots* game using spatial layout. The second graph (right) is a zoomed section rotated by 90°. (Color figure online)

The displayed graph is using the vertex visualization schema for the player's health attribute values (vertex color using traffic light schema: green, yellow, and red). The green and red edges respectively represent the influences that changed the player's experience points (awarded when defeating an enemy) and moments when the player died (red vertex from the edge) and was moved to the restoration unit to be revived (green vertex from the edge). Blue vertices represent activities executed by other characters in the game (*i.e.*, enemies) and blue edges represent chronological order of events or state change in scene objects (*e.g.*, terminals, doors). By analyzing the visualization from Fig. 5, we can see the chronology of events, regions visited by the player, sections where more action happened, where the player engaged in battle, when he/she suffered heavy health loss (vertex color change), and the player's health during each section. For instance, we can infer that the cause of the player death in the middle of the map (near the circle-shaped object that represent a storage cylinder) was because he rushed through the level without waiting to recover health from his small health regeneration trait (sequence of orange followed by red vertices) after most engagements. Other three deaths (three "respawn" red edges in the bottom, leaving the second graph of Fig. 5) were caused by three different engagements (red circles) with the same enemy (blue vertices) in close quarters, leaving the player without enough room to maneuver to dodge the explosive attacks. In this game, we used a screenshot of the scenario with the dimensions of 4,280 × 3,208 for the background, which precisely matches the locations where the events (*i.e.*, activities). This high resolution allows for a higher detail of the game scene when zooming the graph during analysis.

4.2   Bus Traffic Provenance

The second case study is based on bus traffic data analysis in the city of *Rio de Janeiro*. The data used in this research, which includes geographic location tracked from the buses' GPS, is obtained from *DataRio*[2]. *Prov Viewer* is being used in this context to render the data for analysis, allowing the research team to understand the wealth of tracked information. Our tool allows for filtering the data to focus on specific buses or relate the bus delays with ongoing events in the city through their geographic location, speed in the region, and timestamp.

Figure 6 illustrates one of the possible visualizations of the provenance data using *Prov Viewer*. The graph contains 601 vertices and 600 edges. The displayed graph is using a color schema based on the bus speed. Therefore the vertices, which represent on-line GPS information tracked from buses at every minute interval, are colored from red to green according to their (instantaneous) speed at that specific moment, while the blue edges link these vertices in a chronological order. Note that the displayed graph is showing bus data from nine different busses from the same route within a period of two hours.

In the graph from Fig. 6, we can see the buses routes through the city and their respective speeds along the way. Furthermore, we can see that the traffic is better in the region near "*Botafogo*" due to the high concentration of green vertices than "*Urca*" and "*Copacabana*". This type of graph visualization allows the user to quickly indentify the streets where the buses moved slower due to traffic by finding regions in the graph with reddish vertices by looking at the vertex location in the map. Moreover, it is also possible to better understand the extension of the traffic jam and the affected areas by crossing the displayed graph with a graph from another route (*e.g.*, merge the graphs) that also use segments of the same street.

---

[2] *DataRio*: http://data.rio/dataset.

Fig. 6. Provenance Graph rendered on *Prov Viewer* from collected bus traffic data (Color figure online)

5 Conclusions

Graph visualization strategies bring problems related to scalability when dealing with provenance datasets beyond a few hundred nodes. Traditional node-link diagrams can easily become too visually cluttered when dealing with huge provenance data, limiting the user's ability to thoroughly analyze and explore the data. To deal with this problem, *Prov Viewer* offers collapse options that can generate different levels of detail and graph layouts to sort the data and reduce node clustering. *Prov Viewer* also has some basic automatic collapses based on vertex similarity and graph merges, allowing users to omit data and combine different graphs for analysis. Other contributions include the merging of PROV-N data from different files and georeferencing capabilities for provenance information.

Our tool can be configured and used by different provenance applications as a general-purpose provenance visualization tool as it supports graphs that use the PROV-N notation. *Prov Viewer* also supports pre-processing steps, which can be done outside the tool, as long as the final data format is compatible with the PROV-N notation. We showed two case studies from different domains: analysis of digital game sessions and bus traffic data. In both cases, the graph had more than one thousand artifacts (vertices and edges combined). However, the performance starts to degrade after rendering graphs with more than two thousand visible artifacts (*i.e.*, long loading times). Future work includes more complex algorithms to analyze the provenance data and suggest which information can be omitted to reduce the graph to acceptable sizes; more types of graph visualization techniques; summarization techniques; and more graph layouts, including a support for dynamically loading new layouts, or handcrafted ones, in the tool at run-time. We are also working on optimizing the tool to be able to handle rendering huge graphs more smoothly and reducing loading time.

Acknowledgment. The authors thank CAPES, CNPq, and FAPERJ for the financial support.

References

1. Altintas, I., et al.: Kepler: an extensible system for design and execution of scientific workflows. In: Proceedings of 16th International Conference on Scientific and Statistical Database Management, 2004, pp. 423–424 (2004)
2. Bastian, M., et al.: Gephi: an open source software for exploring and manipulating networks. In: Third International AAAI Conference on Weblogs and Social Media (2009)
3. Biton, O., et al.: Querying and managing provenance through user views in scientific workflows. In: IEEE 24th International Conference on Data Engineering, ICDE 2008, pp. 1072–1081 (2008)
4. Callahan, S.P., et al.: VisTrails: visualization meets data management. In: Proceedings of the 2006 ACM SIGMOD International Conference on Management of Data, pp. 745–747. ACM, New York (2006)
5. Cheung, K., Hunter, J.: Provenance explorer – customized provenance views using semantic inferencing. In: Cruz, I., Decker, S., Allemang, D., Preist, C., Schwabe, D., Mika, P., Uschold, M., Aroyo, L.M. (eds.) ISWC 2006. LNCS, vol. 4273, pp. 215–227. Springer, Heidelberg (2006)
6. Diehl, S.: Software Visualization: Visualizing the Structure, Behaviour, and Evolution of Software. Springer, Heidelberg (2007)
7. Ebden, M., Huynh, T.D., Moreau, L., Ramchurn, S., Roberts, S.: Network analysis on provenance graphs from a crowdsourcing application. In: Groth, P., Frew, J. (eds.) IPAW 2012. LNCS, vol. 7525, pp. 168–182. Springer, Heidelberg (2012)
8. Ellson, J., et al.: Graphviz and dynagraph — static and dynamic graph drawing tools. In: Jünger, M., Mutzel, P. (eds.) Graph Drawing Software, pp. 127–148. Springer, Berlin Heidelberg (2004)
9. Hoekstra, R., Groth, P.: PROV-O-Viz - understanding the role of activities in provenance. In: Ludaescher, B., Plale, B. (eds.) IPAW 2014. LNCS, vol. 8628, pp. 215–220. Springer, Heidelberg (2015)
10. Hull, D., et al.: Taverna: a tool for building and running workflows of services. Nucleic Acids Res. **34**(suppl 2), W729–W732 (2006)
11. Jacob, L., et al.: A non-intrusive approach for 2D platform game design analysis based on provenance data extracted from game streaming. In: 2014 Brazilian Symposium on Computer Games and Digital Entertainment, pp. 41–50 (2014)
12. Kohwalter, T.C., Clua, E.G., Murta, L.G.: Game Flux analysis with provenance. In: Reidsma, D., Katayose, H., Nijholt, A. (eds.) ACE 2013. LNCS, vol. 8253, pp. 320–331. Springer, Heidelberg (2013)
13. Kohwalter, T., et al.: Provenance in Games. In: Brazilian Symposium on Computer Games and Digital Entertainment, SBGAMES, pp. 162–171 (2012)
14. Kohwalter, T., et al.: Reinforcing software engineering learning through provenance. In: 2014 Brazilian Symposium on Software Engineering, SBES, pp. 131–140 (2014)
15. Kohwalter, T., et al.: SDM – an educational game for software engineering. In: Brazilian Symposium on Games and Digital Entertainment, SBGAMES, pp. 222–231 (2011)
16. Koop, D., et al.: Visual summaries for graph collections. In: IEEE Pacific Visualization Symposium (Pacific Vis 2013), pp. 57–64. IEEE (2013)
17. Moreau, L., Missier, P.: PROV-DM: The PROV Data Model. http://www.w3.org/TR/prov-dm/
18. Del Rio, N., da Silva, P.P.: Probe-It! Visualization support for provenance. In: Bebis, G., et al. (eds.) ISVC 2007, Part II. LNCS, vol. 4842, pp. 732–741. Springer, Heidelberg (2007)
19. Seltzer, M.I., Macko, P.: Provenance map orbiter: interactive exploration of large provenance graphs. In: TaPP (2011)

Intermediate Notation for Provenance and Workflow Reproducibility

Danius T. Michaelides[1]([✉]), Richard Parker[2], Chris Charlton[2],
William J. Browne[2], and Luc Moreau[1]

[1] Electronics and Computer Science, University of Southampton, Southampton, UK
{dtm,L.Moreau}@ecs.soton.ac.uk
[2] Graduate School of Education, University of Bristol, Bristol, UK
{Richard.Parker,C.Charlton,William.Browne}@bristol.ac.uk

Abstract. We present a technique to capture retrospective provenance across a number of tools in a statistical software suite. Our goal is to facilitate portability of processes between the tools to enhance usability and to support reproducibility. We describe an intermediate notation to aid runtime capture of provenance and demonstrate conversion to an executable and editable workflow. The notation is amenable to conversion to PROV via a template expansion mechanism. We discuss the impact on our system of recording this intermediate notation in terms of runtime performance and also the benefits it brings.

1 Introduction

Reproducibility of scientific results is a key challenge to the modern scientist [1]. Systems built to tackle this often focus on recording provenance, especially scientific workflow systems.

The focus of the EBook project[1] is on a suite of tools called StatJR[2] designed to aid in the use and teaching of statistical analysis techniques with an emphasis on their use in social science. The suite consists of a Web front-end to statistical processes, a command line interface and a dynamic document system, whereby interactive computations can be embedded in a document [2]. They are designed to support the user as their experience and understanding of statistical methods improves by surfacing different levels of detail of the underlying computations. More recently, the suite was enriched by a workflow system that enables the composition of processes from low-level operations to broad methodological steps. The overall aim is to allow users to move seamlessly between the StatJR tools in order to refine the activity they are engaged in, whilst maintaining their context and the choices they have made so far in their interactive computational investigations. Concretely, it is a requirement to be able to capture both the interactive investigations and the batch processing that took place, convert them to editable

---

[1] http://www.bristol.ac.uk/cmm/research/ebooks/.
[2] http://www.bristol.ac.uk/cmm/software/statjr/.

© Springer International Publishing Switzerland 2016
M. Mattoso and B. Glavic (Eds.): IPAW 2016, LNCS 9672, pp. 83–94, 2016.
DOI: 10.1007/978-3-319-40593-3_7

workflows that may be further refined, before being packaged up downloadable web-enabled documents, which support full reproducibility of the computations.

Many scientific workflow tools, such as Taverna [3], Kepler [4] and VisTrails [5], are monolithic "integrated development environments". Instead of locking a user into a single tool, we seek to facilitate their mobility between tools, to allow them to use the best tools for the job. This motivates the need for recording provenance in a manner that allows multiple tools to be used. Our approach is more akin to YesWorkflow [6] allowing multiple tools to be used in the scientific processes.

Furthermore, reproducibility is a key direction of development for many workflow tools. For example, ReproZip [7] enables reproducible experiments by monitoring command-line executions and packaging required resources into a distributable package. Its integration with VisTrails aids reproducibility by creating a suitable workflow of the original experiment for running within VisTrails. Provenance traces can be viewed as a "program" [8,9], which when interpreted, can reproduce results. Our take on this is the ability to translate the trace of a process execution back into an executable specification that is also editable.

The aim of this paper is to present a PROV-based technique to capture provenance at runtime from multiple tools, and provide the capability to automatically convert it into reproducible and editable workflows. Specifically, our contributions are: (*i*) INPWR (Intermediate Notation for Provenance and Workflow Reproducibility), a serialised format for capturing key values logged at runtime, from the various tools; (*ii*) A conversion of INPWR to PROV by means of a template expansion mechanism; (*iii*) A conversion of INPWR into an editable and executable workflow, which when executed would result in the same provenance; (*iv*) A quantitative evaluation demonstrating that the approach is tractable in terms of size of representations and computational costs.

In this paper, we discuss some application requirements in Sect. 2 and our computation model in Sect. 3. In Sect. 4, we introduce INPWR and demonstrate how we capture logs in Sect. 5. We demonstrate how INPWR enables the generation of PROV graph data as well as generation of new workflows in Sect. 6. In Sect. 7 we evaluate the costs of INPWR and go on to look at related work. Finally, we present our conclusions and further work.

2   Application Requirements

In this section we discuss some of the requirements of application to provide some context and motivation for this work.

Guide a reader through steps of an analysis. The system should enable a user to step through a complex analysis. The steps in the analysis could vary in size from broad methodological steps down to low-level operations. They should match the user's cognitive understanding of what is going on.

Adaptable. The user should be able to influence the path taken through an analysis. Analyses should support user input, branching and repetition.

Allow the results to be reproduced. The system should support the reproducibility of the analysis in light of choices made by the user. Specifically: (1) published material - provide supporting evidence for publication (2) automation - rerun the analysis e.g. to verify results or run with a different dataset (3) logbook - be a record of what actions were performed in the analysis for the user to refer/return to.

Ease of authoring. Authoring of an analysis should be available to all types of users. It should be easy to adapt/extend/repurpose an analysis. There should be a tight link between edit and running to facilitate explorative analysis and pedagogy.

From these application requirements, we derive the following technical requirements:

1. Capture information about the steps taken in the analysis into a log in sufficient detail for re-use whilst remaining concise.
2. Be able to transform that log into outputs for different purposes.
3. Transformation of log back into analysis should include user input and unwind branching and repetition. This revised analysis is different to storing the original analysis and any inputs made, as it reflects the exact steps taken to complete the analysis.

3   Computational Model

StatJR uses the Blockly visual programming system [10]. Blockly is designed to aid non-programmers in writing short scripts and as a toolkit for building visual programming language, it focusses on extensibility. Blockly opts to take an imperative programming approach in contrast to the dataflow approach of many scientific workflows. Blocks can be statement blocks or expression blocks and they have the notion of containment of other blocks for scoping and traditional flow control. Statement blocks are composed into a sequence of blocks.

In StatJR, we extend the selection of blocks available to include blocks that perform common statistical processes and blocks operate in the context of a dataset that flows down the chain of blocks. In addition, as blocks can encapsulate large computations, statement blocks can produce named outputs that can be viewed by the user.

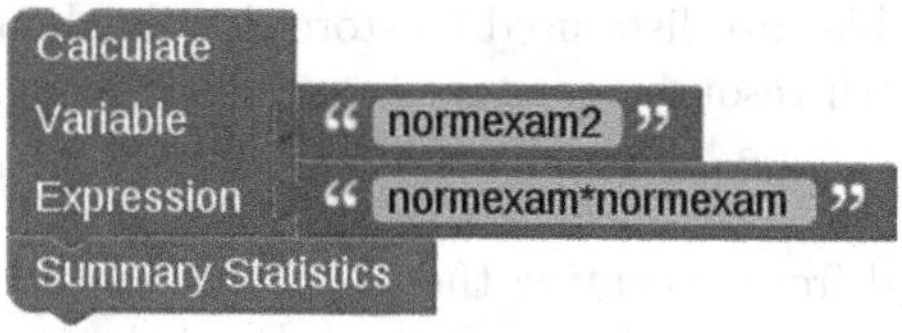

Fig. 1. Simple StatJR workflow.

Variable name	Type	Description
block_instance	uri	identifier for this execution
parent	uri	the parent of this execution
starttime	date	when the block started executing
endtime	date	when the block finished executing
block_uri	uri	refers to the block
block_title	string	the name of the block
block_type	uri	the type of the block
consumed	list of URIs	entities consumed
consumed_at	list of dates	when they were consumed
consumed_name	list of strings	their names
produced	list of URIs	entities produced
produced_at	list of dates	when they were produced
produced_name	list of strings	their names
literal	list of URIs	identifiers of literal values
literal_value	list of strings	their value
literal_type	list of strings	their type

Fig. 2. Binding variables for an execution of a block.

A simple workflow is shown in Fig. 1 which consists of a sequence of two blocks: (1) add a new column (`normexam2`) to current dataset by squaring values in another column (`normexam`) and (2) calculate some summary statistics about the revised dataset. In this example `normexam` is the name of a column in the dataset. The Calculate block generates a new dataset with the additional column and sets it as the dataset for following blocks.

We model the computation in our system in terms of tasks with named inputs and outputs. All tasks and values are uniquely identified. Tasks are invoked by a parent task.

4   INPWR Notation

INPWR captures the salient detail of the execution of a task defined in the previous section and consists of a set of variables and their values as shown in Fig. 2. They fall into two categories; (1) pertaining to information about the task and (2) linking to resources consumed and produced. Tasks have a type, are uniquely identified by the instance URI[3] and link to the block in the original workflow document. The parent task is stored to indicate the task hierarchy. Resources are linked to a task via a named port as with many dataflow workflow systems [11]. Values of literals are also stored in variables. All inputs and outputs (including literals) are given a generated URI with the exception of static resources that are supplied with StatJR (such as datasets). The `consumed`, `consumed_at` and `consumed_name` variables are lists used to store details about the consumption of resources i.e. the nth resource $consumed_n$ was used at $consumed\_at_n$ on the named port $consumed\_name_n$. A similar pattern is used for produced resources and any literals.

INPWR generated from executing the workflow in Fig. 1 is shown in Fig. 3. For clarity uuid references have been renamed. Block 1 represents the sequence

---

[3] We generate UUIDs and use the `urn:uuid:` scheme.

Variable name	Block 1	Block 2	Block 3
block_instance	urn:uuid:1	urn:uuid:2	urn:uuid:8
parent	-	urn:uuid:1	urn:uuid:1
block_uri	rqvik2xqakayemazt813	pgno3ns6cur7ej7yxhju	6fdqrmkq5n8fuq57qfti
block_title	Sequence	Calculate	DatasetSummary
block_type	estatwf:Sequence	estatwf:Calculate	estatwf:DatasetSummary
starttime	2016-02-12T15:12:28.543093	2016-02-12T15:12:28.546712	2016-02-12T15:12:28.679199
endtime	2016-02-12T15:12:29.527988	2016-02-12T15:12:28.677037	2016-02-12T15:12:29.527225
consumed		urn:uuid:3 ① urn:uuid:4 ② estat:datasets/tutorial	urn:uuid:5
consumed_at		2016-02-12T15:12:28.546846 2016-02-12T15:12:28.546846 2016-02-12T15:12:28.546846	2016-02-12T15:12:28.679253
consumed_name		expression column dataset	dataset
produced		urn:uuid:5 urn:uuid:6 urn:uuid:7	urn:uuid:9 urn:uuid:10 urn:uuid:11
produced_at		2016-02-12T15:12:28.676943 2016-02-12T15:12:28.676943 2016-02-12T15:12:28.676943	2016-02-12T15:12:29.527171 2016-02-12T15:12:29.527171 2016-02-12T15:12:29.527171
produced_name		inputs output script.py	script.py inputs table
literal		urn:uuid:3 ① urn:uuid:4 ②	
literal_value		normexam*normexam ① normexam2 ②	
literal_type		xsd:string ① xsd:string ②	

Fig. 3. Example INPWR log for an execution of workflow in Fig. 1 consisting of a sequence (Block 1) of two blocks which adds a new column `normexam2` to a dataset using the expression `normexam*normexam` (Block 2) and generates a summary table (Block 3).

of executing Blocks 2 and 3 (they have Block 1 (`urn:uuid:1`) as parent). Block 2 consumes two literal values "`normexam2`" (the name of the new dataset variable) and "`normexam*normexam`" (an expression the Calculate block passes to an underlying statistics library) as named inputs `column` and `expression` respectively. In this case, the URIs in the consumed variable (marked 1 and 2 in circles) refer to values defined in the 3 variables for literals. Both blocks output intermediate resources such as marshalled inputs and underlying Python code that is generated and executed by our statistical subsystem, in line with project goals of exposing pedagogical material to the user.

5 Capture

The StatJR workflow interpreter was augmented to capture execution information using INPWR. The key points for capture during interpreting a workflow are at the beginning of a block evaluation, at the point its input arguments have been evaluated, at the point when outputs are generated and finally at the end of block evaluation. At each capture point, a subset of variables are captured; we call this a *binding fragment*. The binding fragment is appended to a log along with the type of recording: *begin*, *input*, *output* and *end*.

To generate the complete INPWR log after execution, we iterate over the binding fragment log and use a stack to aid in combining the fragments. A *begin* fragment pushes a new INPWR record onto the stack, filling in values of variables known at block start (i.e. the top 6 variables in Fig. 2). This includes the parent variable which is the value of the `block_instance` variable in the next INPWR record on the stack. *Record input/output* appends values to the `consumed`, `produced` and `literal` variables as appropriate, including the `_at`, `_name`, `_value` and `_type` linked variables. *End* finalises a binding setting the `endtime` variable, pops the INPWR record from the stack, and commits it to the log.

6 Transformations

In this section, we look at how the INPWR log that we captured in Sect. 5 can be transformed into outputs useful in the StatJR system.

6.1 PROV Output via Templates

The PROV-Template system [12] allows the generation of PROV [13] documents by combining a template with a binding. The template is a PROV document which contains variables acting as placeholders for values and a binding document contains values for those variables. A provenance document is created by expanding a template against a binding; templates include special attributes that control this expansion process.

The process log recorded using INPWR is an ordered list of sets of variables, one for each step in the execution. Each set of variables in INPWR are the equivalent of a binding in PROV-Template. Hence, creating a complete PROV graph for an execution of a workflow involves expanding each binding in the INPWR log against a template and merging the resulting documents.

Figures 4 and 5 show an example template in graphical form and PROV-N representation. This PROV document is modelled on the computation model from Sect. 3 and articulates the process hierarchy, entities consumed and produced, and their derivations as well as supplementary information about time and types. In PROV-Template, attributes in the `tmpl` namespace map to specific elements in PROV-DM [13] where the typing does not allow a Qualified Name, for example the attribute `tmpl:startTime` on an Activity corresponds to the activity's start time. Note that in this template, we choose to model literal values as entities and whilst in the template the `var:literal` entity is disconnected, references to it will appear in the `consumed` or `produced` variables and the graph will be connected after expansion. This can be seen in Fig. 6 showing the provenance graph derived from the INPWR log from an execution of the workflow from Sect. 5. In this paper we use a single template for all INPWR log

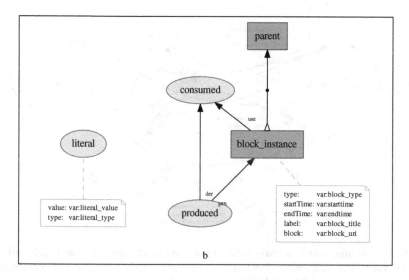

Fig. 4. Graphical representation of a template.

```
document
  prefix tmpl <http://openprovenance.org/tmpl#>
  prefix var <http://openprovenance.org/var#>
  prefix vargen <http://openprovenance.org/vargen#>
  prefix estat <http://purl.org/net/statjr/ns#>
  prefix estatwf <http://purl.org/net/statjr/wf#>

  bundle vargen:b
    activity(var:block_instance, -, -,
             [ tmpl:startTime='var:starttime', tmpl:endTime='var:endtime',
               prov:type='var:block_type', tmpl:label='var:block_title',
                 estatwf:block='var:block_uri' ] )
    activity(var:parent,-,-)
    wasStartedBy(var:block_instance, -, var:parent, -, [tmpl:time='var:starttime'])
    entity(var:consumed)
    used(var:block_instance, var:consumed, -,
         [ tmpl:time='var:consumed_at',
             estat:bindingname='var:consumed_name'] )
    entity(var:produced)
    wasGeneratedBy(var:produced, var:block_instance, -,
                   [ tmpl:time='var:produced_at',
                       estat:bindingname='var:produced_name'] )
    entity(var:literal, [estatwf:value='var:literal_value', estatwf:type='var:literal_type'])
    wasDerivedFrom(var:produced, var:consumed, -, -, -)
  endBundle
endDocument
```

Fig. 5. PROV-N representation of the template in Fig. 4.

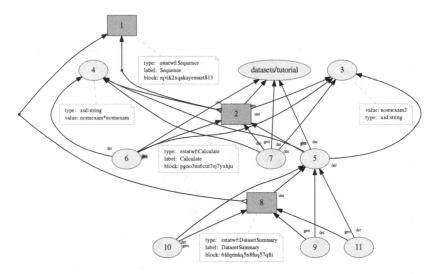

Fig. 6. Provenance graph derived from expansions of the template in Fig. 5 and the INPWR log in Fig. 3. Numbered entities (ovals) and activities (rectangles) correspond to the urn:uuid: URIs in the INPWR log.

entries, however templates could be applied selectively, perhaps based on the value of a variable (`block_type` for instance).

6.2   Workflow Output

The INPWR log captured is sufficiently descriptive to allow conversion to a workflow. Whilst conversion from INPWR back into the original workflow is not possible (due to conditionals), reconstructing the exact execution steps taken has some utility, particularly for publishing reproducible results. In addition, the INPWR log may not have been generated directly by the workflow system, and may instead come from one of the other StatJR tools and so being able to generate a workflow facilitates moving activity between tools in our system.

Blockly uses an XML format to serialise the abstract syntax tree of a Blockly program. Converting an INPWR record to Blockly XML involves creating the appropriate XML node and recursively generating nodes for the consumed resources. A consumed resource is found by searching the outputs of the immediate children of the current block. Special cases occur for sequences, control structures and user input. Reconstruction of sequences is performed by looking for blocks which have the same the parent and then ordering by time. For control structures, special care has to be taken to evaluate any conditions in case they created a side-effect; their results are discarded in the generated workflow. We unwind all loop structures. User input blocks are replaced with literal values that represent the input made.

Figure 7 shows an example workflow (left) and a reconstructed workflow from the INPWR log or a run (right). The workflow (left) consists of a loop asking

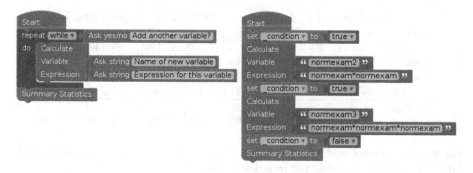

Fig. 7. Workflow (left) enabling the user to iteratively add new variables to a dataset, and resulting workflow reconstruction (right) after two variables were added.

the user whether they want to add a new variable, and a calculate block to construct a new variable based on asking the user the name of the new variable and an expression for it. A variable in this context is a statistical variable i.e. a column in a dataset. This calculate block modifies the currently active dataset by adding the column. This workflow was executed in which the user adds 2 variables (**normexam2** and **normexam3**), answering the "Add another variable?" question **Yes**, **Yes** and **No**. The reconstruction of this run is shown on the right of the figure, with the evaluation. The unwinding of the repeat/while loop can be seen with the repetition of the Calculate block and the condition translated to 3 instances of setting the variable _condition. The values of the loop conditional were inputs made by the user, and were translated to boolean literals **true**, **true** and **false**.

7   Evaluation

To establish that the cost of recording an INPWR log is not too onerous we look at memory and CPU usage when running a selection of workflows. Workflows were based on real-world examples and vary in size from small workflows which, for example, perform linear regression with 3 variables (**reg3**) or generate X-Y plots of multiple variables (**plotloop**) to larger workflows which perform more lengthy analysis (**lemma3** and **big**).

Figure 8 shows some memory usage metrics for the workflows. Python sizes are calculated by traversing the Python structures and applying **sys.getsize()**. The Python fragment sizes equate to the runtime memory overhead. Python records are the post-computation in memory cost and PROV-N records is the cost of serialising to disk. On average, we see a per record overhead of approximately 6 kB during runtime, 3.4 kB post-computation and on disk cost of 1.8 kB per record.

Runtime was measured as the wall-clock time for running each workflow 100 times with and without provenance capture. Figure 9 shows the results and the runtime overhead calculated as percentage.

name	blocks #	records #	fragments #	python	INPWR log python	prov-n	expansion prov-n	variables #
reg3	18	40	308	283,714	177,309	81,126	81,439	1,364
lemma3	74	69	441	414,514	267,197	122,939	97,324	2,082
plotloop	25	75	393	371,821	245,102	120,898	74,557	2,004
big	259	235	1,501	1,360,741	859,482	415,609	305,844	7,088
Average per record	–	–	6	5,962	3,395	1,798	1,436	30

Fig. 8. Memory overhead for a number of workflows (Python memory usage and PROV-N in bytes), including per record averages.

name	no provenance seconds	provenance seconds	overhead %
reg3	1333.16	1334.97	0.14
lemma3	1196.58	1202.45	0.49
plotloop	198.78	200.15	0.86
big	783.61	790.37	0.86

Fig. 9. Runtime overhead of tracking provenance across a selection of workflows - total runtime for 100 runs.

8   Related Work

Many scientific workflow systems capture provenance [14] with a distinction made between prospective and retrospective provenance. VisTrails [5] uses an SQL database for storage of retrospective provenance and an XML serialization for storing prospective provenance. It also records provenance about the evolution of workflows as they are edited. Taverna [3] collects retrospective provenance for use internally with in its workbench and provides export in the form of PROV-O. The noWorkflow system [15] captures provenance information from scripts without the need to instrument them. They use language dependent (primarily Python) methods to capture runtime provenance from of function activations and I/O events. They store their structured data in an SQL database. YesWorkflow [6] provides script authors with an annotation mechanism to describe prospective provenance. Their annotations are placed in language comments to be extracted by YesWorkflow tools; many scientific languages are supported.

Converting workflow traces back into valid workflows was the subject of the third Provenance Challenge [16]. To guarantee losslessness in the conversion from OPM back into a valid Taverna workflows additional annotations are needed [17].

9   Conclusion and Future Work

This paper has introduced an intermediate notation for recording provenance (INPWR) for use across multiple tools in StatJR. INPWR is compatible with existing PROV tools allowing easy generation of PROV graphs. We also demonstrated that INPWR expressive enough to support conversion to executable workflow and we have discussed benefits to our system of being able to do so. We measured the overhead of recording INPWR at runtime and found that it is tractable. The advantages of using INPWR are that it decouples logging from PROV generation and that it is more concise. In addition, whilst it would be possible to convert INPWR to PROV and then to workflow, this would involve complex queries over the PROV graph. We find that with INPWR, the information required is in a more readily accessible structure.

It is clear that in-memory and on-disk management of INPWR lends itself to optimisation, in particular in the presence of large workflows. Whilst we have made no attempt to optimise storing of INPWR logs, one possible avenue is to look at storing them in SQL databases as many workflow systems do.

INPWR logs are amenable to other transforms. For example, D-PROV [11] introduces extensions to PROV to express structural features in typical dataflow models. Generating D-PROV from INPWR would simply involve introducing the new relations to the PROV-Template system. Whilst our generated workflows reproduce the entire execution trace, applying program slicing [18] techniques could lead to more concise workflows for a given output.

Acknowledgements. This research was supported by the UK's Economic and Social Research Council (grant reference ES/K007246/1). Downloadable versions of workflows, provenance and other resources used in this paper can be found at http://dx.doi.org/10.5258/SOTON/393118.

References

1. Stodden, V., Leisch, F., Peng, R.D.: Implementing Reproducible Research. CRC Press, Boca Raton (2014)
2. Yang, H., Michaelides, D.T., Charlton, C., Browne, W.J., Moreau, L.: DEEP: a provenance-aware executable document system. In: Groth, P., Frew, J. (eds.) IPAW 2012. LNCS, vol. 7525, pp. 24–38. Springer, Heidelberg (2012)
3. Wolstencroft, K., Haines, R., Fellows, D., Williams, A., Withers, D., Owen, S., Soiland-Reyes, S., Dunlop, I., Nenadic, A., Fisher, P., Bhagat, J., Belhajjame, K., Bacall, F., Hardisty, A., Nieva de la Hidalga, A., Balcazar Vargas, M.P., Sufi, S., Goble, C.: The Taverna workflow suite: designing and executing workflows of web services on the desktop, web or in the cloud. Nucleic Acids Res. **41**(W1), W557–W561 (2013)
4. Ludäscher, B., Altintas, I., Berkley, C., Higgins, D., Jaeger, E., Jones, M., Lee, E.A., Tao, J., Zhao, Y.: Scientific workflow management and the Kepler system. Concurrency Comput. Pract. Exp. **18**(10), 1039–1065 (2006)
5. Callahan, S.P., Freire, J., Santos, E., Scheidegger, C.E., Silva, C.T., Vo, H.T.: VisTrails: visualization meets data management. In: Proceedings of the 2006 ACM SIGMOD International Conference on Management of Data, SIGMOD 2006, pp. 745–747. ACM, New York (2006)

6. McPhillips, T., Song, T., Kolisnik, T., Aulenbach, S., Belhajjame, K., Bocinsky, R., Cao, Y., Cheney, J., Chirigati, F., Dey, S., Freire, J., Jones, C., Hanken, J., Kintigh, K.W., Kohler, T.A., Koop, D., Macklin, J.A., Missier, P., Schildhauer, M., Schwalm, C., Wei, Y., Bieda, M., Ludäscher, B.: YesWorkflow: a user-oriented, language-independent tool for recovering workflow information from scripts. Int. J. Digital Curation **10**(1), 298–313 (2015)
7. Chirigati, F., Shasha, D., Freire, J.: ReproZip: using provenance to support computational reproducibility. In: Presented as part of the 5th USENIX Workshop on the Theory and Practice of Provenance, Berkeley, CA. USENIX (2013)
8. Moreau, L.: Provenance-based reproducibility in the semantic web. Web Semant. Sci. Serv. Agents World Wide Web **9**(2), 202–221 (2011)
9. Cheney, J., Ahmed, A., Acar, U.A.: Provenance as dependency analysis. Math. Struct. Comput. Sci. **21**, 1301–1337 (2011)
10. Fraser, N.: Blockly: A library for building visual editors. https://developers.google.com/blockly/
11. Missier, P., Dey, S., Belhajjame, K., Cuevas-Vicenttin, V., Ludäscher, B.: D-PROV: extending the PROV provenance model with workflow structure. In: 5th USENIX Workshop on the Theory and Practice of Provenance (TaPP 2013), Lombard, IL. USENIX Association, April 2013
12. Michaelides, D., Huynh, T.D., Moreau, L.: PROV-Template: A Template System for PROV Documents. https://provenance.ecs.soton.ac.uk/prov-template/
13. Moreau, L., Missier, P.: PROV-DM: The PROV data model. World Wide Web Consortium, Recommendation REC-prov-dm-20130430, April 2013
14. Freire, J., Koop, D., Santos, E., Silva, C.T.: Provenance for computational tasks: a survey. Comput. Sci. Eng. **10**(3), 11–21 (2008)
15. Murta, L., Braganholo, V., Chirigati, F., Koop, D., Freire, J.: noWorkflow: capturing and analyzing provenance of scripts. In: Ludaescher, B., Plale, B. (eds.) IPAW 2014. LNCS, vol. 8628, pp. 71–83. Springer, Heidelberg (2015)
16. Simmhan, Y., Groth, P., Moreau, L.: The third provenance challenge on using the open provenance model for interoperability. Future Gener. Comput. Syst. **27**(6), 737–742 (2011)
17. Missier, P., Goble, C.: Workflows to open provenance graphs, round-trip. Future Gener. Comput. Syst. **27**(6), 812–819 (2011)
18. Cheney, J.: Program slicing and data provenance. IEEE Data Eng. Bull. **30**(4), 22–28 (2007)

Towards the Domain Agnostic Generation of Natural Language Explanations from Provenance Graphs for Casual Users

Darren P. Richardson[✉] and Luc Moreau

Electronics and Computer Science,
University of Southampton, Southampton, UK
{dpr1g09,l.moreau}@ecs.soton.ac.uk

Abstract. As more systems become PROV-enabled, there will be a corresponding increase in the need to communicate provenance data directly to users. Whilst there are a number of existing methods for doing this — formally, diagrammatically, and textually — there are currently no application-generic techniques for generating linguistic explanations of provenance. The principal reason for this is that a certain amount of linguistic information is required to transform a provenance graph — such as in PROV — into a textual explanation, and if this information is not available as an annotation, this transformation is presently not possible.

In this paper, we describe how we have adapted the common 'consensus' architecture from the field of natural language generation to achieve this graph transformation, resulting in the novel PROVglish architecture. We then present an approach to garnering the necessary linguistic information from a PROV dataset, which involves exploiting the linguistic information informally encoded in the URIs denoting provenance resources. We finish by detailing an evaluation undertaken to assess the effectiveness of this approach to lexicalisation, demonstrating a significant improvement in terms of fluency, comprehensibility, and grammatical correctness.

1 Introduction

As organisations begin to understand the value of storing and utilising PROV data [13], they will increasingly find scenarios where it is useful to show that data to their users. Where resources allow, the best interfaces to this data will likely be bespoke creations, tailored to the specific needs of the application. However, we speculate that in many cases the resources will not be made available to take this approach, motivating the search for an application-generic way of communicating provenance to casual users.

In this vein, there are already a number of different ways for communicating PROV data to human users in formal [14], diagrammatic [5,17], and linguistic forms [16]. The utility of these various approaches depends on a number of factors but, perhaps, most importantly the user and their familiarity with the intricacies of both PROV and the application context. For example, whilst it is

© Springer International Publishing Switzerland 2016
M. Mattoso and B. Glavic (Eds.): IPAW 2016, LNCS 9672, pp. 95–106, 2016.
DOI: 10.1007/978-3-319-40593-3_8

a very useful tool in a suitable context, it would not be appropriate to use the PROV-N notation to communicate with the vast majority of users. Likewise, the diagrammatic forms of representing PROV are also potentially inaccessible to many users who would perhaps have difficulty understanding mathematical graphs.

A competent speaker of a particular language, on the other hand, is presumably far more likely to understand a well-worded provenance explanation, than understand a diagrammatic representation in a format that they have not previously encountered. Linguistic interfaces are of further use in contexts where a visual interface might be inappropriate, unsafe, or illegal — such as when driving a vehicle.

The main contribution of this work is to extend the state-of-the-art with respect to natural language interfaces for provenance, showing significant improvements in terms of grammatical correctness, fluency, and comprehensibility. This is achieved by introducing techniques from the field of Natural Language Generation (NLG), and using URIs as a source of lexical information. We present an approach to transforming PROV graphs into natural language in an application-generic fashion, resulting in explanations which our evaluation shows are more accessible to a casual user.

After a brief review of related work in Sect. 2, we introduce the PROVglish architecture we have developed to accomplish this in Sect. 3, followed by a deeper explanation of how we extract the necessary linguistic information from the PROV graph in Sect. 4. We then continue by demonstrating the effectiveness of this approach in a formal evaluation in Sect. 5. Finally, in Sect. 6, we conclude with a brief summary of this work's contributions followed by a consideration of possible avenues of future research.

2   Related Work

PROV was standardised as a recommendation of the World Wide Web Consortium in 2013 [13]. The Provenance Working Group, which developed this recommendation, created a human-readable representation for PROV, PROV-N [14], and suggested a diagrammatic representation [17]. These representations — in particular PROV-N — were only intended for developers and implementors already familiar with the PROV data model, rather than for casual users of provenance. Since then, there has been little research published as to how to present provenance to users in a domain-generic way.

At present, interfaces are either being tailor-made for a particular application, such as on the website of *The Gazette*[1], or by integrating the diagrammatic representations into the interface, such as in [23]. One notable exception is [5], in which Sankey diagrams are used to represent provenance in a process-centric way; this approach is probably far more accessible to a casual user than the

---

[1] *The Gazette* is the official public record of the United Kingdom. For an example of their provenance trail, see https://www.thegazette.co.uk/notice/2184651/provenance.

PROV Working Group's diagrammatic approach, but is as yet unable to show provenance in an entity- or agent-oriented manner. Finally, in order to help users understand large-scale provenance datasets, an approach has been developed to generate summaries of a PROV graph [15], which can be displayed using a minimally adapted version of the PROV Working Group diagrams.

As for natural language interfaces, there exists a string-substitution templated approach to generating natural language explanations from provenance data [16], but this is application-specific due to the simple nature of the templates. The NLG research community, on the other hand, has developed more sophisticated approaches to generating texts from data. There are a number of NLG architectures described in the literature, with the two most well-known being the 'consensus' architecture [19], in particular the refined version [20], and the RAGS architecture [12]. The advantage of such architectures is that they allow for the sharing and reuse of architectural components, such as a realisation engine [4]. Within the field, there are also a number of common ways of evaluating NLG systems [11], often involving the use of humans comparing two example sentences across a number of different metrics [6].

There have been a number of attempts to apply NLG techniques to RDF datasets. Some use an ontology to annotate the linguistic information that is needed to perform the transformation of data to text [10], whilst others use a statistical, corpus-based approach [3]. Finally, there has been an attempt to exploit the linguistic information informally encoded in URIs [22], though this was only able to generate very short texts from up to six triples, due to the fact that there are very few constraints on what sorts of information an RDF document can include. PROV, on the other hand, contains a limited set of relationships, as well as information relating to the temporal ordering of events. Our earlier work [21], presented a technique that was able to choose a near-minimal set of templated sentences in a controlled natural language required to fully transform a provenance graph.

3   Generating Explanations from Provenance

We are aware of only one existing technique capable of transforming provenance graphs into text [16]. However, in that case, the approach taken is template-based, using simple string-substitution, and consequently is only as application-generic as the templates it is based on. Here there are two options: either, create templates that would work for all valid provenance graphs, based on the primitives of PROV; or, alternatively, use templates created for a specific application that can take advantage of the additional knowledge one has about the form and structure of the data to be transformed.

The latter, whilst able to produce the most natural-looking sentences, requires more development and maintenance than a general solution. On the other hand, the former, more general, solution has historically been limited to using sentences like: "X was derived from Y, which was a revision of Z." Whilst this sort of language *might* be appropriate when talking about documents, in

PROV an entity can be almost anything, and it may not be appropriate to refer to all things using those terms. To illustrate, a person can be a prov:Entity (as well as a prov:Agent), and it is altogether less usual to refer to people as derivatives of their earlier selves in English, even if this is how they could be represented in a provenance graph.

The existing template-based PROV explainer [16] used a relatively simple string-replacement approach, where the template contained variables that were substituted by values each time the template was expanded. This has the advantage of being simple to implement, and efficient to execute, but makes generating orthographically correct sentences difficult for a number of reasons, such as number agreement or verb conjugation. In order to be able to generate explanations of more complex situations, we decided to explore the use of a more sophisticated template-based architecture drawing on the work of the natural language generation (NLG) research community.

Figure 1 shows the components of our PROVglish architecture, which is based on the 'consensus architecture' [19, 20]. The consensus architecture, whilst having its detractors [12], is so-called because it presents an attempt to describe how

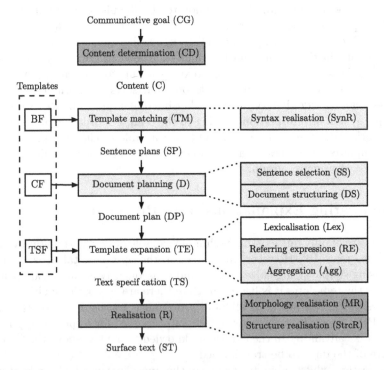

Fig. 1. Provenance explanation generation architecture, PROVglish. Modules are shown in the centre, with the component processes of those modules on the right. The template functions, and their mappings onto modules are shown on the left. Modules in dark grey occur outside of our system; those in light grey occur within our system; and those in white are the focus of the evaluation presented in this paper.

NLG systems are typically constructed, rather than prescribing a model that new systems should adhere to. Our design retains the core pipeline model of this architecture, starting with a communicative goal and resulting in a surface text, but splits and rearranges a number of the intermediate steps to better suit a template-based approach to generation.

One particular advantage of following a common architectural design such as this is that the task can be easily modularised, allowing for the use of off-the-shelf tools. In this case, specifically, it allows us to focus on the areas of NLG that are of particular interest from a provenance perspective, shaded in white in Fig. 1. Those blocks shaded in dark grey, on the other hand, represent parts of the process that are not directly contributing to this research. For example, we were able to use a pre-existing off-the-shelf realisation engine (R) [4], capable of taking text specifications (TS) and producing orthographically-correct surface texts (ST). The first stage in the pipeline, content determination (CD), is where the application decides what provenance to communicate to the user. Because this will vary from application to application, we leave that to individual implementers, with our system providing all the stages from template matching (TM) to template expansion (TE).

3.1 Templates

In the PROVglish architecture templates are comprised of three functions:

Bindings Function (BF). A function that takes the graph and returns a set of sets of bindings. Each set of bindings corresponds to a possible expression of a part of the graph in textual form — a possible sentence. The bindings themselves are values mapped to variable names that will later be used by the coverage function (CF) and text specification function (TSF). Because of the many possible combinations of sentences that could be used to express a graph, many more sets of bindings are generated than are actually necessary to do this.

Coverage Function (CF). A function that returns the subgraph that can be inferred from, or is expressed by the template and a set of bindings — that is, what subgraph would be transformed into text by this template with this set of bindings. Using these coverage sets, we are able to ensure that every explanation generated by our system expresses the entire provenance graph that was passed to it.

Text Specification Function (TSF). A function that takes a set of bindings and returns the sentence as a text specification (TS). This is done by simple template string substitution, but unlike the existing technique allows the realisation engine to handle the much harder task of ensuring that the sentence is orthographically correct.

3.2 The Process of Explanation Generation

Template Matching (TM). In this stage, the bindings function of each template registered in the system is executed over the content provenance graph (C), returning a set of bindings for each pattern in the graph matched by the template. We call the combination of a template and a set of bindings a sentence plan (SP), because together they represent a possible sentence that can be expressed from the content graph (C).

Document Planning (D). This stage is separated into two parts, sentence selection (SS) and document structuring (DS). Sentence selection is the process by which the list of sentence plans (SP) is whittled down to a smaller list; ideally one that is capable of completely expressing the graph with a minimal number of sentences. This is an example of the set-cover problem, and is solved using the greedy algorithm described in [21]. Document structuring (DS) is the process by which the chosen sentences are ordered into a coherent structure, either using a mathematical metrics-based approach, or by using a narrative-based approach such as Rhetorical Structure Theory [8] to guide the structuring.

Template Expansion (TE). comprises three aspects of NLG, though in this work we only focus on the first two, leaving Aggregation (Agg) for further work. Lexicalisation (Lex) and referring expression generation (RE), on the other hand, form one of the most important contributions of this work. Lexicalisation, which will be discussed in more detail in Sect. 4 is the process by which the system decides how each concept in the provenance graph should be mapped onto English words in a general sense, while RE determines how a concept should be referred to in a particular context. For example, a person will commonly be lexicalised by their name, whereas in many sentences it is more appropriate to refer to them by a description, by their contextual situation, or by using some form of anaphoric reference. By choosing these terms, and substituting them into the template, we are able to generate text specifications to be passed into the realiser(R).

4 Extracting Linguistic Information from URIs

One of the major obstacles that is necessary to overcome when generating explanations from data is the matter of obtaining the linguistic information necessary to perform lexicalisation. More simply put: how does one know what to call anything? In RDF, there are ways to formally annotate this linguistic information [10], or one can even encode it less formally in features such as rdfs:label. However, making use of these features for explanation generation would not be application-generic, because these features are not guaranteed to be present in all PROV data. The only features that might contain linguistic information that are guaranteed to be present in a PROV dataset are the URIs that denote each resource.

It is worth noting that URIs, per the RFCs that define them, formally contain no linguistic information that would facilitate natural language generation, as they are intended to be treated opaquely [1]. However, many system developers have created systems that mint meaningful URIs, for a number of possible reasons, such as increasing code maintainability. This means that if one were able to understand how this linguistic information is often informally encoded in URIs, then it would be possible to exploit this information for the purposes of natural language generation. We are not the first to attempt to use URIs in this way [22], but previous attempts were met with limited success due to the fact that there are far fewer constraints on what an RDF document can say, and how it can say it. PROV, on the other hand, is a much smaller domain, limited by a number of constraints, leading us to hypothesise that we might have a greater degree of success. Our investigation has shown this to be the case.

We tested this hypothesis, using the University of Southampton Provenance Store, a PROV repository, as our source of provenance data. From these documents we extracted the URIs denoting all the PROV resources to use as our corpus of PROV URIs. Using this corpus, we were able to develop a regular expression that allowed us to split each URI into its linguistic tokens — this is not as trivial a task as might be expected, as there are a number of approaches people use to compose tokens, with CamelCase and snake_case as just two examples. The expression we settled upon was able to correctly tokenise 96 % of the URIs (2525 out of 2637 distinct URIs). The remaining 4 % would have required a more complex system with an understanding of the English language. The regular expression we used was:

```
[0-9a-fA-F]{10,} | (?:Mc|Mac)?[A-Z][a-z]+ | [A-Z]+s?(?![a-z]) |
[a-z]+ | [0-9]+
```

This expression is able to distinguish tokens that fall into the following categories:

- Hexadecimal numbers of at least 10 characters (this limit was introduced to prevent splitting English words like 'feedback', which is comprised mainly of the characters 'a' to 'f');
- Words beginning with a capital letter, including those with common Scottish name prefixes;
- Acronyms and their plurals;
- Lower case words; and
- Decimal numbers.

Having developed a technique to tokenise the URIs, it became necessary to understand the linguistic role played by each of the tokens. We used an off-the-shelf part-of-speech (POS) tagger to tag the URI tokens according to which role they would play in a sentence — for example, whether the token was a 2nd person present tense verb, or a superlative adjective, etc. Specifically, we used the maximum entropy POS tagger [18] trained on the Penn Treebank corpus [9], which came as the default tagger of the NLTK python library [2]. It was important to verify that the tagger would perform well with tokenised URIs because it was originally trained on standard English texts, and there was no guarantee that it would work with the much shorter, less grammatically correct URI tokens.

However, the performance of the POS tagger was surprisingly good, with it being able to identify the correct specific tag (singular proper noun, present-tense 3rd person verb, superlative adjective, etc.) 62.7 % of the time, and the correct class of tag (whether the token was a noun, verb, adjective, modifier, or a number) 92.3 % of the time. This level of performance indicated that it would be possible to build generation rules using at least the classes of tags, if not the specific tags themselves.

5 Evaluation

Having used the knowledge gained in the investigations described in Sect. 4 to build templates that were able to exploit the linguistic information in URIs, we devised a human experiment, based on common examples in the literature [6,11] to evaluate the effectiveness of this approach relative to a system where this information was not exploited. Consequently, this experiment is centred around a number of sentence pairs generated automatically, where each sentence pair consists of one sentence generated using the URI lexicalisation technique, and an equivalent sentence that was generated without that additional linguistic information. For each sentence pair, the participant was asked to rank them across a number of dimensions: grammatical correctness, fluency of the language, and ease of comprehension. It should perhaps be noted that the KNIGHT study [6] had additional dimensions, but these were excluded because they relate to the structure of an explanation, whereas in this evaluation we were focussing on the performance of individual sentences within a document.

It was our hypothesis that the system exploiting the linguistic information in URIs should have performed better in terms of fluency and comprehensibility. However, it was our expectation that there would be no significant difference in terms of grammatical correctness, because the sentences that were generated without exploiting the linguistic information in URIs were guaranteed to generate grammatically correct sentences. (This is a consequence of the way the templates were constructed.)

We had 15 participants, each comparing 15 sentence pairs, resulting in the collection of 225 individual data-points for each condition (URIs exploited/URIs unexploited), and for each dimension (Grammatical correctness, Fluency, and Comprehension). Participants were not given definitions for each of the dimensions, but rather were asked to answer the questions with respect to their own perceptions of what those terms meant. The participants were drawn from our Electronics and Computer Science department, and the majority were unfamiliar with PROV or provenance annotation.

Table 1 shows the results of these experiments, and Fig. 2a, b, and c clarify the distribution of responses. In addition to those results, when asked simply which sentence they thought was the better explanation, participants indicated the sentence with the URIs exploited 56.5 % of the time, URIs unexploited 29.3 % of the time, and neither the remaining 14.2 % of the time.

Table 1. The results of the study across all sentence pairs and participants, broken down by dimension (Grammar, Fluency, and Comprehensibility), and further broken down by whether the linguistic information in the URIs was exploited or unexploited.

Metric	Grammar		Fluency		Comp.		Combined	
	Exp.	Unexp.	Exp.	Unexp.	Exp.	Unexp.	Exp.	Unexp.
Mean	4.72	4.36	4.65	3.59	4.74	4.13	4.70	4.03
Standard Deviation	1.49	1.28	1.49	1.35	1.48	1.42	1.49	1.39
Difference	+0.36		+1.06		+0.61		+0.67	
p Value	4.8×10^{-5}		2.5×10^{-15}		7.1×10^{-7}		—	
N	225						675	

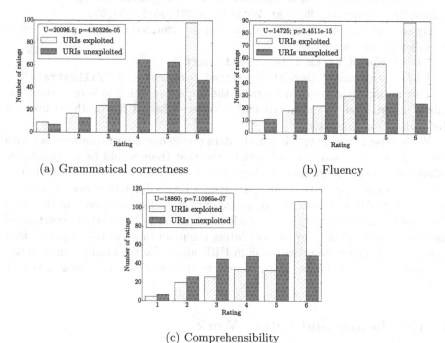

(a) Grammatical correctness   (b) Fluency

(c) Comprehensibility

Fig. 2. Participant responses for each dimension, aggregated across all sentence pairs and participants. Legend shows U-value and p-value obtained from Mann-Whitney U Test. $N = 225$

We used a Mann-Whitney U-test [7] to determine the statistical difference between the condition where the linguistic information in URIs was exploited and the condition where it was not. Across all sentence pairs, and all participants, the system that exploited the linguistic information in URIs performed significantly better in all three dimensions than the system that did not. See Fig. 2a, b, and c. In each case, one can clearly see the difference in distributions from the graphs.

There are a couple of interesting points to be drawn from these results, that cannot be seen from the figures alone. Firstly, not a single participant gave significantly worse ratings for the sentences generated exploiting URIs, across any dimension, when averaged across all sentence pairs.

Additionally, the only sentence pair to perform significantly worse across all three dimensions was pair 8, where the system was confused by the fact that the word 'step' can be both a verb and a noun, resulting in a text specification that was further misinterpreted by the realiser, and where the following two sentences were generated:

URIs exploited: `Vote 1043 0 was executioned step at`
`2011-12-18T01:00:17+00:00`.

URIs unexploited: ' `/data/UpVote1043.0` ' `was generated by`
' `/data/ExecutionStep652` ' `at 2011-12-18T01:00:17+00:00`.

By contrast, one of the sentence pairs that performed best was pair 12, with the following two sentences:

URIs exploited: `Derek illustrated chart 1`.

URIs unexploited: ' `/derek` ' `generated` ' `/chart1` ' `by` ' `/illustrate` '.

This example clearly demonstrates the impact of being able to extract linguistic information — and in particular, verbs — from URIs on the richness of the explanation generated.

With respect to our hypotheses, the data proves our expectations correct with only a single exception: we had anticipated that there would be no significant difference between the grammatical correctness of the sentences produced. In this regard, it would appear that our participants had a different expectation to us as to what makes a sentence grammatically correct. However, even in this case, the system that exploited the linguistic information in URIs still outperformed the system that did not, further validating the main thesis of this paper — that exploiting the linguistic information in URIs allows for the production of better explanations of provenance. With respect to that, the data is supportive on all counts.

6   Conclusions and Future Work

In this paper, we have shown how the use of more sophisticated architectures for natural language generation can be applied to the task of explaining provenance graphs to casual users. In addition to facilitating richer explanations at a lower development cost by using off-the-shelf components for surface realisation, when combined with the exploitation of linguistic information informally encoded in URIs, we were able to generate explanations that performed significantly better in a user evaluation. Our approach is application-generic, and can work with all valid provenance graphs.

At present, our system is only capable of generating single sentence explanations. However, many of the provenance graphs we might wish to communicate with a user are considerably larger than can be reasonably transformed into a single sentence. Consequently, we are now investigating the possibility of generating longer, multi-sentential explanations from larger PROV graphs, as well as from PROV graph summaries [15]. We are exploring the potential role of various narrative theories to the application of structuring these longer texts, with a goal of generating more engaging texts than can be achieved with more conventional, graph-metric-based approaches.

Acknowledgements. Research was sponsored by US Army Research laboratory and the UK Ministry of Defence and was accomplished under Agreement Number W911NF-06-3-0001. The views and conclusions contained in this document are those of the authors and should not be interpreted as representing the official policies, either expressed or implied, of the US Army Research Laboratory, the U.S. Government, the UK Ministry of Defence, or the UK Government. The US and UK Governments are authorised to reproduce and distribute reprints for Government purposes notwithstanding any copyright notation hereon. The investigations and human experiment were subject to ethics approvals ERGO-FPSE-16722 and ERGO-FPSE-16731, and the source data used to generate the sentence pairs was drawn from the Southampton Provenance Store (https://provenance.ecs.soton.ac.uk/store). The research data can be found at http://dx.doi.org/10.5258/SOTON/393255 and http://dx.doi.org/10.5258/SOTON/393257.

References

1. Berners-Lee, T.: Universal Resource Identifiers - Axioms of Web Architecture, Technical note, World Wide Web Consortium (1996). https://www.w3.org/DesignIssues/Axioms.html
2. Bird, S., Loper, E., Klein, E.: Natural Language Processing with Python. O'Reilly Media Inc., Sebastopol (2009)
3. Ell, B., Harth, A.: A language-independent method for the extraction of RDF verbalization templates. In: Proceedings of the 8th International Natural Language Generation Conference, Philadelphia, PA, USA (2014)
4. Gatt, A., Reiter, E.: SimpleNLG: a realisation engine for practical applications. In: Proceedings of the 12th European Workshop on Natural Language Generation, Athens, Greece, pp. 90–93 (2009)
5. Hoekstra, R., Groth, P.: PROV-O-Viz - understanding the role of activities in provenance. In: Ludaescher, B., Plale, B. (eds.) IPAW 2014. LNCS, vol. 8628, pp. 215–220. Springer, Heidelberg (2015)
6. Lester, J.C., Porter, B.W.: Developing and empirically evaluating robust explanation generators: the KNIGHT experiments. Comput. Linguist. **23**(1), 65–101 (1997)
7. Mann, H.B., Whitney, D.R.: On a test of whether one of two random variables is stochastically larger than the other. Ann. Math. Stat. **18**(1), 50–60 (1947)
8. Mann, W.C., Thompson, S.A.: Rhetorical structure theory: toward a functional theory of text organization. Text **8**(3), 243–281 (1988)
9. Marcus, M.P., Santorini, B., Marcinkiewicz, M.A.: Building a large annotated corpus of English: The Penn Treebank. Comput. Linguist. **19**(2), 313–330 (1993)
10. McCrae, J., Spohr, D., Cimiano, P.: Linking lexical resources and ontologies on the semantic web with lemon. In: Antoniou, G., Grobelnik, M., Simperl, E., Parsia, B., Plexousakis, D., Leenheer, P., Pan, J. (eds.) ESWC 2011, Part I. LNCS, vol. 6643, pp. 245–259. Springer, Heidelberg (2011)

11. Mellish, C., Dale, R.: Evaluation in the context of natural language generation. Comput. Speech Lang. **12**(4), 349–373 (1998)
12. Mellish, C., Scott, D., Cahill, L., Paiva, D., Evans, R., Reape, M.: A reference architecture for natural language generation systems. Nat. Lang. Eng. **12**(1), 1–34 (2006)
13. Moreau, L., Missier, P.: PROV-DM: The PROV Data Model. Recommendation of the World Wide Web Consortium (2013). http://www.w3.org/TR/prov-dm
14. Moreau, L., Missier, P.: PROV-N: The Provenance Notation. Recommendation of the World Wide Web Consortium (2013). http://www.w3.org/TR/prov-n
15. Moreau, L.: Aggregation by provenance types: a technique for summarising provenance graphs. In: Proceedings of Graphs as Models 2015 (An ETAPS 2015 Workshop), in Electronic Proceedings in Theoretical Computer Science, London, UK, pp. 129–144 (2015)
16. Packer, H.S., Moreau, L.: Sentence templating for explaining provenance. In: Ludaescher, B., Plale, B. (eds.) IPAW 2014. LNCS, vol. 8628, pp. 278–280. Springer, Heidelberg (2015)
17. PROV Working Group: PROV Graph Layout Conventions, Technical note, World Wide Web Consortium. https://www.w3.org/2011/prov/wiki/Diagrams
18. Ratnaparkhi, A.: A maximum entropy model for part-of-speech tagging. In: Proceedings of the Conference on Empirical Methods in Natural Language Processing, New Brunswick, NJ (1996)
19. Reiter, E.: Has a consensus NL generation architecture appeared, and is it psycholinguistically plausible? In: Proceedings of the Seventh International Workshop on Natural Language Generation, Kennebunkport, ME, pp. 163–170 (1994)
20. Reiter, E., Dale, R.: Building Natural Language Generation Systems. Cambridge University Press, Cambridge (2000)
21. Richardson, D.P., Moreau, L., Mott, D.: Beyond the graph: telling the story with PROV and controlled English. In: Proceedings of the 2014 Annual Fall Meeting of the International Technology Alliance, Cardiff, UK (2014)
22. Sun, X., Mellish, C.: Domain independent sentence generation from RDF representations for the semantic web. In: Proceedings of the Combined Workshop on Language-Enabled Educational Technology and Development and Evaluation of Robust Spoken Dialogue Systems, Riva del Garda, Italy (2006)
23. Toniolo, A., Wentao Ouywang, R., Dropps, T., Oren, N., Norman, T.J., Srivastava, M., Allen, J.A., de Mel, G., Sullivan, P., Mastin, S., Pearson, G.: Assessing the credibility of information in collaborative intelligence analysis. In: Proceedings of the Annual Fall Meeting of the International Technology Alliance, Cardiff, UK, p. 2014 (2014)

Provenance Models and Applications

Versioning Version Trees: The Provenance of Actions that Affect Multiple Versions

David Koop[✉]

University of Massachusetts Dartmouth, Dartmouth, MA, USA
dkoop@umassd.edu

Abstract. Change-based provenance captures how an entity is constructed; it can be used not only as a record of the steps taken but also as a guide during the development of derivative or new analyses. This provenance is captured as a version tree which stores a set of related entities and the exact changes made in deriving one from another. Version trees are generally viewed as monotonic–new nodes may be added but none are modified or deleted. However, there are a number of operations (e.g., upgrades) where this constraint leads to inefficient and unintuitive new versions. To address this, we propose a version tree without monotonicity where nodes may be modified and new actions inserted. We also propose to track the provenance of these tree changes to ensure that past version trees are not lost. This provenance is change-based; it links versions of version trees by the actions which transform the trees. Thus, we continue to track every change that impacts the evolution of an entity, but the actions are split between direct edits and changes to the version tree that affect multiple entity definitions. We show how this provenance leads to more intuitive and efficient operations on workflows and how this hybrid provenance may be understood.

Keywords: Provenance · Version tree · Workflows

1 Introduction

As the number of documents, source trees, and images continues to grow, it is important to understand when and how individual items are related to each other. If a digital entity has changed over time, there are different versions of it, and the relationships between these versions help organize the information they contain. Version graphs encode derivation histories of the entities and may also relate different objects that were derived from a similar source. Usually, these graphs are used to archive past versions, often encoded for efficient storage. However, past versions may also be re-examined and integrated with current and future versions. In most cases, *one* new version is generated when an entity is modified or merged with another version. For example, in versioned source code, a commit defines a single new version with the updates to the files.

A version graph most basically defines when one version is derived from another, but this information need not contain *how* the versions are related.

© Springer International Publishing Switzerland 2016
M. Mattoso and B. Glavic (Eds.): IPAW 2016, LNCS 9672, pp. 109–121, 2016.
DOI: 10.1007/978-3-319-40593-3_9

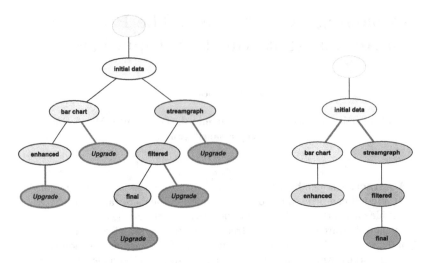

Fig. 1. It is often necessary to update or upgrade collections of related documents or workflows. Even though these changes can be automated, each version must be modified often with the same changes (left, new nodes and edges outlined in red). If we can instead edit the version tree, we can update past changes to reflect the updates (right, modified edges highlighted in red). (Color figure online)

Change-based schemes, however, store the changes that transform one version to another. With this richer history, we can not only understand the difference but also directly edit the change to update the derivative version. When that edit impacts a version that itself has many derivative versions, *all* of those versions are also affected. Such edits can correct past errors, update an old approach, or introduce additional functionality to multiple versions. For example, in a source code version tree, we might replace an algorithm added early in development with a more efficient version. Instead of applying these changes to each branch, we modify the tree itself so branches inherit the update.

While this rewriting of history brings the potential for efficient and intuitive edits over a collection of versions, it also presents the problem of how to preserve the old collection. This is particularly problematic when the past versions are tied to other provenance information. For example, a collection of workflows may need to be upgraded, but if the provenance of past runs is associated with the old versions, we do not want to lose the definitions of them. To address this problem, we suggest *versioning version trees* by storing the evolution provenance of the version tree. Figure 1 shows how this can declutter workflow upgrades. Any version can be obtained by first materializing the version tree and then materializing the version in that tree. To simplify navigation, we propose *links* between a version in one version tree and its "derivative" version in another version tree. Because simple additions to a current version tree can be interleaved with transformations of version trees, the provenance of any single version becomes more involved.

We introduce meta version trees (MVTs), define intuitive operations enabled by the new trees, test their efficiency using synthetic version trees, and discuss the implications in understanding the provenance of entities created and modified in this framework.

2 Preliminaries

2.1 Versioning Background

Keeping track of different versions of documents, code, and workflows is commonplace, but the strategies for doing so have evolved over time. With a central authority for changes, it is possible to fully order the versions according to the time they were submitted. However, distributed version control systems allow changes to be evolve independently from a central repository. Branching allows users to develop new features in a branch, and then merge these changes back into a "master" branch. Version graphs track versions of evolving objects and any merges [5]; merging operations require the history to be represented as a directed acyclic graph. Because we will be leveraging change-based versioning where explicit user changes specify the derivation of a version, we focus on version trees which do not contain merges.

A *version tree* is a tree where each node represents a version of a particular entity (S) and an edge from one version to another indicates that the child version was derived from the parent version. Recall that a tree $T = (V, E)$ is a directed acyclic graph where each node $v \in V$ has at most one edge ending at v. In a version tree, each node v has an associated version S_v. If, for a given v, there exists u such that $(u, v) \in E$, then S_u is the *parent version* of S_v and S_v is a *child version* of S_u. Note that in general, there is no specific restriction on how two versions must relate to each other. A version tree may represent a human-curated understanding of derivations or enforce specific derivation requirements that permits automated construction.

2.2 Change-Based Version Trees

A version tree indicates relationships between versions, but these relationships can be further defined as transformations from one version to another. These functions define the *changes* and may be inferred or prescribed. For example, version control software like svn [17] computes differences between the current and previous version of a file, inferring the lines added and deleted. Thus, a search-and-replace of a single word would be recorded by most version control software as a sequence of line modifications. VisTrails, on the other hand, stores the exact actions it makes when a user changes a workflow [8]. For example, when a module is added to a workflow, the exact detail is recorded. Such prescriptive changes allow greater understanding of the process involved in creating a workflow.

Formally, a change-based version tree $T = (V, E, S_0)$ is a version tree where S_0 is a default version, and for each edge $(u, v) \in E$, there exists an associated function f such that $f(S_u) = S_v$. In other words, f tells us how S_v can be derived from S_u. Associating the function with the edge instead of the node will provide more intuitive operations in manipulating change-based version trees. The root of the change-based tree often corresponds to an empty state, e.g., an empty repository or an empty workflow. In a general version tree, we might need to store the associated version for each node, but a change-based version tree requires storing *only* the edge functions and the default state S_0. Let $P(0, v)$ denote the edges $e_1, \ldots, e_n$ along the path from the root to version v. Then, given a change-based version tree $T = (V, E, S_0)$ and a node v,

$$S_v = f_n \circ \cdots \circ f_1(S_0)$$

where each f_i is the function associated with the edge $e_i \in P(v)$. Although we do not need to store any versions S_v except the default version, we will need to be able to *materialize* any version via the above construction.

In many cases, we may also have inverse functions that allow us to transform from a version to its parent version. Specifically, the *inverse action* f^{-1} associated with an edge (u, v) satisfies $f^{-1}(S_v) = S_u$. This allows greater flexibility in materializing versions as we can move between states in both directions. Note that we may have some actions where inverses exist and others where they do not in the same change-based version tree. If there exists an inverse for *every* edge, we say the change-based version tree is *invertible*. Given an invertible change-based version tree $T = (V, E, S_0)$ and two nodes u and v with common parent p,

$$S_v = f_n \circ \cdots \circ f_1 \circ g_1^{-1} \circ \cdots \circ g_m^{-1}(S_u)$$

where each f_i is the function associated with the edge $e_i \in P(p, v)$ and g_j^{-1} is the inverse associated with the edge $e_j \in P(p, u)$. The construction corresponds to applying inverses up to a common parent p and then applying forward actions down to v.

We can also *compress* edges in a change-based version tree by composing their functions. Specifically, suppose v has a single parent u and a single child w. We can compress edges (u, v) and (v, w) with associated actions f and g, respectively, into a single edge (u, w) with the associated function $g \circ f$. The node v can then be eliminated from the change-based version T.

This allows us, given a set of nodes $\{v_i\}$, to construct a *skeleton* of a change-based version tree T, $\texttt{skel}(T, \{v_i\})$. The skeleton consists of all nodes $\{v_i\}$, the root, and the compressed edges between them. Often selected nodes include those that have been annotated or are at a branch point (have more than one child node).

2.3   Identifiers and Labeling

Unique identifiers make it possible to refer to a particular version, and labels provide users with the ability to annotate versions with memorable titles. For histories with centralized control, integers can be used to identify versions, but when versions may be distributed, we need to assign identifiers that are universally unique. Git uses hashes of content and commits to identify versions [9], but universally unique identifiers (UUIDs) can also be generated randomly with minimal probability of overlap.

In addition to an identifier, each node of a version tree may also be labeled. We will assume that a single label may be associated with each node, but clearly, associating a set of attributes is also possible. Note that labels may change over time; for example, a user who creates an updated version of a workflow may wish to move the label to the new version in the same way as one would overwrite a file with updated information. Formally, all version trees may have an associated labeling function $\mathcal{L} : V \to \Sigma^*$.

2.4   Provenance

Provenance captures how a particular result was achieved—the steps involved in the derivation of that result. Version trees naturally integrate with this goal as they capture dependencies between the different versions. Change-based version trees go further, presenting descriptions of the actions that transform one version to another. Change-based provenance further limits this to a monotonic change-based version tree. In change-based provenance, a user may add new actions to the tree but not edit or reorganize existing actions.

The distinction between change-based provenance [8] and change-based version trees is intentional because the latter offers more latitude in reorganizing or editing. Specifically, change-based provenance seeks to capture the exact changes that occurred and maintain the monotonicity of the tree. Each change is recorded and cannot be relocated or mutated. A change-based version tree requires a function to exist for each edge but does not enforce any restraints how this was derived or inferred. However, in many cases, one can obtain provenance about how an entity was constructed directly from the change-based version tree.

3   Manipulating Change-Based Version Trees

Instead of viewing version trees as a historical, immutable record, we propose operations that allow users to manipulate and update the trees. In the same way that a user might keep versions of code files or workflows, we argue that versions of version trees provide powerful new ways to manipulate collections of entities. Our goal is to allow users to modify the version tree itself. Some operations, like labeling and pruning are agnostic to the versioned entities, but others, like those where changes are being modified, require some understanding of the domain. In either case, an operation takes one version tree and produces another.

At the lowest level, we propose three pairs of primitive operations:

1. ADDNODE, DELNODE: Add/delete a node
2. ADDEDGE, DELEDGE: Add/delete an edge
3. ADDLABEL, DELLABEL: Add/delete a label to/from a specific node

These operations provide the ability to construct any tree T' from any other tree T as in the worst case, we can delete everything from T and add everything from T'. In addition, each primitive operation has a clear inverse which means any change to the tree is invertible. While each action produces another tree, some may produce a degenerate tree where a subtree is not connected to the root.

Using these primitive operations, we can generate higher-level operations that transform the version tree. Two operations that act without any understanding of the versioned entities are relabeling and pruning. Relabeling involves moving a label ℓ from a version u to a version v. This can be accomplished by the pair of actions DELLABEL(u) and ADDLABEL(v, ℓ). Pruning v is a deletion of all nodes and edges in the subtree rooted at v. Again, we can rewrite this in terms of DELNODE and DELEDGE operations.

Other operations that act on the changes in a change-based version tree require some information about the underlying entities being manipulated. These include operations that rewrite past changes or reorganize versions. The *remap* operation takes pairs of changes (f, g) and replaces any instance of f on an edge in the version tree with g. For example, in a version tree of sets, we may wish to replace any occurrences of an element n with n'. Once a matching edge is identified, remap requires a DELEDGE(u, v) operation followed by a ADDEDGE(u, v, g). Since version trees reflect the chronological order of user-initiated changes, reorganizing versions by similarity can aid in producing more compact and more intuitive trees [10]. This reorganization involves moving nodes and rewriting edges.

4   Framework

4.1   Versioning Version Trees

While allowing users to modify version trees grants some intuitive and efficient operations, we lose the original state of the version tree upon modification. Since a new version of the version tree has been created, the same versioning procedures can also be used to manage versions of version trees. Furthermore, since we have identified a set of primitive, invertible operations that change version trees, we can create an invertible change-based version tree to store versions of version trees. While one may question whether a tree is necessary here, the overhead in keeping a tree versus a list is minimal, and thus it seems reasonable to keep all versions of the version trees.

Formally, a *meta version tree* (MVT) $T = (V, E, S_0)$ is an invertible change-based version tree where each edge defines a change to a version tree and S_0 is an empty version tree with only a root node. While the definition is straightforward and parallel to a standard version tree, working with the entities stored by the MVT of version trees comes with more overhead. Specifically, the creation of a new version of an entity triggers a new version in the current version tree, T, which in turn triggers updates to the MVT about the new node and edge added to T. This is represented by *two* new nodes and *two* new edges in the MVT, one pair for the new node and one pair for the new edge in T. With

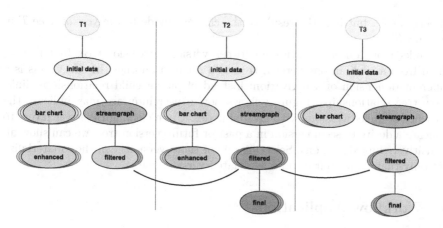

Fig. 2. Three versions of a version tree. Layered nodes indicate the presence of links to older versions (layered left) or newer ones (layered right). Green nodes are linked nodes that change from T1 to T2 or T2 to T3. Note that `filtered` has links to both older and newer versions. (Color figure online)

edge compression, we can package all of these changes together, but there is some extra overhead. Operations on the version trees are encoded as changes as described in the previous section.

Finally, note that with an MVT, identifying a specific version of an entity requires two identifiers—one to identify the version of the version tree and the other to identify the version of the entity in that tree. To materialize this entity, we must first materialize the version tree and then use that version tree to materialize the version of the entity.

4.2 Linking Versions Across Trees

Systems like git and VisTrails have demonstrated that users can understand and interact with trees, but using similar interfaces for a meta version tree would likely be confusing. In a parallel interface, when a user wishes to select a specific object, that user would both choose a version tree and then select a specific version in that tree. As it is cumbersome to keep track of both of these levels—especially as both are trees, we propose an interface where users are encouraged to navigate between trees by identifying a particular version for which they wish to see a previous version in an older version tree.

To track relationships between versions that appear in different versions of the version tree, we propose a *link* that directionally links a version v in one version tree T_1 with a version v' in another version tree T_2. Suppose we have a meta version tree $\mathcal{T}$, a specific tree $T \in \mathcal{T}$, and a specific version $v \in T$. Then if T' is a child version of T and $v' \in T'$, we can define a *link* between v and v' to denote that v' was *indirectly derived* from v via the set of actions that transformed T to T'. In other words, v' is not the result of changes made directly in T', but it is the result of the changes made to the version tree T in deriving T'.

Links allow a user to navigate between versions of version trees by following them from a node in one version tree to a node in another. In effect, this is a different dimension of a derivation; instead of parent-child relationships, links show tree relationships. Figure 2 shows how a user interface may indicate the presence of linked versions with layered nodes. Upon clicking the lower layers to indicate a desire to see a version in a past or future version tree, we can show all transitively linked versions. Selecting one of those versions can then materialize not only that entity but also its associated version tree.

5   Workflow Applications

To demonstrate the potential of versioned version trees, we present intuitive operations they enable in the context of scientific workflows. In this section, we define scientific workflows as composed of computational modules and connections that link an output of one module with an input of another; each module may also have configurable parameters. Thus, changes to the workflow include the addition or deletion of modules, connections, or parameters.

5.1   Bulk Edits and Upgrades

Suppose a user made a number of workflows using a particular module, but decided later that a different module would have worked better. Instead of changing every version that contained the module, a user may instead wish to edit the action where that module was originally introduced, replacing it with the alternate module. Without meta version trees, replacing each version would at least require actions that remove the original module and add the new module, and could also require elements that depend on that module to be deleted and re-added after the change actions.

As software and libraries are updated, it may be necessary for workflows to also be updated to match them [11]. For example, if a library changes the interface for a particular call, we may also need to update the corresponding module. Furthermore, even if the module's interface does not change, it is important that the execution provenance capture exactly the version used. It is common, then, for an older workflow to need an upgrade to reflect the current interfaces. Without MVTs, upgrading an entire version tree can lead to a number of new branches that can drastically alter the appearance of the tree as shown in Fig. 1 (left). When collaborators are working with different package versions (perhaps because they have different operating systems), this can be especially distracting. With MVTs, the upgrades can be encoded as updates to the *changes*, effectively replacing any action that added an old version of a module with a new action that adds the new version of the module as shown in Fig. 1 (right).

5.2   Parameter Exploration

Parameter exploration is often viewed as a transient state whereby a number of versions are explored but only a select few are preserved, added to the version tree, and examined further. Otherwise, the many versions would clutter the version tree. We can store the parameter ranges explored as annotation on the version being explored, but the version tree is only updated when a selected workflow of interest is persisted. Not only is the provenance of unselected workflows lost, but storing information about the exploration in an annotation does not match how a user might manually carry out the same operations.

We propose representing parameter exploration in an MVT by creating an intermediate version tree to uniformly encode all parameter combinations tested and then pruning that version tree to eliminate all non-selected versions. In other words, from a node v of version tree T, we create a version tree T' with nodes $v_0, \ldots, v_n$ as children of v but also each with links to v in T. If a user decides to use v_i for future work, it is persisted as a new version in the resulting version tree T^* but unselected versions are pruned.

5.3   Reorganization

Reorganizing a version tree by moving nodes and rewriting edges may allow a clearer understanding of relationships between workflows and/or a more efficient encoding. The minimization of version trees allows operations that cancel each other out to be removed, leading to a smaller version tree. Refactoring is an operation where nodes are relocated in order to represent the versions with fewer actions [10]. In the original implementation, the reorganized tree was not linked with the starting tree, and this made it difficult to determine which nodes had been moved or edges minimized. Using the actions in MVTs, we can not only link corresponding versions but we can highlight those that changed.

6   Provenance

As how an entity is created or derived is a question about the provenance of that entity, it is important to understand how meta version trees impact an understanding of that entity's evolution. We may either make a very literal interpretation of the origin of an entity or look to project this literal provenance into a form that may be more understandable.

The *literal provenance* of an entity derived from a version tree of version trees is exactly the steps in materializing that entity. Specifically, this is a sequence of actions describing the construction and transformation of the version tree the entity lives in, following the sequence of actions from the path through the version tree that actually construct the entity. While this provenance is correct, and following the steps will create the entity, its use is limited. Literal provenance is a chronological log of all activity in the version tree followed by the materialization of a specific version.

If we wish to dispense with a provenance view that involves multi-layered construction, we must project the operations down to the entity-level. Workflow evolution provenance is the sequence of operations involved in constructing a workflow [8]. While those operations live in a version tree, the provenance for any specific workflow involves only the changes related to that workflow. This is in contrast to literal provenance which keeps track of operations that may be unrelated to the entity in question. If we ignore the other versions of the version tree, we can generate *updated provenance* that is exactly the changes from the path through that tree. However, such a derivation is not accurate when the version tree has been transformed. Suppose a remap operation that mapped change A to Z occurred between T and T'. If the version v in T was created via a sequence BCAE, v' is created via BCZED. However, the change from A to Z was made *after* E and D. Thus, we want the sequences to look like $BCAEA^{-1}Z$.

We define *projected provenance* as the entity-level provenance that seeks to translate the effects of any tree operations into the entity-level while maintaining the correct order. For tree operations like remap, this equates to a inverse-forward sequence as shown in the previous example. In general, we can examine the version before the version tree operation and after and infer the necessary entity-level operations. Note that such provenance introduces actions that did not actually occur. However, it may still be faithful in communicating the evolution of that entity.

7   Evaluation

In addition to providing intuitive operations over collections of versioned entities, meta version trees enable more efficient storage because they do not duplicate the same work in many branches. To evaluate this, we used synthetically-generated version trees and applied remap operations, comparing the resulting trees with those where the remap was applied to individual versions independently.

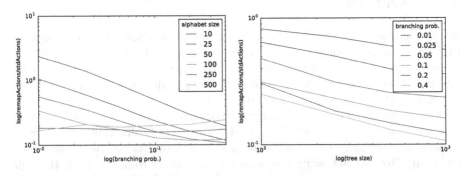

Fig. 3. Results for running remap operations over synthetically generated version trees capturing set manipulation. Generally, remap operations do better on trees with larger alphabets and higher branching probabilities. (Color figure online)

We used sets of integers from a bounded range as the domain with two change actions: add value and delete value. The version trees were randomly generated; each edge was an add or delete value of a randomly selected integer from the range (if the integer was in the set, delete value was inserted, otherwise add value was inserted). Based on a branching probability, the new edge was either appended to the current branch or the start of a new branch from an existing node. Then, a remap which changed a few of the values used in the actions was applied to the tree T. The same remap was also accomplished individually on nodes appearing in the skeleton of T. Tags were generated at a probability of 0.02; the skeleton includes tagged nodes.

We ran tests that combined different branching probabilities (0.01, 0.025, 0.05, 0.1, 0.2, 0.4), alphabet sizes (10, 25, 50, 100, 250, 500), tree sizes (100, 250, 500, 1000), and number of remapped values (1, 2, 4, 8). For each test, the number of new MVT nodes created by the remap operation was compared with the number of MVT nodes created individually. Each of the 576 tests was run 200 times, and the average ratio between the new MVT nodes in the two approaches was computed.

In most cases, remap operations use fewer actions than conventional version updates (see Fig. 3). Interestingly, there are scenarios where the remap fares worse. Specifically, when the alphabet for the set is small, the same integers are being added and deleted over and over so many need to be changed in the remap operation but the replacement at the end of a long branch needs only happen once. For larger alphabets (when items aren't being constantly added and removed), the remap operations needs fewer actions since the operations update multiple branches at once.

8   Related Work

Version graphs have been used in a number of contexts, including source code management (e.g., git [9] and darcs [6]), web content versioning [15], and web services [12]. Conradi and Westfechtel's survey on versioning for software configuration management provides both background and an overview of different approaches for versioning including the distinction between state-based and change-based [5]. Version control system provenance from git can also be represented in the PROV standard [7].

In the context of data management, versioning has focused on data lineage [3,4] and changes over time [14]. Recently, the DataHub project has been working to support collaborative data analysis with a view to versioning evolving datasets [2]. Because of the cost of storing both versions and changes, the project seeks to examine the tradeoff between storing versions and materializing them using change information. Ba et al. describe methods for incorporating uncertainty into version control [1].

The problem of determining impacts and conflicts of operations on versions that are themselves graphs, like workflows, is complicated by the subgraph isomorphism problem. Previous work focused on reorganizing versions by using the given changes [10]. Metrics based on maximal common subgraphs may also be used to compare workflow graphs [13]. Taentzner et al. have investigated versioning graphs and resolving conflicts in software modeling [18]. darcs uses patch theory to reorder and merge different changes [6].

9   Conclusion

We present meta version trees to allow more intuitive and efficient operations on collections of versions. Instead of editing multiple versions individually, users may edit the change and create a new version of the version tree. Future work includes examining applications beyond workflows and considering the process of applying analogies to multiple versions. Specifically, we envision allowing a user to edit a single entity and then propagate those changes to multiple versions. While this could be done using workflow analogies [16], it should be possible to encode the analogy as an edit to the version tree instead.

Another important consideration is potential conflicts introduced by an edited operation. For example, when an action adding a specific value is removed from the version tree, descendant actions that delete that value are invalid. One could check for such conflicts before allowing the operation to proceed, or it might be possible to separate those versions that are affected and put them in a subtree unaffected by the tree modification.

Acknowledgements. The author thanks Juliana Freire for her suggestions and the anonymous reviewers for their helpful comments. This work was supported in part by NSF CNS-1405927.

References

1. Ba, M.L., Abdessalem, T., Senellart, P.: Uncertain version control in open collaborative editing of tree-structured documents. In: Proceedings 2013 ACM Symposium on Document Engineering, pp. 27–36. ACM (2013)
2. Bhattacherjee, S., Chavan, A., Huang, S., Deshpande, A., Parameswaran, A.: Principles of dataset versioning: exploring the recreation/storage tradeoff. Proc. VLDB Endow. **8**(12), 1346–1357 (2015)
3. Bose, R., Frew, J.: Lineage retrieval for scientific data processing: a survey. ACM Comput. Surv. **37**(1), 1–28 (2005)
4. Buneman, P., Khanna, S., Tan, W.C.: Why and where: a characterization of data provenance. In: Proceedings 8th International Conference on Database Theory, pp. 316–330. Springer-Verlag (2001)
5. Conradi, R., Westfechtel, B.: Version models for software configuration management. ACM Comput. Surv. **30**(2), 232–282 (1998)
6. Darcs. http://darcs.net/
7. De Nies, T., Magliacane, S., Verborgh, R., Coppens, S., Groth, P., Mannens, E., Van de Walle, R.: Git2PROV: exposing version control system content as W3C PROV. In: Poster and Demo Proceedings of 12th International Semantic Web Conference (2013)

8. Freire, J.-L., Silva, C.T., Callahan, S.P., Santos, E., Scheidegger, C.E., Vo, H.T.: Managing rapidly-evolving scientific workflows. In: Moreau, L., Foster, I. (eds.) IPAW 2006. LNCS, vol. 4145, pp. 10–18. Springer, Heidelberg (2006)
9. Git. http://git-scm.com/
10. Koop, D., Freire, J.: Reorganizing workflow evolution provenance. In: 6th USENIX Workshop on the Theory and Practice of Provenance (Tapp. 2014) (2014)
11. Koop, D., Scheidegger, C.E., Freire, J., Silva, C.T.: The provenance of workflow upgrades. In: McGuinness, D.L., Michaelis, J.R., Moreau, L. (eds.) IPAW 2010. LNCS, vol. 6378, pp. 2–16. Springer, Heidelberg (2010)
12. Leitner, P., Michlmayr, A., Rosenberg, F., Dustdar, S.: End-to-end versioning support for web services. In: IEEE International Conference on Services Computing, pp. 59–66 (2008)
13. Lins, L.D., Ferreira, N., Freire, J., Silva, C.T.: Maximum common subelement metrics and its applications to graphs. CoRR abs/1501.06774 (2015)
14. Özsoyoğlu, G., Snodgrass, R.T.: Temporal and real-time databases: a survey. IEEE Trans. Knowl. Data Eng. **7**(4), 513–532 (1995)
15. Sabel, M.: Structuring wiki revision history. In: Proceedings 2007 International Symposium on Wikis, NY, USA, pp. 125–130. ACM, New York (2007)
16. Scheidegger, C.E., Vo, H.T., Koop, D., Freire, J., Silva, C.T.: Querying and creating visualizations by analogy. IEEE Trans. Vis. Comp. Graph. **13**(6), 1560–1567 (2007)
17. Subversion (svn). https://subversion.apache.org
18. Taentzer, G., Ermel, C., Langer, P., Wimmer, M.: A fundamental approach to model versioning based on graph modifications: from theory to implementation. Softw. Syst. Model. **13**(1), 239–272 (2014)

Enabling Web Service Request Citation by Provenance Information

Nicholas John Car[✉], Laura S. Stanford, and Aaron Sedgmen

Geoscience Australia, Symonston, ACT 2609, Australia
nicholas.car@ga.gov.au
http://www.ga.gov.au

Abstract. Geoscience Australia (GA) is a government agency that delivers much scientific data via web services for government and research use. As a science agency, the expectation is that GA will allow users of its data to be able to cite it as one would cite academic papers allowing authors of derived works to accurately represent their sources.

We present a methodology for assisting with the citation of web service requests via provenance information recording and delivery. We decompose the representation of a web service request into endurant and occurrent components, attempting to source as much information as possible about the endurant parts as organisations find these easiest to manage. We then collect references to those parts in an endurant 'bundle', which we make available for citation.

Our methodology is demonstrated in action within the context of an operational government science agency, GA, that publishes many thousands of datasets with persistent identifiers and many hundreds of web services but has not, until now, provided citable identifiers for web service-generated dynamic data.

Keywords: Provenance · Web services · Dynamic data citation · PROV-O

1   Introduction and Background

Web service requests are one form of data subsetting, the citation of which has been considered by groups such as the Research Data Alliance's Data Citation Working Group[1] which aimed to "bring together a group of experts to discuss the issues, requirements, advantages and shortcomings of existing approaches for efficiently citing subsets of data". Their approach to solving problems with data subset citation in general is to "adapt a data source for providing identifiable subsets for the long term" [9]. Some of these recommendations are well-known data management practices like the provision of data versioning and timestamping. Others are further from common data management or related practice, such

---

[1] https://www.rd-alliance.org/groups/data-citation-wg.html.

© Springer International Publishing Switzerland 2016
M. Mattoso and B. Glavic (Eds.): IPAW 2016, LNCS 9672, pp. 122–133, 2016.
DOI: 10.1007/978-3-319-40593-3_10

as query normalisation, storage and the assignment of persistent identifiers to checksummed queries to provide long-term immutable query retrieval.

Some of these recommendations require much time and effort to implement which may be appropriate for one-off data subsetting process citation, such as for data quoted in journal articles, but are not appropriate where citations are needed for many subsetting processes that may be run in quick succession, for example, defining the data presented in a web portal's interface where multiple requests to web services for individual data layers have been made.

In this paper we present a provenance-based methodology for web service request citation that is analogous to the citation of a recipe in order to bake a cake: ingredients and methods are recorded and stored and may be used again to recreate the same outputs. The aim is to store as much information as possible about the inputs to the web service request as static datasets in their own right as this will enhance the likelihood of future users to be able to determine how to recreate the request. This methodology will work when it is not possible to store static copies of the request outputs for various reasons, such as data size. It is hoped that this methodology can be retro-fitted into existing web service request scenarios.

This method does require that some well-known data management practices be carried out, such as Recommendations 1–3 in [9]. It also requires other things, such as a provenance data model, a Linked Data platform for data and web services and the registration of certain data items, as outlined in Sect. 2. Variants of this approach are currently being contemplated by large data holders, such as Australia's National Computing Infrastructure [12].

2   Methods

The methodology consists of the following steps for each web service request:

1. **create a standardised representation** of the request's process and actors, decomposed into endurant and occurrent (perdurant) components;
2. **store as much metadata about registered actors** (systems) related to the process as possible in order to place knowledge retention effort into endurant components of the request representation, not occurrent components;
3. **store the representation as a document** with a persistent identifier and refer to it as the citation;
4. **use Linked Data for access to other objects** such as input datasets thus allowing for their retrieval, not just their representation;
5. **provide pre-packaged queries to assemble request citation** information in accordance with data citation conventions.

2.1   Standardised Representation

In order to maximise long-term understanding of process representation, and we use the PROV Data Model [7], an open provenance representation standard by

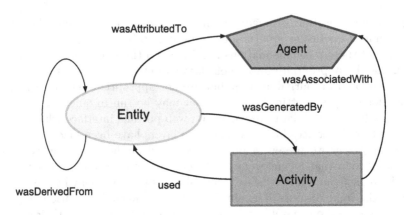

Fig. 1. The basic PROV-O classes and relationships, adapted from https://www.w3.org/TR/prov-primer/.

an open standards organisation, the W3C[2], in its web ontology language (OWL) [10] expression, PROV-O [6]. The basic PROV-O classes and their relations are given in Fig. 1. These classes refer to endurant things (`Entity` & `Agent`) and occurrent (perdurant) things (`Activity`).

We use the basic PROV-O classes to construct a very generic ontology design pattern for data processing, such as web service subsetting, which relates an action (`Activity`) to the data it takes in (`Entity`) and that it produces (`Entity`) in accordance with a procedure (`Plan`, a subclass of `Entity`) and which is attributed to a system (`Agent`). Some small extensions of this model are that the data taken in may be multiple `Entity` objects which may be represented independently or as a single `Collection` class object which is a subclass of `Entity`. All of the pattern's information is grouped together in a document which is represented as a PROV-O `Bundle`, another subclass of `Entity` depicted as a chamfered box. This modelling is shown in Fig. 2. For a web service request process, the procedure could be a set of key/ value pairs within a query string, as often supplied with a Uniform Resource Identifier (URI)[3] or a SPARQL query[4] presented to a SPARQL endpoint or an XML document sent via an HTTP POST request to an Open Geospatial Consortium (OGC)'s Web Feature Service (WFS)[5]); it is the set of instructions to the web service `Agent`.

2.2 Actor Information

In instantiating the design pattern given in Fig. 2 for web service requests, we focus on recording as much information as possible about the endurant parts of

---

[2] World Wide Wed Consortium: https://www.w3.org/.

[3] https://en.wikipedia.org/wiki/Uniform_Resource_Identifier.

[4] https://en.wikipedia.org/wiki/SPARQL.

[5] https://en.wikipedia.org/wiki/Web_Feature_Service.

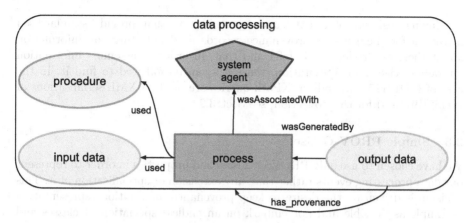

Fig. 2. A template for a web service request using classes from Fig. 1 with the addition of a PROV-O `Plan` class for the procedure , a PROV-O `Bundle` containing the provenance information and a PROV-AQ [5] `has_provenance` property.

the request. This is due to previous analysis [3] of our organisation (see p. 30) that showed we already possessed registers of endurant `Entity` objects, such as datasets and `Agent` objects such as web services, but not of occurrent `Activity` objects. From discussions we have had with four other Australian science agencies that use web services (CSIRO, Bureau of Meteorology, Department of the Environment) this situation is typical. Such a focus then on endurants means agencies wishing to adopt this methodology are likely able to do so by extending existing systems, rather than creating new ones.

While dataset registers, sometimes known as catalogues, are familiar to many data delivery agencies, `Agent` registers are not. Before this work, our organisation provided a list of all the web services it delivers publicly on a web page (http://www.ga.gov.au/data-pubs/web-services/ga-web-services) and in this way, the web services are considered `Entity` objects, however, as previously indicated, our modelling considers them `Agent` objects, given that their actions *use* and *generate* data. We recognise that `Agent` objects are properly defined by roles and are not essences thus our register of `Agent` objects is really a register of `Entity` objects. We model endurant `Agent` objects as `prov:Agent rdfs:subClassOf prov:Entity`, as allowed by PROV-O.

In order to enable our web services to be referred to as `Agent` objects via Linked Data methods, we have created a register for them; the information about the datasets they access is stored as links to items in the dataset register. For interoperability reasons, the information model used for our organisation's dataset and web service agent registers is ISO19115-1 [4] compliant. While this is not an RDF-based information model, class instances (`Entity` and `Agent` objects) are individually identified via URIs and human (HTML) and machine (XML)-readable metadata for each object is given, thus it is somewhat compatible with Linked Data methods.

Having registers of `Entity` and `Agent` objects that provide standardised metadata for them means provenance records need not store any information about them other than their URI and that, in order to assemble information for web service data use citation, the URIs can be followed to find it. In the case of ISO19115-1 metadata, XPath queries are used on XML serialisations of it (ISO19115-3) for this collection, see Sect. 3.2.

2.3   Simple PROV-O Use

We have chosen to use only PROV-O classes and properties in order to represent our data processing events rather than any extension or specialisation of it. This decision is driven by the desire to keep provenance information representation as simple as possible and not embark on an endless speciation of classes and properties for every conceivable scenario to be represented.

2.4   Provenance Information Storage

The PROV-O `Bundle` containing information representing a data processing event is stored by a provenance store product, known as PROMS Server [2], within an RDF database using a *named graph*[6] based on the `Bundle`'s URI which is assigned (minted) by the provenance store. This ensure the `Bundle` information is identifiable and remains associated as it would be in a document, despite being merged into the RDF database which provides cross `Bundle` querying capabilities. Since the provenance store mints the `Bundle`'s URI, access to that `Bundle` is available RESTfully (via the `Bundle` URI) as well as via SPARQL queries against the RDF database.

A `Bundle` can be linked to by the `entity` that it describes the provenance for using the PROV-AQ [5] methodology's `has_provenance` property.

2.5   Citation Queries

Information within these `Bundle` objects can be used with human-readable citations similar to those for referencing academic publications in order to supply useful information about web service outputs. We have adapted a simple citation template from the Bioregional Assessment Programme [1], a project our agency has participated in, which is structured as follows:

`{DATASET_REF}`: `{DATASET_OWNER}` `({YEAR})` `{DATASET_TITLE}`.
`{DATASET_TYPE}` `Viewed` `{DD MMM YYYY}`, `{DATASET_URI}`

A specific example from [8], p. 62, is:

`Dataset 3: Australian Government Department of the Environment (2013) Australia World Heritage Areas. Bioregional Assessment Source Dataset. Viewed 19 April 2015`, http://data.bioregionalassessments.gov.au/dataset/4927789b-7ba7-4a77-b6fc-be1b29b6590c.

---

[6] https://en.wikipedia.org/wiki/Named_graph.

3 Results

Our methodology is demonstrated in action within the context of our operational government science agency, Geoscience Australia (GA), that has published many thousands of datasets with persistent identifiers and many hundreds of web services but has not, until now, provided citable identifiers for web service-generated dynamic data.

In the following two subsections, we show how the information required to satisfy our requirements for a web service request citation can be collected at either the client or server side of the request. In both scenarios, we consider a request made to a geospatial web service by a Virtual Laboratory (VL). VLs are online scenario processing tools that marshal data from various sources, such as web services or user input, and then makes processing routines on that data available with managed processing (cloud) resources. In these scenarios, the VL can represent any sophisticated, automated, web service client. Figure 3 shows a VL client using data generated by a web service request 'WS output data' alongside other data to generate VL outputs. This figure will be referred to in the following subsections.

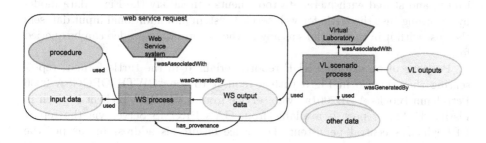

Fig. 3. A Virtual Laboratory using web service request and other data

3.1 Demonstration, Client-Side Recording

In previous work some of these authors were involved with, a particular Virtual Laboratory known as VHIRL[7] had functions added to its code allowing it to log its operations using PROV-O according to the general pattern of Fig. 2 [11]. Once logged (recorded in an RDF document) VHIRL is then able to send the information to any PROV-O-compliant provenance store; the store need not be associated with the data supplier. As per any client external to a web service provider ad without access to its internal information, VHIRL was able to know about the following objects from Fig. 3:

– the procedure – this is the web service request query it is making;
– the WS output data – the data the client receives;

---

[7] Virtual Hazard Impact & Risk Laboratory: http://www.vhirl.net.

– some information about the WS process – at least approximate `Activity` class
  `prov:wasStartedAt` & `prov:wasEndedAt` values;
– all values directly associated with the client such as other data, the client
  outputs (VL outputs) and client `Agent` details.

VHIRL and other web service clients may not necessarily know details about
the web service system `Agent` directly – some may be inferred by the web service
endpoint – and they are unlikely to know the identity of, or any details for, the
input data to the web service request. Given the establishment of an `Agent`
register (see Subsect. 2.2), we have added code to VHIRL and other similar VLs
that records the identity (URI) of the web service `Agent` and we now derive its
endpoint from that via an XPath query of its metadata, rather than recording
it directly. Likewise, the client may look up URIs for the input datasets to the
web service by querying the `Agent` metadata since our organisation's policy is to
explicitly associate every published web service with the datasets it draws from.
This layer of indirection has the added bonus for system operations of allowing
us to alter web service endpoint locations without breaking VL or other client
functionality.

Since all datasets associated with registered web services are themselves registered and stored with metadata too, clients can satisfy the Fig. 2 data model
by recording just the URIs for web service system and additional input datasets
they use with it in their actions as any further information needed can be queried
for.

Portions of an example RDF report, serialised in the turtle format, representing the scenario in Fig. 3 with a request to the "CWTH OPGGSA 2006
Petroleum Blocks AMB2001a" web service from a VHIRL VL client is given in
Listing 1. This report is available from GA's PROMS Server via the report
URI which a central persistent ID service ensures is addressable as per the
listing (http://pid-test.geoscience.gov.au/dataset/provenance/e1b2eb), regardless of server location within the organisation.

Listing 1. Example RDF document generated by a web service client

```
@prefix  : <http://pid-test.geoscience.gov.au/dataset/provenance/> .
@prefix rdfs: <http://www.w3.org/2000/01/rdf-schema#> .
@prefix xsd: <http://www.w3.org/2001/XMLSchema#> .
@prefix prov: <http://www.w3.org/ns/prov#> .
@prefix proms: <http://promsns.org/def/proms#> .
@prefix gadata: <http://pid-test.geoscience.gov.au/dataset/> .
@prefix gasrv: <http://pid-test.geoscience.gov.au/service/> .

:e1b2eb a prov:Bundle;
    rdfs:label "VL Report"^^xsd:string;
    prov:wasAssociatedWith gasrv:VHIRL;
    prov:generatedAtTime "2016-02-17T14:27:04"^^xsd:dateTime.

:7d7ae2 a prov:Activity;
    prov:wasAssociatedWith gasrv:CWTH_OPGGSA_2006_Petroleum
      _Blocks_AMB2001a;
    prov:used
```

```
    gadata:132cbd8e−b004−0670−e053−12a3070add7e ,
    gadata:184c15be−3f59−da6e−e053−10a3070a6b6b ,
    gadata:184c15be−3f5b−da6e−e053−10a3070a6b6b ,
    : bf683c ;
 prov:generated   :1 ef37b ;
 prov:startedAtTime  "2016−02−17T14:10:17"^^xsd:dateTime ;
 prov:endedAtTime  "2016−02−17T14:27:02"^^xsd:dateTime .

:bf683c a prov:Plan ;
 rdfs:label "WS request query string"^^xsd:string ;
 prov:wasAttributedTo gasrv:VGL ;
 prov:value "SERVICE=WFS&VERSION=1.1.0&REQUEST=GetFeature
 &MAXFEATURES=3&SRSNAME=urn:ogc:def:crs:EPSG:6.9:4283&
 BBOX=−38.7204/104.4244/−39.2583/105.4896"^^xsd:string .

:1ef37b a prov:Entity ;
 rdfs:label "Pet. Blks WS Output"^^xsd:string ;
 prov:generatedAtTime "2016−02−17T14:13:06"^^xsd:dateTime ;
 prov:has_provenance  :e1b2eb .
```

The definition of the web service request output dataset shown in Listing 1 (1ef37b) does not contain a URI to an external register as that dataset's data, the results of the request, has not been stored anywhere, therefore we only have a representation of it as a **Entity** in the PROMS Server provenance store with no PROV-O **value** component. The procedure/query **Plan** object in this example also has no representation in an external register but does have its value recorded using the PROV-O **value** property. If the query was too large to be stored as a text string, it could have been stored in an external repository, perhaps a simple text repository that uses URIs/URLs for file identification, such as the GitHub version control repository[8].

In order to generate a web service request citation from the code in Listing 1, as per the format given in Subsect. 2.5, the following mapping logic is used:

- {DATASET_REF} – Supplied by the document containing the citation;
- {DATASET_OWNER} – an **Agent** which the web service **Agent** acted for, determined by inferencing;
- {YEAR} – the year the request was made, i.e. the year of **prov:generated AtTime**;
- {DATASET_TITLE} – "Output of the" + WS **Agent** label + "Web Service", or other static text preferred by the generator;
- {DATASET_TYPE} – "Web Service request outputs", or other static text preferred by the generator;
- {DD MMM YYYY} – **prov:generatedAtTime** of request output data;
- {DATASET_URI} – the URI of the **Entity**.

The mapping logic results in the following human-readable request citation:

`VHIRL Virtual Laboratory (2016). Outputs of the CWTH OPGGSA 2006 Petroleum Blocks AMB2006a Web Service. Web Service request outputs.`

---

[8] http://github.com.

Viewed 17 Feb 2016, http://pid-test.geoscience.gov.au/dataset/provenance/
1ef37b

The logic as to *when* to generate a web service request citation is an issue
for the configuration of the client. In the case of VHIRL, a decision was made
to allow its users [11] to opt in for provenance reporting allowing them to run
scenarios without it and to turn it on as required. It is conceivable that other
VLs participating in sensitive operations would report provenance by default.

3.2   Demonstration, Server-Side Recording

Where a client application may not have the sophistication required to allow
provenance recording as per VHIRL in the above Subsection, it is possible for
the web service owner to enable clients to complete the data model as per Fig. 3
by storing some request log information entirely at the server side of the request
and making it available via another web service. Recording information in this
way obviates the need for the client-side activity provenance recording but, of
course, imposes additional work on the web service owners.

On the server side (the web service request infrastructure), we know about:

– the procedure – captured in web log files;
– the WS process – `prov:wasStartedAt` & `prov:wasEndedAt` and other values
  also captured in web log files;
– the WS system – whether registered or not, this is known to the WS provider;
– input data – known to the WS provider

We do not know about the WS output data directly (we could reproduce it
but we don't capture it) and we don't know any details of external clients such
as the VL in the example in Fig. 3.

As per client-side capture, it behoves us to record information about `Agent`
objects thus the establishment of a register (Subsect. 2.2) is still a requirement.
Its establishment provides the links between WS requests and the input datasets
they use. We then mine web logs for information about the procedure.

In order to capture web server log information for GA procedures and WS
process information, we:

– **capture all the web requests** made of GA web services at a single point
  via web server logs;
– **filter the logs** to retain only 'interesting' requests, i.e. those likely to be
  from data using applications, not system maintenance requests which are in
  the majority. This is accomplished by techniques such as discarding requests
  from specific IP address ranges and certain User Agents;
– **associate the filtered log entries with WS `Agent` objects** via an endpoint
  look-up;
– **store the associated log entries in a provenance store** as per Fig. 4.

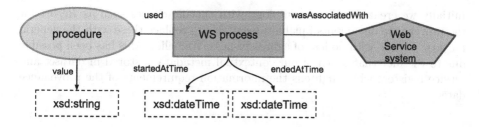

Fig. 4. The web requests repository objects (using PROV-O & XSD classes)

Having completed these actions, we have a combined repository for `Activity` objects (WS processes) and one type of `Entity` object (procedures). The provenance store acts as a register for both of these types of objects which can then be accessed via URI and via SPARQL queries.

To generate citations, users whose clients have performed web service requests need to discover the particular web service request entry in the provenance store relevant to them and then assemble data as per Fig. 2's data model by extraction from the provenance store and from the `Agent` register's metadata. They will likely be able to find request entries based on combinations of date range and web service metadata matching.

4   Discussion and Conclusions

Here we have shown that loosely-coupled client and server systems without knowledge of each other's internals can record the information needed to meet a particular data model and that the information collected can produce both machine and human readable citation forms. While client recording produces the most direct result, it is not always possible and, where it is not, web log records linked to an `Agent` register can be used.

The decomposition of web service requests into parts with the endurant ones stored as per common dataset and system metadata methods allows the occurrent parts of the request to be represented with minimal metadata only. Storage volumes for the information needed for web service request citations as recorded by clients are not onerous as Listing 1 shows indicating the client method is scalable. The server method is scalable insofar as an organisation has the appetite for filtered log storage volumes.

How web service request citations are used is a matter outside of scope for this work. We can imagine VHIRL metadata outputs containing input data citations provided alongside its "VL outputs", as per Fig. 3 that could be made available to its users in order for them to properly reference their experiments. For the server scenario, citation use could occur when users of the web services request dataset transparency information in retrospect.

PROV-O Specialisation. Regarding the specialisation of PROV-O: we have found it unnecessary to subclass the general-purpose ontology for this work.

Initially we created our own ontology with specific classes such as *Report* for the provenance documents but have been able to replace these with the general purpose *Bundle* with no loss of expressiveness. We believe this has been possible due to the fact that much of our contextual metadata is stored in dataset and service registers which lightens the information requirements of the provenance data.

5   Future Work

These methodologies comfortably accommodate data-delivering web services but do not deal with web processing service or similar which require sophisticated procedures to operate. It can be imagined that such services could be accommodated with an extension of the `Plan`-as-input-data pattern shown here.

We have started using the Data Provider Node Ontology (DPN-O) [13] to capture information about web service *Agent* objects rather than ISO19115-1 *Service* records. ISO19115-1 use is not tightly bound to reference metadata such as vocabularies nor does it prescribe explicit range values for many fields. We are implementing DPN-O with service classification vocabularies that we believe will preserve knowledge of service types and roles over time, even when the specific versions and brands have been forgotten.

We hope to soon link our public dataset (`Entity`), `Agent` and provenance metadata registers together into a single federated register for our agency using specialisations of the Linked Data Platforms Vocabulary[9] and Registry vocabulary[10]. This will aid typed object discovery in general as it will allow human or machine users to discover the endpoints to registers containing classes of object by "following their nose" from the top-level register. Thus they will not need to be directly informed of register endpoints for requests that require information from multiple registers, only their required objects' classes.

References

1. Bureau of Meteorology. Bioregional Assessments (2015). http://www.bioregional assessments.gov.au
2. Car, N.J., Woodman, S.: The Provenance Management System (PROMS) (2016). http://promsns.org/wiki/proms
3. Peter Fitch, N.J., Car, D.L.: Organisational provenance capacity implementation plan: a report to geoscience Australia. Technical report, CSIRO, Black Mountain, ACT (2015)
4. ISO. ISO 19115-1: 2014 Geographic information - Metadata - Part 1: Fundamentals. International Standards Organisation, Geneva, Switzerland (2014)
5. Klyne, G., Groth, P. (eds.): PROV-AQ: Provenance Access and Query, April 2013. http://www.w3.org/TR/prov-aq/

---

[9] https://www.w3.org/ns/ldp.
[10] http://www.epimorphics.com/public/vocabulary/Registry.html.

6. Lebo, T., Sahoo, S., McGuinness, D. (eds.): PROV-O: ThePROV Ontology, April 2013. http://www.w3.org/TR/prov-o/
7. Moreau, L., Missier, P. (eds.): PROV-DM: The PROV Data Model (2013). http://www.w3.org/TR/prov-dm/
8. Mitchell, P., O'Grady, A.P., Bruce, J., Slegers, S., Welsh, W.D., Aryal, S.K., Merrin, L.E., Holland, K.L.: Description of the water-dependent asset register for the Maranoa-Balonne-Condamine subregion. Product 1.3 for the Maranoa-Balonne-Condamine subregion from the Northern Inland Catchments Bioregional Assessment. Technical report, Department of the Environment, Bureau of Meteorology, CSIRO and Geoscience Australia, Canberra, ACT, Australia (2015)
9. Rauber, A., Asmi, A., Van Uytvanck, D., Pröll, S.: Identification of reproducible subsets for data citation, sharing and re-use (draft). Technical report, Research Data Alliance (2015)
10. W3C OWL Working Group. OWL 2 Web Ontology Language Document Overview, 2nd edn. (2012)
11. Wise, C., Car, N.J., Fraser, R., Squire, G.: Standard provenance reporting and scientific software management in virtual laboratories. In: Weber, T., McPhee, M.J., Anderssen, R.S. (eds.) MODSIM 2015, 21st International Congress on Modelling and Simulation, pp. 634–640. Modelling and Simulation Society of Australia and New Zealand, Gold Coast (2015)
12. Wyborn, L., Car, N., Evans, B., Klump, J., Australia, G.: How do you assign persistent identifiers to extracts from large, complex, dynamic data sets that underpin scholarly publications? Geophys. Res. Abstr. EGU Gen. Assembly 18, 2016–11639 (2016)
13. Yu, J., Leighton, B., Car, N.J., Seaton, S.: The eReefs data brokering layer for hydrological and environmental data. J. Hydro. Inf. (2016, in press)

Modelling Provenance of Sensor Data for Food Safety Compliance Checking

Milan Markovic[1(✉)], Peter Edwards[1], Martin Kollingbaum[1], and Alan Rowe[2]

[1] Computing Science, University of Aberdeen, Aberdeen AB24 5UA, UK
{milan.markovic,p.edwards,m.j.kollingbaum}@abdn.ac.uk
[2] Rowett Institute of Nutrition and Health,
University of Aberdeen, Aberdeen AB21 9SB, UK
a.rowe@abdn.ac.uk

Abstract. The Internet of Things (IoT) is resulting in ever greater volumes of low level sensor data. However, such data is meaningless without higher level context that describes why such data is needed and what useful information can be derived from it. Provenance records should play a pivotal role in supporting a range of automated processes acting on the data streams emerging from an IoT-enabled infrastructure. In this paper we discuss how such provenance can be modelled by extending an existing suite of provenance ontologies. Furthermore, we demonstrate how provenance abstractions can be inferred from sensor data annotated using the SSN ontology. A real-world application from food-safety compliance monitoring will be used throughout to illustrate our achievements to date, and the challenges that remain.

1 Introduction

The Internet of Things (IoT) concept refers to the seamless integration of physical objects, sensors and mobile devices into the information network. The IoT encompasses numerous technologies, services and standards and is seen by many as the cornerstone of the emerging ICT market. Such devices are becoming ever cheaper and easier to deploy; for example, CAO Gadgets[1] market a range of low power plastic tags able to measure temperature, humidity and motion. Due to their low cost, there is now significant potential for technologies such as these to be used in a range of applications that require routine data capture, condition monitoring and behavioural tracking. One such application is monitoring of food safety compliance.

In its 2015–2020 strategic plan, the UK's Food Standards Agency observes that: "It is the responsibility of people producing and supplying food to ensure it is safe and what it says it is". Non-compliance with food storage and handling

---

The research described here was funded by an award made by the RCUK IT as a Utility Network+ and the UK Food Standards Agency. We thank the owner and staff of Rye & Soda restaurant, Aberdeen for their support throughout the project.

[1] http://www.wirelesstag.net/.

M. Mattoso and B. Glavic (Eds.): IPAW 2016, LNCS 9672, pp. 134–145, 2016.
DOI: 10.1007/978-3-319-40593-3_11

guidelines presents a significant risk to individuals and society as a whole. As an illustration, *campylobacter* is the most common cause of bacterial food poisoning in the UK, and each year is estimated to be responsible for 280,000 cases of food poisoning - at a cost of around £900M to the economy. As a result there is now considerable interest in the use of technologies such as low-cost wireless meat probes as a means to monitor cooking processes. It is now perfectly possible to imagine a future restaurant kitchen in which a suite of sensors monitor food from the moment it arrives until it is served to a customer, with automated systems alerting staff to take appropriate action when necessary, and providing management information to aid staff training and reduce wastage.

Provenance has an important role to play in documenting entities representing real physical objects, and their relationship to activities as part of a food preparation workflow. Given descriptions of workflow plans (i.e. prospective provenance documenting expected behaviour) and records of actual events (i.e. retrospective provenance documenting what really happened), provenance can help support compliance analysis - by determining whether expected food safety protocols have been followed. For example, whether chilled food has been stored within the correct temperature limits (typically 1–5 °C).

While the W3C recommendation for provenance capture PROV[2] is suitable for modelling the retrospective part of a provenance record (i.e. workflow execution) it does not support descriptions of workflow plans [MM12]. Approaches such as D-PROV [MDB+13], ProvOne [CVLM+14], and P-PLAN [GG12] have all proposed extensions to the PROV model, to enable more detailed descriptions of such plans. These extensions typically introduced new concepts to describe workflow structures in terms of expected workflow steps and corresponding inputs and outputs. As part of our work on the SC-PROV model [Mar16,MEC13] we expanded on these earlier efforts, by providing a means to document constraints (e.g. preconditions) that might be associated with individual steps of a workflow plan. The ability to represent such constraints is especially relevant within the food safety domain, where frameworks such as HACCP (Hazard Analysis and Critical Control Point) define process workflows in terms of critical limits associated with the various workflow steps. Currently, monitoring of HACCP based workflows in commercial kitchens is predominantly a manual exercise and relevant records (e.g. temperature readings) are stored off-line.

In this paper, we argue that by enhancing IoT technology we can automate HACCP compliance monitoring, and facilitate other activities such as data exchange with appropriate government agencies. To support this, we describe an ontological model for recording prospective and retrospective provenance in the food safety domain. Furthermore, we demonstrate the utility of this model in the context of automated provenance generation for food safety compliance checking using a set of real sensor observations and sample inference rules.

The remainder of this paper is structured as follows: Sect. 2 discusses relevant related work in the provenance, semantic sensing and food safety arenas; Sect. 3 describes the HACCP model in terms of its key elements, before Sect. 4

---

[2] https://www.w3.org/TR/prov-dm/.

discusses a provenance model (FS-PROV) tailored to the food safety domain; Sect. 5 outlines an experimental deployment into a commercial kitchen. Using examples drawn from this real-world setting, we then discuss how provenance assertions are inferred from sensor data (Sect. 6), and how a range of queries can be used to check HACCP compliance (Sect. 7). The paper concludes with a discussion highlighting issues and future directions (Sect. 8).

2   Related Work

Work in the provenance literature includes generic models for recording provenance (e.g. PROV [MM12]) and mechanisms for publishing plans and execution traces of scientific and social computation workflows (e.g. P-PLAN [GG12], D-PROV [MDB+13], ProvONE [CVLM+14], and SC-PROV [Mar16]). While the PROV specification could be used to record execution traces of food preparation workflows, the resulting provenance records would be limited in terms of their utility - due to the lack of information about the structure of the workflow plans, and configuration details of individual workflow tasks (e.g. HACCP constraints). Missier et al. [MDB+13] previously highlighted these limitations of PROV and proposed the D-PROV extension (which in turn later served as a starting point for the ProvONE extension). D-PROV and ProvONE provide a vocabulary for annotating execution traces of data-driven scientific workflows with descriptions of data-dependencies based on the planned data flow, but do not provide generic concepts for modeling constraints associated with workflow elements. Garijo and Gil [GG12] proposed a PROV extension called P-PLAN that focuses on describing abstract workflows in the form of *p-plan:Step*(s) and *p-plan:Variable*(s) to support modelling of diverse workflow structures. Steps represent the various planned activities that need to be executed, while variables represent the expected inputs and outputs of these activities. A step can refer to one or more activities recorded by PROV in the retrospective provenance record. This enables a provenance record to capture variant execution traces of the same plan. SC-PROV further extended P-PLAN with a vocabulary for describing various *sc-prov:Condition*(s) that might be associated with a step. In addition, it provides a means for capturing the parameters associated with such conditions, and the outcome of evaluation of these conditions during the workflow execution (i.e. a record of whether the condition was satisfied or not). This is modelled in a retrospective provenance record using *sc-prov:EvaluationContext*. This concept binds an *sc-prov: Condition* to a single instantiation of a *p-plan:Step*, and to the evaluation result represented as a *prov:Entity*. While the SC-PROV model supports modeling of constraints associated with individual steps, it is not able to associate constraints with variables. This is required to accommodate the HACCP view of constraints (e.g. cooked meat should have a core temperature of greater than 75 °C).

The Semantic Sensor Network ontology (SSN) [CBB+12] represents the state-of-the-art in sensor metadata models and includes support for characterisation of sensor hardware devices, sensor observations, and links between sensor capabilities and features of interest in the real world. In our view, SSN has been under-utilised in the IoT arena, where it could provide a useful platform for further standards development. Previous work [CCT14] defined alignments between the SSN and PROV-O ontologies, along with mechanisms for inferring provenance of sensor data. However, the richness of SSN descriptions for individual sensor readings can be seen as an obstacle to scalability and it is therefore necessary to consider how much of the ontology to use in any given setting. The volume of sensor observations likely in any application setting (e.g. food safety monitoring) also means that it is essential to find a way to identify and record abstractions, such as key events.

3 Food Safety and The HACCP Model

The HACCP model focuses attention on a set of critical food preparation factors. *Hazards* are anything that may introduce harm to customers, which can be microbiological, chemical or physical. *Control Measures* are ways to prevent or control hazards. For example, the survival of harmful bacteria in food, which may cause food poisoning, can be controlled by thorough cooking. *Control Measures* can be associated with a "Critical Limit". For example, food is considered to be cooked properly if the core temperature reaches at least 75 °C. Other aspects of the HACCP system encompass record keeping and verification to ensure that measures are being consistently applied. Businesses are expected to create and document their own house rules to reflect food safety working practices and articulate hazards, control measures, critical limits, etc. An example food preparation workflow is depicted in Fig. 1. The example illustrates part of a typical food preparation workflow where steps (e.g. storage and cooking) are associated with relevant HACCP constraints.

To support compliance checking of HACCP-based food safety workflows, it is necessary to answer queries such as the following: **Q1:** *How long has this meat item been stored in compliance with HACCP guidelines for chilled storage?* **Q2:** *How long did this food item spend outside chilled storage before being cooked?* and **Q3:** *When was this food item first cooked in accordance with HACCP guidelines?*

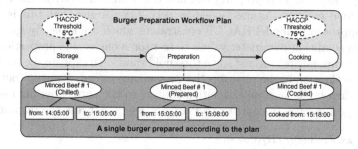

Fig. 1. A sample food preparation plan and corresponding instantiations of the plan concepts.

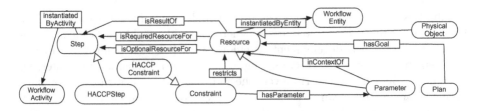

Fig. 2. An illustration of the core FS-PROV concepts for modelling provenance of HACCP-based food preparation workflows and their execution.

In the next section, we describe how a suite of existing provenance vocabularies can be extended to support such queries.

4 Modelling Provenance of a HACCP Workflow

To enable modelling of HACCP-based food preparation workflows, we have extended three existing ontologies, namely PROV-O[3], SC-PROV-O[4] and P-PLAN[5]. PROV-O was selected for its suitability as a means to model the retrospective workflow provenance. P-PLAN was used to model prospective provenance of a workflow, and these capabilities were further extended with concepts from SC-PROV-O in order to represent plan constraints and their evaluation results during a workflow execution. Figure 2 illustrates the core concepts of the FS-PROV ontology[6] (we will use the *fs* prefix when referring to these concepts in the text). FS-PROV extends the various ontologies through definition of subclasses of existing concepts with the alignments specified in Fig. 3. The core concepts include definitions of planned food handling activities (*fs:Step*) and expected physical and virtual items (*fs:Resource*) that are required and produced by individual steps. In order to capture compliance requirements, we use the concept *fs:HACCPConstraint* together with the description of a physical property (*fs:Parameter*) of an item used and/or produced by the step of a workflow plan. In contrast with the SC-PROV model, *fs:Constraint* can also be associated with *fs:Resource* (e.g. the product of a cooking step) via a binding property *fs:restricts*. This property can link constraints directly to the representation of food entities. As mentioned in Sect. 2, we argue that this is a more suitable approach to model HACCP constraints which are typically specified in the form of condition-parameter values to test some observable properties (e.g. a core meat temperature) against some threshold values. To capture the results of a condition evaluation in the retrospective provenance record, *fs:entity* (not shown in Fig. 2) then binds *sc-prov:EvaluationContext* to the corresponding instantiation of an *fs:Resource*. In contrast to P-PLAN, we do not link the instantiations

---

[3] https://www.w3.org/TR/prov-o/.

[4] https://w3id.org/abdn/socialcomp/sc-prov.

[5] http://vocab.linkeddata.es/p-plan/.

[6] https://w3id.org/abdn/foodsafety/fs-prov.

Fig. 3. Alignment between the concepts of FS-PROV and concepts originating from PROV-O, SC-PROV-O, and P-PLAN.

of planned concepts via a functional relationship to only one template description (i.e. *p-plan:Step* or *p-plan:Variable*). Instead, we define relationships in the opposite direction (see *fs:instantiatedByActivity* and *fs:instantiatedByEntity* in Fig. 2). This enables independent modelling of various abstractions of workflow plans (e.g. a more detailed plan for the purposes of kitchen monitoring and less detailed for the food safety authority - without the inclusion of sensitive data) that can then be linked to the same execution trace. Furthermore, we defined the *fs:inContextOf* property to capture the relation between constraint parameters (e.g. surface temperature) and a particular resource. The *fs:hasGoal* was introduced to annotate the final output of a workflow plan (e.g. a cooked burger).

5   Experimental Deployment

As part of our experimental setup, we deployed 10 wireless tags from CAO Gadgets[7] and a wireless meat probe from Corintech[8] into a commercial kitchen in Aberdeen, UK. We focused on gathering temperature sensor data that related to three specific steps within a food preparation workflow: storage of raw burgers in their chilled state, preparation of the raw burgers, and cooking. Using the deployed sensors we collected data from two distinct experimental scenarios: *Scenario1* - kitchen staff complied with the HACCP temperature constraints for storage and cooking of minced beef; and *Scenario2* - staff deliberately violated these constraints.

Limitations on our experiments were caused by both hygiene and technological restrictions. The wireless tags could not be attached directly to the meat product or be used during cooking. As a result, continuous monitoring of the transition of the raw meat product into its fully cooked state with one type of sensor was not possible. While in its raw state, burgers were contained within a plastic bag with a wireless tag attached on the outside (Fig. 4 - left). A meat probe was then used to record the core meat temperature during cooking (Fig. 4 - right). A common precondition for all scenarios explored in our experiment was that the tracked burgers had been placed into the fridge at least two hours before the commencement of each experiment. The first part of the experiment focused on the collection of the "good" data. Chefs were asked to cook six burgers[9]. All burgers were kept at the correct temperature while in storage and they

---

[7] http://wirelesstag.net/.

[8] http://www.corintech.com/.

[9] Four burgers were cooked separately and two burgers were cooked at the same time.

Fig. 4. Wireless tag attached to a pack containing a single raw burger (left). Wireless meat probe used to measure the core temperature of a burger during cooking (right).

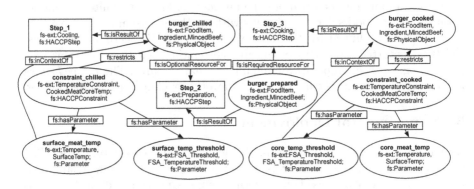

Fig. 5. An illustration of the plan concepts used in our burger tracking experiments.

were also cooked according to the HACCP constraint requiring that the core meat temperature should exceed 75 °C. In the second part of the experiment, we simulated non-compliance by asking the chef to under-cook four burgers. This provided us with sample sensor data from which HACCP compliance should not be inferred. In the next section we describe how the provenance records reporting compliance with HACCP constraints were generated.

6   Inferring Retrospective Provenance

The execution trace of our food preparation workflow was inferred using low-level sensor data and static descriptions of the workflow plan (e.g. HACCP constraint thresholds). Raw sensor data collected during the deployment were annotated using the SSN ontology. Each sensor reading (*ssn:Observation*) was associated with a specific *ssn:Sensor* (e.g. a temperature sensor) represented as an instance of an *ssn:SensingDevice*. We assumed that each food item (i.e. a burger) that was tracked within our IoT system was described by a unique URI. This was

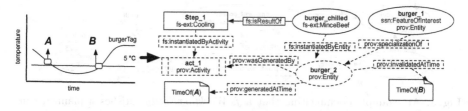

Fig. 6. An illustration of observed temperature variations in relation to a HACCP limit (left) and their relationship to inferred provenance annotations (dashed lines in the graph on the right).

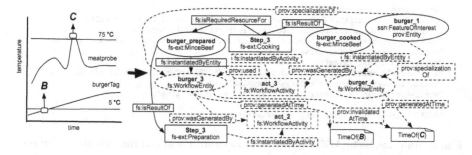

Fig. 7. An illustration of observed temperature variations in relation to HACCP limits (left) and their relationship to inferred provenance annotations (dashed lines in the graph on the right).

used to represent an *ssn: FeatureOfInterest*[10] of an *ssn:Observation* produced by *ssn:Sensor*(s) (e.g. observations produced by wireless tag1 had a feature of interest http://example.org/meatItem1).

An extended FS-PROV ontology[11] (namespace fs-ext) was used to describe a domain-specific food preparation plan required for the experimental deployment. Figure 5 illustrates the manually populated ontology with instances for a three-step burger preparation plan and includes: three instances of *fs: HACCPStep* (i.e. storage, preparation and cooking), two instances of *fs: HACCPConstraint* (i.e. constraint on chilled meat, and constraint on cooked meat), four *fs: Parameters* (i.e. observed surface and core temperatures, and thresholds) and three instances of *fs-ext:MincedBeef* (i.e. *fs:Resources* representing the changing states of burgers within the workflow from chilled to cooked).

The FS-PROV-based provenance abstractions were created using SPARQL INSERT queries that implemented rules to recognise events from low-level sensor data (see Figs. 6 and 7). To infer provenance entities indicating that a burger

---

[10] The meat probe sensor data had to be manually annotated with the feature of interest (i.e. the meat item for which the core temperature was measured) as the current design of the probe does not support automatic recognition of probed items.

[11] https://raw.githubusercontent.com/m-markovic/FoodSafety-Data/master/fso_extended.ttl.

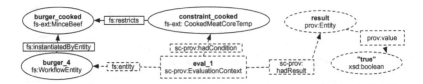

Fig. 8. An example documenting that a *fs:WorkflowEntity* satisfies a planned constraint.

```
SELECT ?item ?start ?finish

WHERE {

?storageStep a fs-ex:Storage.
?resultResource fs:isResultOf ?storageStep;fs:instantiatedByEntity ?result.
fs-ex:HACCPTempConstraintChilledFood fs:restricts ?resultResource.
?result a fs:WorkflowEntity;prov:specializationOf ?item; prov:generatedAtTime ?start.
?result prov:invalidatedAtTime ?finish.
?evaluationContext fs:entity ?result.
?evaluationContext sc-prov:hadCondition fs-ex:HACCPTempConstraintChilledFood.
?evaluationContext sc-prov:hadResult ?evaluationResult.
?evaluationResult  a fs:WorkflowEntity; prov:hasValue "true".

VALUES (?item) {(<http://example.org/meatItem1>)} }
```

Fig. 9. An example SPARQL query to retrieve start and end time for the entity representing a food item in a chilled state.

was in a chilled state (i.e. instantiations of the *burger_chilled* resource in Fig. 5), we used the first observation which reported meat surface temperature falling below the corresponding HACCP threshold. Similarly, an observation reporting meat surface temperature rising above the HACCP was used to infer a new provenance entity representing a burger in a preparation stage and at the same time the "chilled entity" was invalidated using the *prov:InvalidatedAtTime* assertion. Entities representing cooked burgers were generated at the point when an observation from a meat probe reported core temperature above the corresponding HACCP threshold. At the same time the entities describing a burger in a preparation stage were updated with the *prov:InvalidatedAtTime* assertion.

As a result of our approach, entities representing burgers in their chilled and cooked state were only inferred if the corresponding HACCP constraints were satisfied. To record this, we generated additional annotations noting that a corresponding HACCP constraint had been satisfied (Fig. 8).

7   Querying Food Provenance

The query presented in Fig. 9 can be used to retrieve the times when a meat item (identified by a specific URI) was observed to comply with the HACCP temperature constraint for chilled storage. By using this approach, we were able to construct additional queries and successfully retrieve evidence which recorded whether a food item was in compliance with relevant HACCP constraints throughout the storage, preparation and cooking stage. When no evidence of compliance was recorded (e.g. a burger was under-cooked) the corresponding query returned no results. To evaluate our provenance queries we generated a gold standard data set based upon a researcher's observations of the kitchen activities; this was then used to cross-check the results provided by the sample provenance queries.

It is important to recognise that from the HACCP-based provenance perspective, the activities recorded in the provenance record do not necessarily mirror the events observed in the physical kitchen environment. To illustrate this point, consider a situation when a food item is removed from chilled storage. Staff would immediately consider this item as no longer being stored in a chilled state. However, the item might still maintain a temperature below the HACCP threshold for some time after leaving the fridge. In the provenance record the item would therefore remain in the chilled storage state for some time (until its temperature rose beyond the HACCP limit).

To illustrate the utility of the FS-PROV model, we have compared the number of triples required to describe the provenance abstractions to the number of triples required to describe the raw sensor data using SSN (see Fig. 10). We used JENA's[12] *OntModel* to store annotated sensor data using the SSN concepts described earlier in this paper (see Sect. 6).

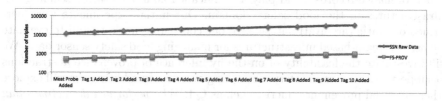

Fig. 10. A comparison of the number of SSN triples required to characterise the sensor data vs. the corresponding FS-PROV provenance assertions.

The provenance model (with model specification set to *OWL_MEM_RDFS_INF*) was firstly loaded with an extended FS-PROV ontology (i.e. the workflow plan) and this was followed by addition of inferred retrospective provenance for each of the observed meat items. From our results, it is clear that FS-PROV based provenance abstractions can significantly reduce the number of triples required to capture compliance of HACCP-based workflows. However, this approach also forces us to consider the trade-off between storing abstractions vs. the original sensor data, which would enable re-evaluation of compliance. In addition, it raises additional questions regarding the reliability of tools that generate such abstractions. FS-PROV could potentially re-use other SC-PROV concepts (e.g. *sc-prov:ParameterCollection*) to record instantiations of parameter values (e.g. temperature readings). However, it may be necessary to introduce new

---

[12] https://jena.apache.org.

mechanisms to decide what parameter values should be recorded. For example, we might have recorded three sensor readings (i.e. HACCPConstraint parameter instantiations) that prove that a food item was cooked (e.g. readings from a meat probe over a period of 30 s). However, we might have recorded thousands of observations that prove the compliance of a food item being in its chilled state (e.g. readings from a wireless tag over a period of 2 days). If we recorded all the parameter instantiations that correspond to the compliance of an entity with the HACCPConstraint for chilled storage, we would be negating the benefits in terms of storage requirements. Alternatively, if only a subset of readings (e.g. the readings just before and after an entity entered the chilled state) were recorded, new classes or properties would be required to record that these were only a sample of the observed sensor data. During our experiments we encountered various issues with sensor accuracy and sampling rates. While information about sensor calibration and measurement errors can be recorded as part of the SSN descriptions of raw data, we did not consider these in our work, and they remain challenges for the future.

8   Conclusions and Future Work

In this paper we have outlined a promising approach that can be used to generate provenance abstractions of food safety sensor data. We have demonstrated that provenance records could play a significant role in facilitating scalable IoT infrastructures in the food safety domain. Our initial experiments were performed on static (archival) datasets. In our continuing work we aim to evaluate the use of stream-based infrastructures for managing food safety sensor data. We will investigate the feasibility of on-the fly inference of provenance abstractions to support real-time food safety monitoring systems. In addition, we will explore other potential provenance queries such as **Q4:** *Who performed the activity that influenced this food item?* **Q5:** *Why was the activity that influenced this food item performed?* and **Q6:** *Where were the food preparation activities performed?* To answer Q4, the sensors would have to be able to identify the agent (e.g. chef) who performed a particular activity involving the tracked food item. Such information could then be captured within a provenance record by associating an agent with a relevant activity such as an instantiation of the cooking step. To answer Q5 and Q6, a provenance record would have to include descriptions of activities that triggered the creation of entities which represent changing states of a food item. For example, an activity representing a customer order would trigger the activity representing the instantiations of the individual planned steps such as preparation and cooking. The activities could then be linked using *prov:atLocation* to a location where they were executed, for example, to a specific restaurant.

Acknowledgment. The research described here was funded by an award made by the RCUK IT as a Utility Network+ (EP/K003569/1) and the UK Food Standards Agency. We thank the owner and staff of Rye & Soda restaurant, Aberdeen for their support throughout the project.

References

[CBB+12] Compton, M., Barnaghi, P., Bermudez, L., García-Castro, R., Corcho, O., Cox, S., Graybeal, J., Hauswirth, M., Henson, C., Herzog, A., Huang, V., Janowicz, K., Kelsey, W.D., Le Phuoc, D., Lefort, L., Leggieri, M., Neuhaus, H., Nikolov, A., Page, K., Passant, A., Sheth, A., Taylor, K.: The SSN ontology of the W3C semantic sensor network incubator group. Web Semant. Sci. Serv. Agents World Wide Web **17**, 25–32 (2012)

[CCT14] Compton, M., Corsar, D., Taylor, K.: Sensor data provenance: SSNO and PROV-O together at last. In: Terra Cognita and Semantic Sensor, Networks, pp. 67–82 (2014)

[CVLM+14] Cuevas-Vicenttín, V., Ludäscher, B., Missier, P., Belhajjame, K., Chirigati, F., Wei, Y., Dey, S., Kianmajd, P., Koop, D., Bowers, S., Altintas, I.: Provone: a PROV extension data model for scientific workflow provenance (2014). http://vcvcomputing.com/provone/provone. html

[GG12] Garijo, D., Gil, Y.: Augmenting PROV with plans in P-PLAN: scientific processes as linked data. In: Proceedings of the Second International Workshop on Linked Science 2012 - Tackling Big Data. CEUR (2012)

[Mar16] Markovic, M.: Utilising provenance to enhance social computation. Ph.D. thesis, University of Aberdeen (2016)

[MDB+13] Missier, P., Dey, S., Belhajjame, K., Cuevas-Vicenttin, V., Ludaescher, B.: D-PROV: extending the prov provenance model with workflow structure. Technical report, School of Computing Science, Newcastle University (2013)

[MEC13] Markovic, M., Edwards, P., Corsar, D.: Utilising provenance to enhance social computation. In: Alani, H., Kagal, L., Fokoue, A., Groth, P., Biemann, C., Parreira, J.X., Aroyo, L., Noy, N., Welty, C., Janowicz, K. (eds.) ISWC 2013, Part II. LNCS, vol. 8219, pp. 440–447. Springer, Heidelberg (2013)

[MM12] Moreau, L., Missier, P.: PROV-DM: The PROV data model. W3C Recommendation (2012). http://www.w3.org/TR/prov-dm/

Modelling Provenance Collection Points and Their Impact on Provenance Graphs

David Gammack[1], Steve Scott[2], and Adriane P. Chapman[2(✉)]

[1] Marymount University, Arlington, VA, USA
dgammack@marymount.edu
[2] The MITRE Corporation, McLean, VA, USA
{slscott, achapman}@mitre.org

Abstract. As many domains employ ever more complex systems-of-systems, capturing provenance among component systems is increasingly important. Applications such as intrusion detection, load balancing, traffic routing, and insider threat detection all involve monitoring and analyzing the data provenance. Implicit in these applications is the assumption that "good" provenance is captured (e.g. complete provenance graphs, or one full path). When attempting to provide "good" provenance for a complex system of systems, it is necessary to know "how hard" the provenance-enabling will be and the likely quality of the provenance to be produced. In this work, we provide analytical results and simulation tools to assist in the scoping of the provenance enabling process. We provide use cases of complex systems-of-systems within which users wish to capture provenance. We describe the parameters that must be taken into account when undertaking the provenance-enabling of a system of systems. We provide a tool that models the interactions and types of capture agents involved in a complex systems-of-systems, including the set of known and unknown systems in the environment. The tool provides an estimation of quantity and type of capture agents that will need to be deployed for provenance-enablement in a complex system that is not completely known.

Keywords: Provenance · Lineage · Agent Based Modelling · Modelling and simulation · Complex systems

1 Introduction

Provenance, the record of creation, update and activities that influence a piece of data, is used to: understand if data was produced correctly (according to published methodology, or according to policy); detect suspicious behavior within complex systems; and, enable trust during cross-organizational collaboration [3]. The utility of the provenance stream for these purposes is tied to what information is actually collected, and how far through the system the provenance can "see".

Approved for Public Release #16-0858. The authors' affiliation with The MITRE Corporation is provided for identification purposes only, and is not intended to convey or imply MITRE's concurrence with, or support for, the positions, opinions or viewpoints expressed by the author.

© Springer International Publishing Switzerland 2016
M. Mattoso and B. Glavic (Eds.): IPAW 2016, LNCS 9672, pp. 146–157, 2016.
DOI: 10.1007/978-3-319-40593-3_12

In our experience, when approached by government organizations seeking to become provenance aware, the first question becomes: How much of the system must be provenance aware in order to utilize the provenance data stream in the desired manner? One of the first considerations is how many capture agents are needed to have good coverage of the system of systems. The next question is, which system(s), if provenance-capture enabled, will give the most "bang for the buck"?

In other words, an analysis of the system of systems with the utility of the final provenance data stream is required to put capture points at appropriate places. Unfortunately, in many cases, the "full workflow" isn't known because of *system complexity* and *human cognitive load*. In the case of *system complexity*, large numbers of systems exist to form a complex system of systems and no one person knows all systems and their interactions. The people required to administer a system know about their system, but not who is using it or why. The running joke in one IT center: Q: "How do you know who is using your system?" A: "Turn it off and listen in the hallway to who starts screaming." Meanwhile, the users of the system, see it merely as a tool and have no knowledge where the underlying data resides and what other systems may be called by the backend. Additionally, *human cognitive load* also plays a part in creating an inaccurate picture of the system-of-systems. When asked, users can faithfully recite their top-used tools, but become increasingly vague and forgetful of lesser used systems.

In this work, we extend a modelling tool designed to simulate the provenance data stream within a complex system of systems, with varying types and distributions of capture agents. The original work [12] was limited in that it allowed a user to specify the *number* of systems in a system-of-systems, but merely arranged that number upon a grid and randomly assigned how provenance was captured at each point. This work is a marked divergence from [12]; it is designed to take in the major systems used in a workflow that can be described with fidelity by users. It also models the "grey areas", those parts of the system that are not well-remembered or documented. The modelling tool allows a user to specify the known systems, and how they are expected to connect. Using this as a base, the tool will run simulations over that base with augmentations of "grey systems". The contributions of this paper are as follows:

1. A simulation tool that analyzes how much provenance is captured in a system of systems, including expansion of those systems to unknown and unspecified "grey systems".
2. A real-world use case from the US healthcare system that motivates the need for anticipating "grey areas" in provenance capture.
3. An application of the tool that shows how the system performs over likely scenarios.

Section 2 discusses related work, in particular capturing provenance, and Agent Based Modelling. In Sect. 3, we present foundations that describe the complex system of systems and motivate this work. Section 4 contains a real world US healthcare use case. The architecture of our system and details on its implementation are in Sect. 5, while in Sect. 6, the model is executed over various sample systems. Finally, in Sect. 7 we conclude and highlight future work.

2   Related Work

Provenance has been touted as a tool to assist with scientific collaboration [19, 20, 25]. Unlike the system-of-systems we describe above, most of these systems [4, 20, 25, 29] constrain the user to a single management system. Many "execution platforms" can be used, but with a central management system and user-defined system-of-systems, provenance tracking can occur with a single capture point within these workflow managers. [3, 9] describe provenance-based techniques for assessing data trustworthiness. However, in order to use the provenance, as described above, it must be captured.

2.1   Provenance Capture

As described in [10], we note that there are classes of provenance capture agents.

Coordination-points: In some systems-of-systems, there are "coordination points". Coordination points are systems or software that provide natural bottlenecks. Typically, these are systems that help order, transmit and manage data and jobs. Examples of current coordinate point capture points include MapReduce [24], UNIX kernel [22], GIT [23], and Enterprise Service Bus (ESB) [2]. Workflow (and yes/no workflow) management systems such as [4, 20, 25, 29] are also good coordination-points. Dynamic instrumentation has the same effect as a coordination point on a given system [26].

Application-based: In some cases, an application is so heavily used that it is beneficial to expend the resources to capture provenance information from just that application. Examples include [5, 11, 21].

Manual: Many standards, such as [1], include provenance as components of the required metadata; in many instances, much of that information is populated by hand by a data curator. Unless the user is particularly motivated to capture provenance, manual capture points have very low capture rates. Of particular interest are hybrid approaches in which the application itself is somewhat provenance-enabled, but the user makes the final decision as to what is important and needs to be stored [19].

Provenance reconstruction work, such as [16] is not considered in this work since the accuracy of this provenance is not always equal to that obtained via making applications and systems provenance aware.

2.2   Provenance Simulation

There have been several efforts to simulate provenance information. Typically, these revolve around creating samples of provenance artifacts. [8] creates sample provenance graphs based on workflows and user rules. The PLUS system [3] has DAGAholic, a tool that creates provenance graphs of specified size, connectivity, sub-graph patterns (tree, star, etc.). Sample provenance graphs such as [7, 10] are available on GitHub ProvBench. To our knowledge, there is no simulator that simulates capture points for a system of systems.

2.3   ABMs

Agent-Based Models (ABMs) are a type of distributed computational simulation in which a set of autonomous, goal-seeking, perceptive agents interact with each other and with their environment in order to achieve some outcome. ABMs originated in the field of computer science, in particular with multi-agent system (MAS) and distributed artificial intelligence (DAI). In DAI applications, a problem is defined such that it can be addressed in parallel by the efforts of multiple independent agents. In MAS applications, a number of agents address a problem in parallel by passing messages among one another in a shared environment. ABMs combine the parallel and distributed inter-agent communications of MAS applications with two-dimensional Cellular Automata (CA) models that are used to form an artificial landscape with which the agents may interact as well [13].

ABMs have been used in a variety of domains, including computational economics [27], auction markets [14], social network analysis [17, 18], and public policy modeling [6], to name a few.

In this study, an ABM is used as a computational platform to study the capture of provenance information in a complex system of systems. The model consists of an abstract landscape containing a network of arbitrarily connected agents, where the agents are used to represent systems in an interconnected set of systems that share data. The network also includes provenance monitoring agents as well, which represent systems that are capable of detecting and logging provenance relevant transactions. As time progresses in the simulation, information artifacts flow through the network, and are subject to simulated update events which may or may not be observed by a provenance monitoring agent, depending on the configuration of the original network and the placement of provenance monitoring capabilities in the network. The ABM is used as a modeling platform to study the interactions among systems in order to provide quantitative metrics on the level of provenance obtained with a particular distribution of provenance capture agents. Based on analysis of the simulated information flow, a predefined agent connection topology, and a particular placement of provenance monitoring systems in the simulation, various provenance management topologies can be quantitatively compared and evaluated.

3   Foundations

To reiterate the problem, when looking to understand a system of systems, interviews and code reviews are performed to understand systems touched and their interactions. The techniques uncover a set of found, known systems, N_F, and their interactions, E_F. We assume that the actual graph of interconnected systems, S, is:

$$S \supseteq (N_F, E_F)$$

S may also contain grey systems (i.e., those that are not well-remembered or documented), N_G, and as yet unfound connections E_G. Thus, the number of systems in the system of systems, S, is bounded by:

$$|N_F| \leq |N| \leq |N_F| + |N_G|$$

Meanwhile, the number of interactions, I, possible is bounded by:

$$|E_F| \leq |I| \leq (|N_F| + |N_G|)^2$$

Each I is an interaction between systems over which data may flow during the execution of a user's tasks; each I represents a possible edge in a provenance graph. Even with low numbers of grey systems, there can be large numbers of interactions that are missing from the provenance record. [10] contains provenance datasets that highlight how a poor choice in capture agents create holes in the provenance record and re-enforce the grey system's absence from the record. Unfortunately, as we discuss in subsequent sections, the systems-of-systems we are concerned about have a large number of N_F and a possibly large number of N_G. In addition, each system, either known or grey, has the potential to be provenance-enabled through a capture agent. We utilize the general categories described in Sect. 2: coordination point, application, and manual.

The goal is to determine where the best systems are to place capture agents, and type of capture agent. We assume that capture agents are expensive to build, deploy and maintain, and thus wish to minimize the number of capture agents while still capturing "good" provenance. There are several choices for "good provenance", depending on the desired usage of the provenance. An example set of "good" evaluations could be:

- 100 % of all provenance is captured
- 80 % of all possible provenance is captured
- At least 1 complete path between a source and sink exists

In the degenerate case, if we assume that every system in S can only support an application-based capture point, then it is easy to determine the minimum number of capture agents by inspection. If "good" is complete provenance, then every system must be provenance enabled; if "good" is 1 path from source to sink, then the shortest path can be provenance-enabled, etc. However, the problem quickly becomes trickier. Assuming that any system can be made a coordination point, that is, it can record the provenance for itself and all systems connected to it, then asking if there is a way to capture complete provenance in fewer than k capture points becomes the NP-complete Vertex Cover problem. For this reason, we utilize a modelling and simulation approach.

4   Use Case: Provenance in the US Healthcare System of Systems

In the US Healthcare system, key stakeholders include Patients, Providers, Payers, and Public Health. Each stakeholder has different incentives, and each maintains information about medical events, but at different levels of detail and for various reasons.

The medical records and associated healthcare information illustrate the problems found in data provenance in a complex system of systems.

Consider the situation in which a patient is seeking medical care for a non-acute condition, for which an episode of care typically spans 6-8 months and involves coordination with generalists and specialists. Assume that the patient has medical insurance coverage under a private plan or a state sponsored health care exchange managed under the Affordable Care Act (ACA). Assume too, that the patient's main provider is part of a hospital-based physician's group. The patient first seeks care from his primary care physician. An initial set of medical records is generated based on this encounter. Based on a preliminary diagnosis, the patient is referred to two specialists and to a lab. The lab and one of the specialists is also a part of the hospital-based group. Because the traffic between these entities is high, the IT and physicians understand how the patient's record gets passed between them. If provenance capture was desired, it would be trivial to analyze these interactions and find the appropriate provenance capture points. Unfortunately, the second specialist and the special lab she sent our patient to are not in the hospital's network; it is unlikely that either of these systems would be remembered for inclusion in a large-reaching provenance system. Assume the patient is advised to seek physical therapy, and choses to do so close to work, not at the hospital. Again, the patient's medical record is passed to the physical therapist, but the therapist in effect runs a grey system – one essential to tracking the movement of the patient's record, but outside the well-worn and understood tracks of the hospital's in-network system. Figure 1 shows the movement of the patient's health record, and both the known and grey systems in the complex system of systems.

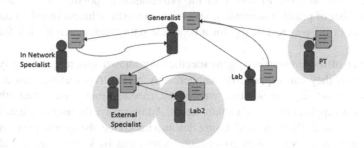

Fig. 1. Depiction of the medical record as it moves through providers. Some providers modify the record and send it back to the generalist's system. Others become an off-shoot. Systems in grey are part of the complex system of systems, but are not easily identified.

5   The Model and Tool

The provenance capture simulator is built using NetLogo [28]. It has two operating modes: default, as described in [12] and user-assisted as we describe here. The model incorporates:

- Types of capture agents:
  - Coordination points capture provenance for themselves and any systems that interact with them.
  - Application-based capture provenance for themselves only.
  - Manual provenance capture based on a human recording the provenance. We assume that humans are lazy provenance agents, and only capture 10 % of the time.
  - None: no capture agent exists in this system.
- Known systems, N_F, as specified by the user.
- The interactions between the known system, E_F.
- The capture agent type for each known system, chosen from: coordination point, application, manual, or none.
- A set number of unknown, grey, systems, $|N_G|$.
- A maximum number of possible connections between grey systems.
- The average number of connections a grey system may have, as specified by the user.
- A user defined number of coordination-point application-based, manual and do-nothing capture agents to be distributed among the grey systems.
- The probability a piece of data will be directed along a new path. Data will always go through the set paths, and probability of P that it will also move down a second or third path at any node that has a degree >1.

Our goal is to produce provenance streams that are useful. Obviously, usefulness is defined by the ultimate usage of the provenance data stream. For instance, for intrusion detection, seeing as close to 100 % of the provenance as possible would detect the greatest number of possible anomalies. Determining trustworthiness based on data path similarity as in [9] we are looking for a complete path from source to sink for every data item.

The user of the simulation system specifies the known systems, and the types of capture agents they can support. Remember, only certain types of systems can be a coordination point (e.g. service bus, web proxy, message router, etc.), and otherwise can only be an application-based capture agent. Additionally, the user can specify how the systems are actually connected. Using this as a backbone, the system then randomly generates grey systems and their connections across that backbone. Figure 2 shows a sample execution.

Using this execution, and defining the allowed number and type of application agents, the output provenance can be analyzed to see if it meets the user's specification of "good" provenance. The simulation itself runs through permutations of grey system configurations, allowing the best, worst and average amount of provenance a given system of systems can capture to be highlighted.

6 Results and Discussion

The point of this section is to show that the tool can be run over any user-specified system-of-systems with different configurations, connections, grey-systems and capture agents. To this end, the tool is run on a standard laptop, and realistic system configurations were used, although chosen with little attention to the systems themselves. The system was run on a Mac with OSX 10.9.5 4. The system has a core processor speed of 2.7 GB with 16 GB RAM. Despite being run on a modest laptop, the simulations took on average less than a minute to run.

In an attempt to find descriptions of real, complex systems-of-systems, we turn to pre-defined workflows in myExperiment [15]. While all of the workflow technologies have strong provenance capture as discussed in Sect. 2, and have no need to analyze what systems involved may need capture agents, the workflows themselves provide a nice, bounded set of realistic system configurations. To showcase this tool, we chose first 5 workflows from myExperiment that satisfied the "runnable" facet, and chose 1 path from source to sink to represent known systems. All others are considered grey systems. Within the known systems, any system with >3 edges in the workflow, is considered a coordination-point. For all other known systems, we rotate through application-based, manual and none, assigning them at random to the known systems. Figure 2 shows an example workflow from myExperiment that was translated into known and unknown systems. We chose a path from source to sink as the known systems. The remaining systems we circled in grey. When actually executing the tool over this description, the edges between grey systems will be lost and substituted in randomly, since by definition we do not know any of the grey systems or their interactions. Table 1 describes the workflows chosen for the tool showcase.

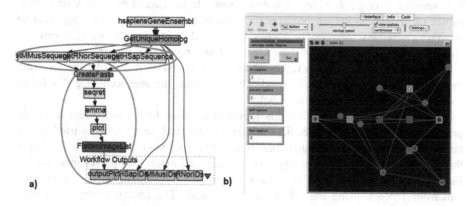

Fig. 2. (a) Sample of a myExperiment workflow, BiomartAndEMBOSSAnalysis. The grey systems in this case are demarked by grey circles; (b) A sample execution of the tool using the systems in 2a. Colored boxes and circles are known systems and grey systems respectively. Along the left, the user can specify the number of coordination-points, application-based and manual capture points to be used amongst the grey systems during the permutations, or the system can run through permutations randomly choosing capture types. (Color figure online)

Table 1. The MyExperiments wokflows used to create reasonable system of system connections for showcasing the tool

	Name	Total systems	$|N_F|$	Known Coord/App/Manual/None	$|N_G|$	Grey coord-point
1	Trivial US Healthcare Example	6	3	1/1/1/1	3	0
2	Unnested_qtl_pathway_3 by Antoon Goderis	12	4	1/1/1/1	8	1
3	BiomartAndEMBOSSAnalysis by Alan Williams	13	5	1/2/1/1	8	1
4	EBI_ClustalW2 by Hamish McWilliam	21	4	2/1 /1/1	17	1
5	PathwaysandGeneannotationsforQTLregion by Paul Fisher	61	8	2/2/2/2	53	8

Using this sampling of complex system of systems, we can explore the functionality of the tool. First we take #3 and #5 from Table 1 and show how user knowledge and graph connectivity can impact how easy or hard it is to get "good" provenance.

Figure 3 shows snapshots of runs for #3 and #5 in which we vary the ratios of capture agent types. We do not show all combinations of coordination-point, application-based, manual and no capture, just a small selection. For graph #3, almost half of the systems are known, and those known systems form a direct path from source to sink (see Fig. 2). Given the assignment of coordination points, the set of known provenance systems is guaranteed to meet the criteria of two of our "good" provenance metrics (at least 1 path through the graph, and 80 % provenance captured). Figure 3a shows this in detail. No matter the provenance capture points deployed in the unknown systems, "good" provenance capture given what is known about the system is very likely. In other words, the tool provides a checkpoint for whether the user must invest more time and effort hunting down and provenance enabling the last few grey systems that may exist. In this case, the answer is a resounding "no" and the user may feel confident that the provenance from her system of systems is "good". On the other hand, the execution over graph #5 tells a different story. In the case of #5, only a very small subset of systems is known (e.g. because a user has just started exploring what to provenance-enable). Figure 3b shows a spread of possible distributions of coordination-points, application-based, manual and no capture through the grey systems. While the ratios chosen represent the same spread as in Fig. 3a, the resulting provenance is not necessarily as good. The tool helps the user recognize that better consideration of grey systems is in order.

Although it is expected that this tool will be used by an individual trying to provenance enable a very specific complex system, and hence will be used as we described above, varying numbers and types of capture points, we wish to highlight that the tool can function over any setup of size and number of provenance graphs. Figure 4 shows the amount of provenance captured when running each complex system from Table 1, using the following arrangement. The known systems and their capture types is fixed. Of the grey systems, 10 % are coordination points, 30 % are application-based, 30 % are manual and 30 % are no capture agent defined. As is expected, our very simple graph #1 that has only a few grey systems does very well. It is supported by the larger number of systems that are known and provenance enabled. At the other end of the spectrum is graph #5 that has a greater set of grey systems than

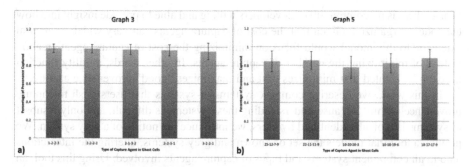

Fig. 3. (a) Workflow 3 from Table 1 run with varying ratios of capture types; (b) Workflow 5 from Table 1 run with varying ratios of capture types. The x-axis indicates the quantity of each type of capture agent: no capture – manual capture – application-based – coordination point.

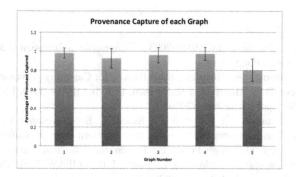

Fig. 4. Each graph from Table 1 has been run with grey system capture agents in the following ratio: 10 % coordination point, 30 % application-based, 30 % manual, 30 % no capture.

known systems. In other words, the tool can help a user estimate how much provenance will be captured in a complex system, and allow the user to determine if that is good enough.

7 Future Work and Conclusion

Until now, we have made the assumption that all provenance capture agents cost the same amount to implement and maintain, and we are merely attempting to maximize the provenance captured while reducing the overall number of required provenance capture agents. Unfortunately, this assumption is incorrect. In our experience, creating a provenance capture agent for a commercial off the shelf (COT) tool, such as Palantir[1] or SpectorSoft [10], is harder and more costly than open source (OS), such as MuleSoft ESB [2] because the code is proprietary and not always easily accessible.

---

[1] www.palantir.com.

Worse, there is no community of developers willing and able to provide insight into how the code is organized. Given that the cost of capture agents can vary widely, a natural extension to this model would focus on minimizing the cost of capture agent creation instead of minimizing the number of capture agents. In other words, a utility function needs to be created that minimizes cost and maximizes "good" provenance capture.

In this work, we describe complex systems-of-systems that users wish to capture provenance within. Because understanding these systems is difficult, and only a subset of systems is typically identified by users, we introduce the notion of a grey system. We provide a tool that models the set of known and grey systems, altering the interactions among all component systems and types of capture agents involved. Using this tool, an estimation of quantity and type of capture agents that will need to be deployed can be found.

References

1. North American Profile of ISO19115:2003 - Geographic Information - Metadata. NAP Metadata Working Group (2005)
2. Allen, M.D., Chapman, A., Blaustein, B., Seligman, L.: Capturing provenance in the wild. In: McGuinness, D.L., Michaelis, J.R., Moreau, L. (eds.) IPAW 2010. LNCS, vol. 6378, pp. 98–101. Springer, Heidelberg (2010)
3. Allen, M.D., Chapman, A., Seligman, L., Blaustein, B.: Provenance for collaboration: detecting suspicious behaviors and assessing trust in information. In: CollabCom (2011)
4. Altintas, I., Barney, O., Jaeger-Frank, E.: Provenance collection support in the Kepler scientific workflow system. In: Moreau, L., Foster, I. (eds.) IPAW 2006. LNCS, vol. 4145, pp. 118–132. Springer, Heidelberg (2006)
5. Asuncion, H.U.: Automated data provenance capture in spreadsheets, with case studies. Future Gener. Comput. Syst. **29**, 2169–2181 (2013)
6. Bankes, S.C.: Tools and techniques for developing policies for complex and uncertain systems. Proc. Natl. Acad. Sci. **99**, 7263–7266 (2002)
7. K. Belhajjame, J. Zhao, D. Garijo, A. Garrido, S. Soiland-Reyes, P. Alper, O. Corcho: A workflow PROV-corpus based on taverna and wings. In: Khalid Belhajjame, J.M.G.-P., Sahoo, S. (eds.) ProvBench (2013)
8. Caron, C., Amann, B., Constantin, C., Giroux, P.: WePIGE: the WebLab provenance information generator and explorer. In: EDBT (2014)
9. Dai, C., Lin, D., Kantarcioglu, M., Bertino, E., Celikel, E., Thuraisingham, B.: Query processing techniques for compliance with data confidence policies. In: Jonker, W., Petković, M. (eds.) SDM 2009. LNCS, vol. 5776, pp. 49–67. Springer, Heidelberg (2009)
10. Coe, G.B., Doty, R.C., Allen, M.D., Chapman, A.: Provenance capture disparities highlighted through datasets. In: Theory and Practice of Provenance (2014)
11. Conover, H., Ramachandran, R., Beaumont, B., Kulkarni, A., McEniry, M., Regner, K., Graves, S.: Introducing provenance capture into a legacy data system. IEEE Trans. Geosci. Remote Sens. **51**, 5098–5104 (2013)
12. Gammack, D., Chapman, A.: Provenance tipping point. In: Theory and Practice of Provenance (2015)
13. Gilbert, N., Terna, P.: How to build and use agent-based models in social science. Mind Soc. **1**, 57–72 (2000)

14. Gode, D., Sunder, S.: Allocative efficiency of markets with zero-intelligence traders: market as a partial substitute for individual rationality. J. Polit. Econ. **101**, 119–137 (1993)
15. A. Goderis, D. De Roure, C. Goble, J. Bhagat, D. Cruickshank, P. Fisher, D. Michaelides, F. Tanoh: Discovering scientific workflows: the myExperiment benchmarks. In: IEEE Transactions on Automation Science and Engineering (2008)
16. Groth, P., Gil, Y., Magliacane, S.: Automatic metadata annotation through reconstructing provenance. In: Third International Workshop on the role of Semantic Web in Provenance Management (2012)
17. Jackson, M.: The stability and efficiency of economic and social networks. In: Jackson, M.O. (ed.) Advances in Economic Design, pp. 319–361. Springer, Heidelberg (2003)
18. Jackson, M., Watts, A.: The evolution of social and economic networks. J. Econ. Theor. **106**, 265–295 (2002)
19. Lerner, B., Boose, E.: RDataTracker: collecting provenance in an interactive scripting environment. In: Theory and Practice of Provenance (2014)
20. McPhillips, T., Song, T., Kolisnik, T., Aulenbach, S., Belhajjame, K., Bocinsky, K., Cao, Y., Chirigati, F., Dey, S., Freire, J., Huntzinger, D., Jones, C., Koop, D., Missier, P., Schildhauer, M., Schwalm, C., Wei, Y., Cheney, J., Bieda, M., Ludaescher, B.: YesWorkflow: a user-oriented, language-independent tool for recovering workflow information from scripts. Int. J. Digit. Curation **7**, 92–100 (2015)
21. Missier, P., Chen, Z.: Extracting PROV provenance traces from Wikipedia history pages. In: EDBT (2013)
22. Muniswamy-Reddy, K.-K., Holland, D.A., Braun, U., Seltzer, M.I.: Provenance-aware storage systems. In: USENIX, pp. 43–56 (2006)
23. De Nies, T., Magliacane, S., Verborgh, R., Coppens, S., Groth, P., Mannens, E., Van de Walle, R.: Git2PROV: exposing version control system content as W3C PROV. In: Proceedings of the 12th International Semantic Web Conference (2013)
24. Park, H., Ikeda, R., Widom, J.: RAMP: a system for capturing and tracing provenance in MapReduce workflows. VLDB **4**, 1351–1354 (2011)
25. Scheidegger, C.E., Vo, H.T., Koop, D., Freire, J. Silva, C.: Querying and re-using workflows with VisTrails. In: SIGMOD (2008)
26. Stamatogiannakis, M., Groth, P., Bos, H.: Looking inside the black-box: capturing data provenance using dynamic instrumentation. In: Ludaescher, B., Plale, B. (eds.) IPAW 2014. LNCS, vol. 8628, pp. 155–167. Springer, Heidelberg (2015)
27. Tesfatsion, L.: Agent-based computational economics: modeling economies as complex adaptive systems. Inf. Sci. **149**, 262–268 (2003)
28. Wilensky, U.: NetLogo. Center for Connected Learning and Computer-Based Modeling, Northwestern University, Evanston, IL (1999). http://ccl.northwestern.edu/netlogo
29. Wolstencroft, K., Haines, R., et al.: The taverna workflow suite: designing and executing workflows of Web Services on the desktop, web or in the cloud. Nucleic Acids Res. **41**, w557–w561 (2013)

System Demonstrations

Yin & Yang: Demonstrating Complementary Provenance from noWorkflow & YesWorkflow

João Felipe Pimentel[1]([✉]), Saumen Dey[2], Timothy McPhillips[3],
Khalid Belhajjame[4], David Koop[5], Leonardo Murta[1], Vanessa Braganholo[1],
and Bertram Ludäscher[3]

[1] Universidade Federal Fluminense, Niterói, Brazil
jpimentel@ic.uff.br
[2] University of California, Davis, Davis, USA
[3] University of Illinois, Urbana-Champaign, Champaign, USA
[4] Université Paris-Dauphine, Paris, France
[5] University of Massachusetts, Dartmouth, USA

Abstract. The noWorkflow and YesWorkflow toolkits both enable researchers to capture, store, query, and visualize the provenance of results produced by scripts that process scientific data. noWorkflow captures prospective provenance representing the program structure of Python scripts, and retrospective provenance representing key events observed during script execution. YesWorkflow captures prospective provenance declared through annotations in the comments of scripts, and supports key retrospective provenance queries by observing what files were used or produced by the script. We demonstrate how combining complementary information gathered by noWorkflow and YesWorkflow enables provenance queries and data lineage visualizations neither tool can provide on its own.

1 Introduction

Methods for harvesting provenance information from scripts and runs of scripts have been of great recent interest to the provenance research community, and the resulting tools have received increasing attention from users of scripting languages in the natural sciences. Some of these approaches are language-specific, e.g., noWorkflow[1] [4,5] (Python) and RDataTracker [2] (R scripts), while others are language-independent, e.g., YesWorkflow[2] [3] and LLVM/SPADE [7]. Using such tools often entails annotating the scripts [2,3], monitoring executing scripts as they run [4,7], or both.

Approaches that do not require annotation, such as noWorkflow (NW), rely on the structure of the code itself to build prospective and retrospective provenance graphs. NW includes the actual function and variable names in the prospective provenance records, and it depends on records of run-time function

---

[1] For "not only Workflow", emphasizing that scripts need provenance tracking, too.
[2] Which can be read as "Yes, scripts can be workflows, too!".

© Springer International Publishing Switzerland 2016
M. Mattoso and B. Glavic (Eds.): IPAW 2016, LNCS 9672, pp. 161–165, 2016.
DOI: 10.1007/978-3-319-40593-3_13

calls to capture the retrospective provenance of script outputs. Consequently, the less meaningful variable and function names are in a script, the less clear the provenance query results and visualizations will be to scientists using the script. noWorkflow thus excels where Python programs are engineered for maintainablity, testability, code reuse, and long-term user support.

YesWorkflow (YW) is an example of a tool that largely ignores the code portions of a script, and instead depends on script authors (or users) adding annotations via comments in scripts. YW annotations declare the scientifically significant steps implemented by code blocks in a script, and the routes of dataflow between these steps. Annotations optionally assign meaningful names to actual (often obscurely named) code-level entities. Consequently, YesWorkflow users need not rename variables, move code into functions, or otherwise refactor scripts that already have been used to produce results (research transparency requires disclosure of the scripts actually used). YW users can capture provenance from a working script without incurring the regression testing costs that refactoring entails. YW thus provides benefits even when scripts are written rapidly in the course of competitive, time-critical research, and when researchers employ scripts that they do not intend to maintain further or to distribute and support.

Given the contrasting aims of noWorkflow and YesWorkflow and the differences in the approaches they take, it is not surprising that each supports queries and visualizations that the other cannot support on its own [1]. Here we show that there are provenance artifacts of great interest to researchers that only a combination of YW and NW provenance can produce. Achieving this combination requires mapping between common entities in both provenance models, and jointly querying the provenance information represented by each system. We refer to the joint provenance model, the system-spanning queries, and the resulting visualizations collectively as YW*NW.

2 Example Queries: noWorkflow, YesWorkflow, and YW*NW

We use the Python script described by McPhillips et al. [3] to demonstrate the kinds of provenance queries NW, YW, and the combination of both support. This script simulates acquisition of diffraction images during macromolecular X-ray crystallography experiments involving multiple samples. The script reads previously measured data quality statistics for each sample from an input spreadsheet; rejects samples that do not meet a minimum quality criterion; and for each accepted sample produces raw and corrected diffraction images according to a data collection strategy that depends on properties of the samples. Although the script only simulates data collection, the order of task execution, the sequence of data production events, and the resulting pattern of dependencies between input, intermediate, and final data items closely mimic those of a real experiment [8]. Queries that probe these dependencies are therefore illustrative of meaningful uses for provenance information. The complete script, marked up with YW annotations, is available on GitHub [6]; a more complete explanation is provided in [3].

noWorkflow. Examples of **prospective** provenance queries of this script that NW supports include: *What functions does the top-level function call? Are any functions defined in the script not called by the top-level function?*

NW can answer **retrospective** provenance queries about runs of this script, such as: *What values did the variable* rejected_sample *take during writes to files referred to by the* rejection_log *variable? What files were written during calls to the* transform_image *function? How many files were written while the* accepted_sample *variable had the value* DRT240*? What variables carry values returned by the* calculate_strategy *function to calls to the* collect_next_image *function? What parameters to the top-level function can effect the results returned by calls to* calculate_strategy*?*

NW also can answer queries about the execution context: *Which user executed the script? What version of Python was used?*

YesWorkflow. YW provenance queries refer to annotated code blocks (workflow steps) rather than to Python functions, and to data names declared via YW annotations instead of to Python variables. Queries of **prospective** provenance supported by YW include: *What are the names of steps that comprise the top-level workflow implemented by the script? What data is output by the* collect_data_set *step? What code blocks provide input directly to that step? What data is* corrected_image *(in)directly derived from?*

YW can also answer some **retrospective** provenance queries [3], including: *What samples did the run of the script collect images from? What energies were used during collection of images from sample* DRT240*? Where is the raw image from which corrected image* run/data/DRT322/DRT322_10000eV_001.img *is derived? Are there any raw images for which there are* **no** *corresponding corrected images?*

Querying the Combined YW*NW Provenance. Queries that must be answered by combining NW and YW provenance generally involve references both to Python functions or variables *and* to code blocks or data declared via YesWorkflow annotations. Examples include: *Can the* sample_id *output of the* collect_data_set *step ever produce values other than those provided via the* accepted_sample *input to this step? What Python functions may be called as part of the* calculate_strategy *step? What was the set of* energies *produced by the* compute_strategy *step for sample* DRT322*?*

As these queries demonstrate, the combination of NW and YW provenance enables code-level entities such as Python functions and variables to be queried in terms of data and workflow steps meaningful to the user (and vice versa). Such queries are useful for understanding runs of the script in ways that neither NW nor YW enable on their own. Generalizing these queries yield meaningful visualizations of the full lineage of any product of the script. Consider the hybrid YW*NW provenance graph in Fig. 1, showing the lineage of a specific output image. This lineage graph can be constructed as a subgraph of the original YW

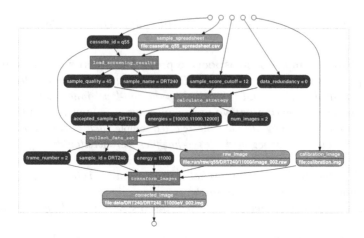

Fig. 1. Hybrid of YW prospective provenance and NW retrospective provenance: nodes and edges comprise the subgraph of the YW model of the script upstream of a single corrected_image; values in nodes are extracted from the NW runtime records of corresponding variable values leading to a particular image.

model [3] (restricted to predecessors nodes upstream of the corrected_image result node), which is then augmented with NW retrospective provenance; see [6] for details and the YW*NW integration queries.

Because the questions scientists have about runs of scripts often can be answered in terms of lineages of data products, YW*NW queries and visualizations promise to be of great value to researchers. Moreover, using noWorkflow and YesWorkflow jointly does not entail the major adaptations to code often needed to run existing software in scientific workflow management systems. Indeed, YW*NW provides many benefits of provenance management without requiring working code to be refactored at all.

3   Demonstration

In our demonstration we will highlight the benefits of harvesting, querying, and visualizing provenance with noWorkflow in conjunction with YesWorkflow. Starting with a directory containing just the example script and input files, we will (1) highlight how YW annotations can be visualized as prospective provenance using YesWorkflow; (2) run the script using noWorkflow and relate the resulting data file names and locations to the YW prospective provenance; (3) query the script and its outputs using noWorkflow and YesWorkflow separately to illustrate what each tool can do on its own; and (4) execute joint YW*NW queries that determine the lineage of a single data product and produce visualizations analogous to the one in Fig. 1.

A companion GitHub repository for this demonstration is available, along with an expanded version of this short demo description [6]. The repository includes the data collection script discussed above; the files produced by a run of this script; the provenance information produced by noWorkflow and YesWorkflow; and helper scripts for running the queries mentioned above and for producing Fig. 1. noWorkflow and YesWorkflow themselves are both available on GitHub and can easily be installed.

References

1. Dey, S., Belhajjame, K., Koop, D., Raul, M., Ludäscher, B.: Linking prospective and retrospective provenance in scripts. In: Theory and Practice of Provenance (TaPP) (2015)
2. Lerner, B., Boose, E.: RDataTracker: collecting provenance in an interactive scripting environment. In: Theory and Practice of Provenance (TaPP). Cologne, Germany (2014)
3. McPhillips, T., Bowers, S., Belhajjame, K., Ludäscher, B.: Retrospective provenance without a runtime provenance recorder. In: Theory and Practice of Provenance (TaPP) (2015)
4. Murta, L., Braganholo, V., Chirigati, F., Koop, D., Freire, J.: noWorkflow: capturing and analyzing provenance of scripts. In: Ludaescher, B., Plale, B. (eds.) IPAW 2014. LNCS, vol. 8628, pp. 71–83. Springer, Heidelberg (2015)
5. Pimentel, J., Freire, J., Murta, L., Braganholo, V.: Fine-grained provenance collection over scripts through program slicing. In: International Provenance and Annotation Workshop (IPAW), Washington D.C. (2016)
6. Pimentel, J.F., Dey, S., McPhillips, T., Belhajjame, K., Koop, D., Murta, L., Braganholo, V., Ludäscher, B.: Yin & Yang: demonstrating complementary provenance from noWorkflow & YesWorkflow. In: Mattoso, M., Glavic, B. (eds.): IPAW 2016. LNCS, vol. 9672, pp. 161–165 (2016). Technical Report & Demo. https://github.com/gems-uff/yin-yang-demo
7. Tariq, D., Ali, M., Gehani, A.: Towards automated collection of application-level data provenance. In: Theory and Practice of Provenance (TaPP) (2012)
8. Tsai, Y., McPhillips, S.E., González, A., McPhillips, T.M., Zinn, D., Cohen, A.E., Feese, M.D., Bushnell, D., Tiefenbrunn, T., Stout, C., Ludäscher, B., Hedman, B., Hodgson, K.O., Soltis, S.M.: AutoDrug: fully automated macromolecular crystallography workflows for fragment-based drug discovery. Acta Crystallogr. Sect. D: Biol. Crystallogr. 69(5), 796–803 (2013)

MPO: A System to Document and Analyze Distributed Heterogeneous Workflows

Kesheng Wu[1(✉)], Elizabeth N. Coviello[2], S.M. Flanagan[2],
Martin Greenwald[3], Xia Lee[2], Alex Romosan[1], David P. Schissel[2],
Arie Shoshani[1], Josh Stillerman[3], and John Wright[3]

[1] Lawrence Berkeley National Laboratory, Berkeley, CA 94720, USA
kwu@lbl.gov
[2] General Atomics, P.O. Box 85608, San Diego, CA 92186-5608, USA
[3] Massachusetts Institute of Technology, Cambridge, MA 02139, USA

Abstract. Large scientific experiments and simulations produce vast quantities of data. Though smaller in volume, the corresponding metadata describing the production, pedigree, and ontology, is just as important as the raw data to the scientific discovery process. Driven by the application needs of a number of large-scale distributed workflows, we develop a metadata capturing and analysis system called MPO (short for Metadata, Provenance, Ontology). It seamlessly integrates with most data analysis environments and requires a minimal amount of changes to users' existing analysis programs. Users have the full control of how to instrument their programs to capture as much or as little information as they desire. Once captured in a database system, the workflows can be visualized and studied through a set of web-based tools. In large scientific collaborations where the workflows have been built up over decades, this ability to instrument the complex existing workflows and visualize the key interactions among the software components is tremendously useful.

1 Introduction

Datasets collected from scientific experiments and generated from computations typically go through numerous analysis steps on their paths to become scientific knowledge. These processes of data generation, conversion, manipulation and transformation are often formalized and codified into sequences of steps known as workflows. In this analysis process, we distinguish the raw data from its metadata. Though the metadata is typically much smaller in volume than the raw data, it contains critical information such as how the raw data is organized, and how the numbers and strings in the data are to be interpreted. In this work, we pay particular attention to two specific type of metadata known as provenance and ontology [1, 2].

© Springer International Publishing Switzerland 2016 (outside the US)
M. Mattoso and B. Glavic (Eds.): IPAW 2016, LNCS 9672, pp. 166–170, 2016.
DOI: 10.1007/978-3-319-40593-3_14

When all steps of a data analysis process is performed within a single workflow management system, the workflow management system often has a way of capturing the provenance information [3, 4]. However, there are many active research collaborations with decades of history and large collections of workflows that are not on any of the modern workflow management systems. In addition, a large workflow might involve an extended collaboration and span a number of different computer systems, where no single workflow management system could reach all of the disparate parts. In such a case, scientists have to manually enter the critical pieces of metadata crossing system boundaries. Manually entering metadata requires scientists to break their attention on the data analysis process and potentially decreases their productivity, which diminishes the chance that metadata will be entered in a timely manner if at all. Furthermore, there is no easy way to enforce a consistent ontology in such a distributed environment. Inconsistencies in terminology used in describing the workflows and data products could cause confusion in their later uses, and reduce the value of the data products, which further reduce the motivation for users to enter metadata about their work. Clearly, automating the metadata capturing and ensuring a consistent ontology are essential to address these difficulties. The key challenge is to do these on an arbitrarily complex workflow in a distributed environment.

Our answer to the distributed metadata capture problem is a system that works with any computing platform; captures information from workflows executed anywhere; and requires a minimal amount of modifications to the existing workflow components. The system is known as MPO, a shorthand for Metadata, Provenance, and Ontology[1] [5]. The MPO software consists of a data model, an API for capturing information, a database for storing the captured information, and a web service for analyzing the captured information [6]. Workflows are represented as directed acyclic graphs, providing explicit information about the relationships between workflow data and actions. This graphical representation is accessible anywhere through a web front-end [5–8]. This brief introduction to the demonstration explains the current status of the design, development and testing of the system.

2 MPO System Architecture

In this section we review the basic architecture and key components of MPO software. We will describe the key new features in the next section.

MPO is designed to allow scientists to capture information about their divergent workflows from anywhere. We design the MPO software system as multi-tier web services. It defines a RESTful [9, 10] API that can be easily accessed from a variety of programming languages used by MPO clients. The building blocks of the MPO system includes: (1) Database; (2) API Server and Event Server; (3) Interactive UI server; and (4) Clients. The heart of the system is a set of web servers: API Server, Event Server, and the Interactive UI Server. The API server communicates with a Database system to store the persistent data. A client may communicate with the API server or the UI

---

[1] MPO project documentation and software are available at <https://mpo.psfc.mit.edu/>.

server. Those that directly communicate with API server are "Native Application" clients, while those that communicate with the UI server are web clients.

The MPO database stores all persistent information as MPO entities such as Data Objects, Activities, and Connections. Currently, PostgreSQL is chosen for the database server. However, the MPO database schema is general enough that the database server could be replaced. The generality is helpful in separating the database implementation from design of user functionality. The team is fortifying this separation by implementing Object Relational Mapping (ORM) with the SQLAlchemy toolkit[2].

The MPO API server exposes its services via RESTful API. The basic entities in the MPO data model are represented with corresponding RESTful resources [10]. The API server utilizes the Model View Controller (MVC) design pattern, and it has been constructed using Flask which is a lightweight micro web application framework written in Python. The MPO event server is an additional service that runs side-by-side with the API server. It is implemented by utilizing the MDSplus [11] system's event features and provides asynchronous events for real-time updates by clients.

3   Advanced Features in MPO

Now that we have described the basic components, we next describe the new features that support analysis and exploration of workflows and ontology.

The MPO interactive UI server provides visualization and interactive browsing of the MPO data via the web browser interface. This interface presents MPO data objects and their relationships, while focusing on the main entities: Workflow, Data Object, and Activities. The searchable fields are based on general workflow metadata descriptors including creation time range, workflow name, description, the author's username, and so on; an example is shown in Fig. 1. The searchable ontology fields are based on the user-defined ontology terms. To reduce the size of the querying interface, only the terms used in the displayed work-

Fig. 1. An example of MPO filter, with part of the workflow screen.

flows will be available for the ontology filter selection. The UI presents these fields in an intuitive and organized manner, grouped by their ontology hierarchy with additional information such as the count of associated workflows using each term. Users can click

---

[2] SQLAlchemy is available at http://www.sqlalchemy.org/.

to toggle the checkboxes next to the desired ontology term(s) to modify the selection. For example, one could find a list of all available workflows with a given list of ontology terms or keywords in their descriptions.

Large collaborations such as those in high-energy physics and fusion could last for a number of decades. Workflows developed in the early years of these projects are gradually evolved to adapt to the new science objectives, new computing hardware and new software infrastructure. In this process, not only the steps of workflows change, but also the terminology and ontology. It is important to support the evolution of terminology and ontology. Our support for ontology evolution takes a practical route, where changes that are more likely to appear in the real applications are supported first. Based on our interactions with application scientists, we observe that the most likely change to ontology in physical sciences is the addition of some terms. This is typically created by the introduction of a new experimental device, a new technique for data collection and analysis, or a new approach to study some physical phenomenon. Our initial attempt at supporting ontology evolution is therefore to add ontology instances without modifying the structure of the ontology tree. Work is planned to support additional functions as the need arises.

4 Summary

The MPO system automates the documentation of scientific workflows and associated information; its functionality is independent of the workflow orchestration and execution mechanisms. It organizes and visualizes documented workflows and related metadata. The recent versions of MPO have a number of advanced workflow search and manipulation functions as well as some rudimentary ontology operations. In addition, we have implemented advanced capability to support efficient searches over thousands of workflows and developed the Container concept to allow users to operate on subtrees and supernodes. The source code of MPO is available to the public[5]. The team is setting up web resources for more users to try out the system and is reaching out to more users.

References

1. Marinho, A., et al.: ProvManager: a provenance management system for scientific workflows. Concurr. Comput. Pract. Exp. **24**(13), 1513–1530 (2012)
2. Kondylakis, H., Plexousakis, D.: Ontology evolution without tears. Web Semant.: Sci. Serv. Agents World Wide Web **19**, 42–58 (2013)
3. Altintas, I., Barney, O., Jaeger-Frank, E.: Provenance collection support in the Kepler scientific workflow system. In: Moreau, L., Foster, I. (eds.) IPAW 2006. LNCS, vol. 4145, pp. 118–132. Springer, Heidelberg (2006)
4. Davidson, S.B., et al.: Provenance in scientific workflow systems. IEEE Data Eng. Bull. **30** (4), 44–50 (2007)
5. Schissel, D.P., et al.: Automated metadata, provenance cataloging and navigable interfaces: ensuring the usefulness of extreme-scale data. Fusion Eng. Des. **89**(5), 745–749 (2014)

6. Wright, J.C., et al.: The MPO API: a tool for recording scientific workflows. Fusion Eng. Design **89**(5), 754–757 (2014)
7. Greenwald, M., et al.: A metadata catalog for organization and systemization of fusion simulation data. Fusion Eng. Design **87**(12), 2205–2208 (2012)
8. Abla, G., et al.: The MPO System for Automatic Workflow Documentation. Fusion Engineering and Design (2016 to appear)
9. Richardson, L., Ruby, S.: RESTful Web Services. O'Reilly Media, Sebastopol (2008)
10. Fielding, R.T., Taylor, R.N.: Principled design of the modern Web architecture. ACM Trans. Internet Technol. **2**(2), 115–150 (2002)
11. Stillerman, J., et al.: MDSplus data acquisition system. Rev. Sci. Instrum. **68**(1), 939–942 (1997)

Joint IPAW/TaPP Poster Session

PROV-JSONLD: A JSON and Linked Data Representation for Provenance

Trung Dong Huynh[✉], Danius T. Michaelides, and Luc Moreau

Electronics and Computer Science, University of Southampton,
Southampton SO17 1BJ, UK
{tdh,dtm,l.moreau}@ecs.soton.ac.uk

Abstract. In this paper, we propose a representation for PROV in JSON-LD, the JSON format for Linked Data, called PROV-JSONLD. As a JSON-based format, this provenance representation can be readily consumed by Web applications currently supporting JSON. As a Linked Data format, at the same time, it also represents provenance data in RDF using the PROV ontology. Hence, it is suitable for usages in both the Web and the Semantic Web.

1 Introduction

PROV provenance currently can be serialised in a number of representations: PROV-N, PROV-XML, PROV-JSON, or in a RDF serialisation using the PROV Ontology (PROV-O).[1] The latter, arguably, is most suitable for Linked Data, given that they can be readily consumed by existing Semantic Web tools and comes with the semantic grounding provided by PROV-O. There are, however, two main challenges for web-based applications when consuming PROV provenance represented in RDFs: (1) Many web applications are built to be lightweight, working mainly with simple data formats like JSON,[2] not the semantically rich RDF data model; (2) there are different, valid ways of representing PROV in RDF and such applications typically do not have the capability to infer canonical provenance information from such flexible representations. The JSON-LD format[3] partly addresses the first challenge by encoding RDF data in JSON. However, serialising RDF data into JSON-LD does not always produce JSON data in an expected structure, thus, necessitating the capability to understand the RDF data model to correctly interpret the data.

Against this background, we propose a new representation for PROV based on JSON-LD, called PROV-JSONLD, to address the above challenges. Specifically, PROV-JSONLD specifies a number of rules for representing PROV provenance in JSON-LD to provide a predefined data structure for PROV in JSON. As a JSON-based format, PROV-JSONLD can be easily consumed and processed

---

[1] See https://www.w3.org/Submission/prov-json/ for PROV-JSON and https://www.w3.org/TR/prov-overview/ for the other PROV representations.

[2] The JavaScript Object Notation (JSON): https://tools.ietf.org/html/rfc7159.

[3] JSON-LD: https://www.w3.org/TR/json-ld/.

© Springer International Publishing Switzerland 2016
M. Mattoso and B. Glavic (Eds.): IPAW 2016, LNCS 9672, pp. 173–177, 2016.
DOI: 10.1007/978-3-319-40593-3_15

by web applications and clients that are already supporting JSON without the need for the to understand the RDF data model. Moreover, with the emerging popularity of JSON databases, PROV-JSONLD allows provenance information to be stored along with application data as-is. As a Linked Data format, PROV-JSONLD is fully compatible with the RDF data model and PROV-O. As such, it can be readily processed by existing tools built for Linked Data and the Semantic Web. Last but not least, PROV-JSONLD was designed to serialise individual PROV records, as units of information in PROV, wholly into separate JSON objects. By so doing, the format enables the processing of large amount of provenance data in a stream-like fashion, which is not currently possible with PROV-JSON or other RDF serialisations.

2   JSON-LD Representation for PROV

PROV-JSONLD is a variant of JSON-LD designed with the following key principles: (1) for every type of PROV record, there is only one way to represent it in PROV-JSONLD; (2) each PROV record is wholly contained in one JSON object; and (3) except from the active JSON-LD context, no other information outside the JSON object is required to interpret the record.

2.1   Encoding a PROV-JSONLD Document

A PROV-JSONLD document is a self-contained package of PROV records in the form of a JSON-LD document. We provide the **PROV-JSONLD context** at https://provenance.ecs.soton.ac.uk/prov.jsonld to disambiguate terms used by PROV-JSONLD and map them to IRIs. It defines:

- prov: and xsd: prefixes (similarly predefined in PROV-N).
- The expected data types of PROV properties used in PROV-JSONLD.
- Simplified terms for all PROV-O properties used by PROV-JSONLD, e.g. entity for prov:entity, activity for prov:activity, and so on.
- Special terms introduced by PROV-JSONLD (listed in Table 1).

A PROV-JSONLD document optionally starts with the @context object, providing a reference to the PROV-JSONLD context above and the definition for any extra prefix. A default namespace can also be provided in the context's @base property. The PROV records packaged by the document go into its @graph array, each in a separate JSON object.

```
1   { "@context": [
2       "https://provenance.ecs.soton.ac.uk/prov.jsonld",
3       { "@base": "http://example.org/",
4         "foaf": "http://xmlns.com/foaf/0.1/" }
5     ],
6     "@graph": [ ] }
```

Listing 1: The basic structure of a PROV-JSONLD document.

2.2   Encoding a PROV Record

Each PROV record is serialised into a single JSON object in a @graph array. All the constituents of the PROV record become properties of the node as follows:

- The **identifier** (if present) becomes the identifier of the node (@id property).
- The **type** of the record, e.g. Activity, Derivation, becomes the **first** type of the node. Additional types are added to the @type array if they are valid IRIs; the remaining types become prov:type property of the node.
- **PROV attributes** are mapped into the corresponding PROV-O properties.
- **Additional attributes** become properties of the node.

```
1   { "@graph": [
2       { "@id": "exg:correct1", "@type": "prov:Activity",
3         "startedAtTime": "2012-03-31T09:21:00.000+01:00",
4         "endedAtTime": "2012-04-01T15:21:00.000+01:00"
5       } ] }
```

Listing 2: An Activity record in PROV-JSONLD.

For PROV elements, applying the above PROV-JSONLD encoding rules is straightforward. With PROV relations, however, there are some exceptions due to the multiple ways of representing them in RDF. In order to ensure a unique JSON structure for each type of PROV relation and that each relation record be encoded wholly in a single node, PROV-JSONLD only uses the qualified form of a PROV relation. Doing so, however, creates two encoding challenges.

First, although PROV-O defines classes for the qualified relations, the ontology does not specify a property to relate those qualified relations to the "subject" of the relations. Instead, for each qualified relation, it defines a qualification property to link the subject to the qualified relation in that order. In order to encode the subject in the same node as the relation, we introduce reverse properties using the @reverse mechanism provided by JSON-LD. Specifically, the subject of a PROV relation becomes a property of the node encoding the relation according to Table 1.

In addition, for Revision, Quotation, and PrimarySource records, which are sub-types of Derivation, PROV-JSONLD represents them as Derivation records with an additional types (prov:Revision, prov:Quotation, and prov:PrimarySource, respectively). This is to enable web applications, which typically do not have inference capabilities, to interpret such records as Derivation records when consuming PROV-JSONLD. Listing 3 below illustrates the encoding rules above for a Revision record. Note that this record does not have an @id property as it does not have an identifier; and the entity_derived property is a reverse property.

Table 1. PROV-JSONLD terms and their (reverse) PROV-O predicates

PROV-JSONLD terms	PROV-O qualification properties	PROV record
entity_generated	prov:qualifiedGeneration	Generation
entity_derived	prov:qualifiedDerivation	Derivation
entity_invalidated	prov:qualifiedInvalidation	Invalidation
entity_attributed	prov:qualifiedAttribution	Attribution
activity_using	prov:qualifiedUsage	Usage
activity_started	prov:qualifiedStart	Start
activity_ended	prov:qualifiedEnd	End
activity_associated	prov:qualifiedAssociation	Association
informed	prov:qualifiedCommunication	Communication
delegate	prov:qualifiedDelegation	Delegation
influencee	prov:qualifiedInfluence	Influence

```
1  {  "@graph": [
2       { "@type": ["prov:Derivation", "prov:Revision"],
3         "entity_derived": "exg:dataset2",
4         "entity": "exg:dataset1",
5         "hadActivity": "exg:correct1"
6       } ] }
```

Listing 3: A Revision record in PROV-JSONLD.

The second encoding challenge is that PROV-O does not define a qualified relation for Specialization, Alternate, and Membership; as a result, those records require special encoding rules. The only way to represent them in RDF is with the prov:specializationOf, prov:alternateOf, and prov:hadMember properties, respectively. For those records, PROV-JSONLD encodes them in single nodes by using the "subject" of such a relation as the node's identifier and the "object" as the value of the appropriate property from the three above. There is no @type or any additional property for those nodes as they are not allowed by PROV. For example, the PROV-N statement alternateOf(exg:dataset2, exg:dataset1) is represented in PROV-JSONLD as:

{ "@graph": [{ "@id":"exg:dataset2", "alternateOf": "exg:dataset1" }] }.

2.3   Encoding a PROV Bundle

Provenance records can be bundled into a named set called a bundle. Following examples in the PROV-O specification, PROV-JSONLD uses named graphs to represent a named set of PROV records. In particular, PROV-JSONLD represents a PROV bundle similarly to the way a PROV document is encoded in

Sect. 2.1. In this case, however, the @graph array is paired with an @id property, which encodes the bundle's identifier.

3   Conclusions

In this paper, we propose a new representation for PROV based on JSON-LD. Given its compatibility with both JSON and the RDF data model, in addition to being amenable to stream processing, PROV-JSONLD has a vast range of useful applications. We believe that its introduction will contribute positively to the adoption of PROV as the provenance standard of choice in Linked Data and Web applications alike.

Provenance as Essential Infrastructure
for Data Lakes

Isuru Suriarachchi[✉] and Beth Plale

School of Informatics and Computing, Indiana University, Bloomington, IN, USA
{isuriara,plale}@cs.indiana.edu

Abstract. The Data Lake is emerging as a Big Data storage and management solution which can store any type of data at scale and execute data transformations for analysis. Higher flexibility in storage increases the risk of Data Lakes becoming data swamps. In this paper we show how provenance contributes to data management within a Data Lake infrastructure. We study provenance integration challenges and propose a reference architecture for provenance usage in a Data Lake. Finally we discuss the applicability of our tools in the proposed architecture.

1 Introduction

Big Data has brought about recognition in industry and research alike that data can be profitably mined for insight and forecasts. Data from numerous sources (e.g., clickstream, sensor data, social media, server logs) are being brought together. The Data Lake [5] has been introduced as an infrastructure which supports broader analysis on various types of data from different sources. It can store unstructured, semi-structured, and structured data at scale and support data transformations by integrating Big Data processing frameworks such as Apache Hadoop[1] and Apache Spark[2]. As the Data Lake does not enforce a schema at the time of ingest, scientists can easily dump data from various sources and process them only when necessary. This "dump everything" nature in a Data Lake increases the flexibility of data storage. However without some level of organization, the popular literature goes, the Data Lake will turn into a data swamp [2]. Transformations performed on data products in a Data Lake write their results back into the lake. A data product can go through number of transformations during its lifecycle within a Data Lake. Critical focus of our attention is on using provenance and lineage information in Data Lakes to avoid data swamps.

We propose two use cases to motivate the study of provenance in a Data Lake. *Use Case 1*: Suppose sensitive data are ingested by a scientist into a Data Lake. By definition of the data lake, the sensitive data will likely undergo schema translation before being used by someone else. Can provenance be used to determine whether the schema and schema translation process change the

---

[1] http://hadoop.apache.org/.
[2] http://spark.apache.org/.

© Springer International Publishing Switzerland 2016
M. Mattoso and B. Glavic (Eds.): IPAW 2016, LNCS 9672, pp. 178–182, 2016.
DOI: 10.1007/978-3-319-40593-3_16

sensitivity level of the data? Can this be determined quickly enough to take appropriate action, and if so, what actions should be taken? *Use Case 2*: Using provenance to assess-respond in real time: Repeating a Big Data transformation in a Data Lake is expensive due to high resource and time consumption. Can we use live streaming provenance from experiments to monitor them real time and identify the faults early in the execution?

2   Provenance Capture in a Data Lake

If a Data Lake could somehow ensure that every data product in the lake is connected with its provenance starting from the origin, critical traceability can be achieved. This is challenging because a data product may go through different distributed processing systems during its lifecycle. Processing frameworks used around a Data Lake can include batch processing systems, stream processing systems, traditional workflow engines or even legacy scripts. These frameworks may or may not produce provenance by default. Even if there are provenance collection techniques [1] for certain systems, they may use their own ways of storing provenance or use different standards. Therefore generating integrated provenance traces is tough. Stitching techniques [3] exist which bring all provenance traces into a common model and then integrate them together. However there are certain limitations in such techniques like loss of information during conversions and higher computation overheads for large provenance graphs which are common in Data Lakes. In addition to that, real time provenance integration (use case 2) can not be achieved by such post processing techniques. As a solution for this provenance integration problem, we propose a central provenance collection system to which all distributed components within the Data Lake stream provenance events. For each transformation, the data scientist who writes the data processing code can instrument her code to generate provenance at all needed steps.

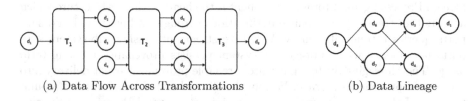

(a) Data Flow Across Transformations   (b) Data Lineage

Fig. 1. Provenance for series of transformations

Provenance is commonly represented as a directed acyclic graph ($G = (V, E)$). A node ($v \in V$) can be an activity, entity or agent while an edge ($e = \langle v_i, v_j \rangle$ where $e \in E$ and $v_i, v_j \in V$) represents a relationship between two nodes. In our provenance collection model, a provenance event always represents an edge in the provenance graph. For example, if process p generates the data product d, the provenance event adds a new edge ($e = \langle p, d \rangle$ where $p, d \in V$) into the provenance graph to represent the 'generation' relationship between activity p and entity d. When all systems connected to the Data Lake continue to send provenance events, the central provenance collection system keeps adding new edges into the provenance graph. Provenance integration across distributed components is guaranteed by using unique identifiers for all data products within the Data Lake. As a simple example, consider the data flow diagram in Fig. 1a. The data product d_1 is subjected to transformation T_1 and it generates data products d_2 and d_3 as results. T_2 uses d_3 together with a new data product d_4 and generates d_5, d_6 and d_7. Finally T_3 uses d_6 and d_7 and generates d_8 as the final output. When all three transformations T_1, T_2 and T_3 have sent provenance events, complete provenance graph is created in the central provenance collection system. Figure 1b shows the provenance graph which represents the data flow when queried for final output d_8. Details like scientists involved, configuration parameters and environment information (CPU speed, memory capacity, network bandwidth etc.) can also be captured as provenance.

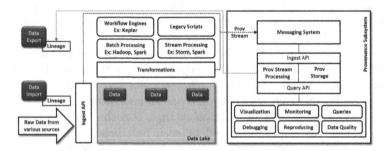

Fig. 2. Provenance for Data Lakes: reference architecture

Figure 2 shows the reference architecture that we propose for Data Lakes based on the provenance integration technique discussed above. Provenance Stream Processing and Storage component is the heart of this architecture which accepts the stream of provenance notifications through its Ingest API and supports queries through its Query API. Live stream processing sub-system supports live queries while storage sub-system persists provenance for long term usage. The Messaging System guarantees reliable provenance event delivery into the central provenance storage. Various distributed transformation tools around the Data Lake stream provenance events into the central Provenance Subsystem. Transformation logics have to be instrumented to capture provenance at required granularity. In order to capture information about the origins of the data products, provenance must be captured at the Ingest. Some data products may carry their previous provenance information which should be integrated as well. Scientists may export data products from the Data Lake in some situations. Such data products should be coupled with their provenance for better usage. Usage subsystem shows how provenance collected around the Data Lake can be used for different purposes. Both live and post-execution queries over collected provenance with Monitoring and Visualization helps in scenarios like the two use cases that we discussed above. There are other advantages as well such as Debugging and Reproducing experiments in the Data Lake.

Komadu [4] is a W3C PROV based provenance collection framework whose design and API are not coupled to any specific system and can be used as a general provenance collection framework. Capturing provenance from distributed applications is made easy with Komadu as it does not depend on any global knowledge about the system. This makes it applicable in the above architecture to capture provenance in a Data Lake. Komadu provides connectors to plug its Ingest API with the RabbitMQ[3] messaging system. The Komadu toolkit includes efficient client libraries for java and javascript applications which minimize instrumentation overhead. Provenance storage system in Komadu is designed based on a relational data model and implemented using MySQL. Ingested provenance events are asynchronously processed and stored in relational tables. Graph generation is delayed till query time to reduce computation at ingest time. Komadu toolkit comes with a Cytoscape[4] plugin as well which can visualize generated provenance graphs.

3   Final Remarks and Future Work

Although Komadu seems to fit well in our reference architecture for provenance capture in a Data Lake, it supports only queries over stored provenance and lacks live provenance stream processing. Fine-grained provenance captured from massively parallel systems can produce large amounts of provenance data that leads to the "Big Provenance" problem [6]. As future work, we plan to combine a series of Big Data transformations to replicate a Data Lake environment and apply our reference architecture into the system using Komadu to see how it performs. We focus on solving the Big Provenance problem using real time provenance stream processing algorithms which reduce the amount of stored provenance.

Acknowledgement. This work is funded in part by a grant from the NSF, ACI-0940824.

References

1. Akoush, S., Sohan, R., Hopper, A.: Hadoopprov: towards provenance as a first class citizen in mapreduce. In: TaPP, pp. 11:1–11:4 (2013)
2. Chessell, M., Scheepers, F., Nguyen, N., van Kessel, R., van der Starre, R.: Governing and managing big data for analytics and decision makers (2014). http://www.redbooks.ibm.com/redpapers/pdfs/redp5120.pdf
3. Missier, P., Ludascher, B., Bowers, S., Dey, S., Sarkar, A., Shrestha, B., Altintas, I., Anand, M., Goble, C.: Linking multiple workflow provenance traces for interoperable collaborative science. In: WORKS, pp. 1–8, November 2010

---

[3] http://www.rabbitmq.com/.
[4] http://www.cytoscape.org/.

4. Suriarachchi, I., Zhou, Q., Plale, B.: Komadu: a capture and visualization system for scientific data provenance. J. Open Res. Softw. 3(1) (2015)
5. Terrizzano, I., Schwarz, P.M., Roth, M., Colino, J.E.: Data wrangling: the challenging journey from the wild to the lake. In: CIDR (2015)
6. Wang, J., Crawl, D., Purawat, S., Nguyen, M., Altintas, I.: Big data provenance: challenges, state of the art and opportunities. In: Big Data, pp. 2509–2516 (2015)

Provenance-Based Retrieval: Fostering Reuse and Reproducibility Across Scientific Disciplines

Lucas Augusto Montalvão Costa Carvalho[1](✉), Rodrigo L. Silveira[2],
Caroline S. Pereira[2], Munir S. Skaf[2], and Claudia Bauzer Medeiros[1]

[1] Institute of Computing, University of Campinas (UNICAMP), Campinas, Brazil
{lucas.carvalho,cmbm}@ic.unicamp.br
[2] Institute of Chemistry, University of Campinas (UNICAMP), Campinas, Brazil
rodrigolsilveira@gmail.com, caroline013@gmail.com, skaf@iqm.unicamp.br

Abstract. When computational researchers from several domains coop-
erate, one recurrent problem is finding tools, methods and approaches
that can be used across disciplines, to enhance collaboration through
reuse. The paper presents our ongoing work to meet the challenges posed
by provenance-based retrieval, proposed as a solution for transdisciplinary scientific collaboration via reuse of scientific workflows. Our work
is based upon a case study in molecular dynamics experiments, as part
of a larger multi-scale experimental scenario.

1 Introduction

Scientific workflows play an important role in data-centric scientific experiments
[1] to speed up the construction of new experiments, and foster collaboration
through reuse of workflow fragments. This is specially complicated when scientists work in distinct domains, due to heterogeneity in vocabularies, methodologies, perspectives of solving a problem and granularity of objects of interest.

Our work is concerned with meeting the needs of such a heterogeneous
research environment, and is based on our ongoing experience with the CCES[1]
(Center for Computational Engineering and Science). CCES congregates experts
from 6 different domains – Computer Science, Chemistry, Physics, Biology,
Applied Mathematics and Mechanical Engineering.

We are helping these scientists to work together via construction and sharing of workflow fragments. However, this is complicated because of the intense
heterogeneity of the domains involved.

To meet reusability and transdisciplinary challenges we designed a
provenance-centric software architecture to support workflow reuse. We will
implement a prototype of the architecture to validate our proposal, running
a case study from Molecular Dynamics Simulation [2] (involving both chemists
and physicists working each at distinct aspects of the problem).

In our approach, provenance, provided by a scientific workflow system, is
semantically enhanced with domain ontologies. This enriched information is then

---

[1] http://www.escience.org.br.

M. Mattoso and B. Glavic (Eds.): IPAW 2016, LNCS 9672, pp. 183–186, 2016.
DOI: 10.1007/978-3-319-40593-3_17

used to support flexibility in workflow retrieval and adaptation across collaborating teams. As discussed further in the paper, provenance information serves as a basis for a wide (new) range of workflow retrieval parameters; furthermore, it allows scientists to assess quality of a workflow fragment.

2   Related Work

Most of the work related to workflow repositories relies on keyword-based retrieval where a user-provided keyword is matched against terms in a workflow's title, workflow's tags or textual description, e.g., myExperiment[2].

Alternatively, semantics-based retrieval mechanisms rely upon semantic annotations which is the process of annotating resources with semantic metadata, using ontologies. The main problem is that annotations require high user effort to describe a workflow, e.g., [3] by augmenting workflow specification, this approach supports workflow retrieval.

Provenance-based retrieval is found in [4] which adopts the ProvONE[3] model. The work of [5] adopts OPM (Open Provenance Model)[4] and takes advantage of keeping the trace of how abstract workflows are instantiated into workflow instances, to assist users in designing new workflows. In Janus [6], domain-specific ontologies are used to annotate the more traditional "domain agnostic" provenance representation of Taverna workflows.

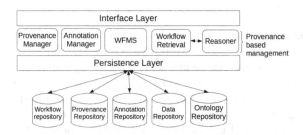

Fig. 1. Architecture of W2SHARE

3   W2SHARE: Architecture and Prototype

The architecture of our framework is shown in Fig. 1. It is composed of three main layers - interface, provenance-based management, and persistence. Through the interface, scientists can design, semantically annotate and search for (sub)workflows using multiple modes. The persistence layer is responsible for ensuring independence between the middle layer and several repositories. The

---

[2] http://myexperiment.org.

[3] http://vcvcomputing.com/provone/provone.html.

[4] http://openprovenance.org/model/opmo.

core of the architecture is the middle layer (Provenance-based Management) and its semantics retrieval capabilities. This is supported by semantic annotations of: (1) the workflows and their components; and (2) the provenance traces generated by the WFMS. The cross disciplinary search of workflows of interest is based on combining these annotations, emphasizing provenance aspects.

While ontologies have been proposed to enrich provenance data (see [6]), this has not yet been exploited to support the selection/retrieval of appropriate workflow fragments. The use of provenance information to help workflow retrieval appears in [4,5], but these solutions do not fully meet our needs.

The Provenance Manager module is based on extending the work of [7]. It extracts information from provenance traces provided by the WFMS, storing their metadata in the Provenance Repository. It interacts with the Annotation Manager to support annotation of these traces. Annotated provenance is subsequently used by Retrieval mechanisms.

The Annotation Manager is responsible for generating semantic annotations of workflow components (interacting with the WFMS and the Persistence layer) and of provenance information (interacting with the Provenance Manager and the Persistence layer). It also manages the Ontology Repository and feeds the Reasoner. This module is also responsible for connections to other Linked Open Data repositories. This makes it possible to retrieve properties of data which are not explicitly represented in annotated data.

Workflow retrieval combines several kinds of semantics-based mechanisms, taking advantage of annotations managed by the Annotation Manager. The approach to be used to rank the results is still under investigation. However our idea is to use data quality assessment to provide information to the ranking algorithm.

The Inference Reasoner expands knowledge of workflow and provenance annotations through Linked Open Data principles. Moreover, it allows additional relationships among annotated items, this offers possibility to search for concepts which are not explicit in annotation.

4   Case Study - Molecular Dynamics

Our case study concerns molecular dynamics (MD), where simulations are used in material sciences, computational engineering, physics and chemistry.

A typical MD simulation experiment receives as input the structure, topology and force fields of the molecular system and produces molecular trajectories as output. Simulations are subject to a suite of parameters, including thermodynamic variables.

Simulations involve both the atomistic modeling, employed by computational physicists and chemists, and the modeling techniques mostly adopted by engineers to treat problems at the macroscopic scales.

To implement a MD [2] simulation, first, we manually analyzed a suite of scripts designed by physiochemists to translate them into Taverna workflows. Its inputs are the protein structure (PDB: 8CEL), the simulation parameters and force field files. Next, we executed the workflow in Taverna. Then, we will use the annotation facilities provided by our future prototype to annotate workflow components used and provenance data generated by Taverna. To perform annotations, we also have to create an ontology with help of experts, since no such ontology exists.

Once all these (annotated) items are stored, we could then proceed with workflow retrieval. Examples of future search requests include: workflows that uses a protein or a liquid solution; or that are derived from a specific and more abstract workflow; or that involve a specific module; or that were designed by groups based in a certain region or workflow authors.

5   Conclusions and Ongoing Work

This paper presented a provenance-based software infrastructure to enable scientists to reuse and repurpose experiments, modeled as workflows, across different disciplines. We show how we are meeting the challenges faced by CCES to convert script-based experiments into scientific workflows, and subsequently navigate through the workflow repository to find the "most appropriate" workflow fragment. There are many challenges in taking advantage of workflows to support transdisciplinary collaboration. We have chosen semantically enriched provenance information as a basis for workflow retrieval in this context, given the many benefits that can be gained from exploring such information. Our prototype implementation and ontology modeling are ongoing work.

Acknowledgments. Work partially financed by FAPESP (2014/23861-4) and FAPESP/CEPID CCES (2013/08293-7).

References

1. Cohen-Boulakia, S., Leser, U.: Search, adapt, and reuse: the future of scientific workflows. ACM SIGMOD Rec. **40**(2), 6–16 (2011)
2. Silveira, R.L., Skaf, M.S.: Molecular dynamics simulations of family 7 cellobiohydrolase mutants aimed at reducing product inhibition. J. Phys. Chem. B **119**(29), 9295–9303 (2014)
3. Gil, Y., Kim, J., Florez, G., Ratnakar, V., González-Calero, P.A.: Workflow matching using semantic metadata. In: 5th K-CAP, pp. 121–128. ACM (2009)
4. Cuevas-Vicenttín, V., Ludäscher, B., Missier, P.: Provenance-based searching and ranking for scientific workflows. In: Ludaescher, B., Plale, B. (eds.) IPAW 2014. LNCS, vol. 8628, pp. 209–214. Springer, Heidelberg (2015)
5. Zhai, G., Lu, T., Huang, X., Chen, Z., Ding, X., Gu, N.: Pwmds: a system supporting provenance-based matching and discovery of workflows in proteomics data analysis. In: IEEE 16th CSCWD, pp. 456–463. IEEE (2012)
6. Missier, P., Sahoo, S.S., Zhao, J., Goble, C., Sheth, A.: *Janus*: from workflows to semantic provenance and linked open data. In: McGuinness, D.L., Michaelis, J.R., Moreau, L. (eds.) IPAW 2010. LNCS, vol. 6378, pp. 129–141. Springer, Heidelberg (2010)
7. Malaverri, J., Santanche, A., Medeiros, C.B.: A provenance-based approach to evaluate data quality in eScience. IJMSO **9**(5), 15–28 (2014)

Addressing Scientific Rigor in Data Analytics Using Semantic Workflows

John S. Erickson$^{(\boxtimes)}$, John Sheehan, Kristin P. Bennett,
and Deborah L. McGuinness

Rensselaer Polytechnic Institute, Troy, NY, USA
erickj4@rpi.edu
http://tw.rpi.edu

Abstract. New NIH grants require establishing *scientific rigor*, i.e.
applicants must provide evidence of strict application of the scientific
method to ensure robust and unbiased experimental design, methodology, analysis, interpretation and reporting of results. Researchers must
transparently report experimental details so others may reproduce and
extend findings. Provenance can help accomplish these objectives; analytical workflows can be annotated with sufficient information for peers to
understand methods and reproduce the intended results. We aim to produce enhancements to the ontology space including links between existing ontologies, terminology gap analysis and ontology terms to address
gaps, and potentially a new ontology aimed at integrating the higher
level data analysis planning concepts. We are developing a collection
of techniques and tools to enable workflow recipes or plans to be more
clearly and consistently shared, improve understanding of all analysis
aspects and enable greater reuse and reproduction. We aim to show that
semantic workflows can improve scientific rigor in data analysis and to
demonstrate their impact in specific research domains.

Keywords: Provenance · Ontologies · Scientific rigor · Reproducibility

1 Introduction

The NIH now requires most research grant applications to address four areas
related to scientific rigor and transparency. [1] One way to accomplish these
objectives is to annotate analytical workflows with enough information to enable
others to accurately reproduce the published results. Our team is evaluating and
extending ontologies, processes and infrastructure that will enable data scientists
to meet these rising standards of scientific rigor and transparency without stifling
scientific creativity, innovation and productivity. Our aim is to demonstrate that
semantic workflows provide an essential framework for addressing these pressing
needs. [2,3]

A data analytics workflow typically draws from multiple data sources, selects
subsets, applies preparatory transformations, and applies a series of existing and
novel data analysis algorithms and/or statistical tests that produce results in

© Springer International Publishing Switzerland 2016
M. Mattoso and B. Glavic (Eds.): IPAW 2016, LNCS 9672, pp. 187–190, 2016.
DOI: 10.1007/978-3-319-40593-3_18

the form of data, tables, visualizations and statistics; each workflow step likely also depends upon setting certain hyperparameters. Given the many steps and interdependencies in data analytics workflows, the high standards for reporting results will not be met by sharing data and code accompanied by only *ad hoc* descriptions of their use. To understand and reproduce another team's analytical results, a complete analysis "recipe" or plan[1] must be captured, including the underlying choices and assumptions embedded in the analysis. The entire analytical workflow including comments, data transformations, descriptions of computational blocks, and specific parameter settings for algorithms are necessary for scientific reproducibility and rigor.

2   Background and Technical Motivation

A number of scientific workflow management systems[2] exist to implement and execute analytical processes and to capture provenance, including low-level descriptions of processes executed and the details of computed results [7]. Dedicated platforms require data analysts to implement their analytical processes within the tool rather than through familiar environments, e.g. R, MATLAB or Python. noWorkflow [8] simplified the capture and analysis of scripted workflow provenance by capturing the details and low-level descriptions of executed scripts, making provenance easier to produce and more accessible to other researchers. YesWorkflow [9, 10] introduced a markup-based approach enabling metadata about workflow structure and intent, including explanations of code blocks and parameter settings, to be captured using embedded annotation within the workflow script.

The use of domain-appropriate comments within scripts as the basis for provenance metadata simplifies documenting workflows and enhances reproducibility, while integrating the production of provenance with the data analytics process. *In situ* workflow analysis systems do not yet enable data analysts to include rich contextual and linking information. Augmenting these tools with semantic technologies including RDF[3], PROV-O[4], and ProvONE [11] will enable richer context and linking to be captured, improving workflow understandability and reuse potential. The focus should be on fine-tuning the captured "prospective provenance"[5] from practical data analysis scripts such as in R, MATLAB and Python; developing utilities to produce metadata descriptions compliant with best-practice Web provenance standards (esp. PROV-O compliant RDF); and developing applications based on the resulting enhanced workflow metadata to further the reproducibility objective. We are developing approaches rooted in semantic technology for extending domain knowledge graphs with workflow provenance metadata that will facilitate referencing workflows from reported results, as well as the discovery of relevant workflows.

---

[1] W3C PROV-O refers to these as "plans." http://www.w3.org/TR/prov-o/#Plan.

[2] For example: Kepler [4], Taverna [5], WINGS [6], etc.

[3] https://www.w3.org/RDF/.

[4] https://www.w3.org/TR/prov-o/.

[5] "Prospective provenance" refers to a workflow's "plan" or "recipe." See [12].

3 Transparent Data Analytics for Scientific Rigor

Workflow analysis tools (e.g., noWorkflow, YesWorkflow) have advantages over dedicated workflow management systems by providing transparency "inside" the boundaries of data analysis scripts. These tools enable richer, more meaningful workflow descriptions and support the capture of critical workflow metadata without burdening the coder; the data analyst can typically convert comments to provenance within an hour.

Most state-of-the-art workflow tools that capture provenance emphasize scientific rigor as an inherent part of the workflow. Future workflow management systems must link to authoritative domain science ontologies as well as ontologies that appropriately express analytical concepts, thereby enhancing interoperability across research projects. We aim to produce workflow ontology enhancements to include links between existing ontologies, terminology gap analysis and ontology terms to address gaps, and potentially a new ontology aimed at integrating higher level data analysis concepts.[6]

We are pursuing opportunities for supporting scientific research through the creation of infrastructure and systems that understand not just what analysis was planned and what was executed, but also how the records of those analysis plans and executions may connect to, and be leveraged by, other scientific work. *Our motivating hypothesis is this: if a knowledge graph of analytics workflows can be built with more declarative representations and with support for comparisons, not only will transparency and reproducibility be improved, but fundamentally new capabilities based on the workflow metadata will be realized.*

4 Ontologies for Scientifically Rigorous Workflows

Semantic representation, reasoning, and query tools, along with provenance standards, can connect workflows to specific scientific domains and enable robust query and inference. We are exploring options for the practical semantic representation of scientific workflows based on established standards. We seek to improve the validation and extension of ontologies that capture workflow provenance, especially ProvONE. We are connecting to data analysis ontologies (e.g., STAT-O[7]) to leverage community standard vocabularies. Our aim is to demonstrate the value *to domain scientists* of representing scripted scientific workflows as semantic workflows. Our motivating use cases involve collaborative projects. Our goal is to represent enough content to capture similarities and differences in analytic approaches to determine where efforts might be combined and/or where they are incompatible, and ultimately to capture a shared, scientifically rigorous description of the intended process.

---

[6] We know of no ontology that enables scripted workflow processes accomplishing semantically similar tasks to be annotated in the same way using the same vocabulary.

[7] http://stato-ontology.org/.

We are developing tools that will enable workflow plans to be more clearly and consistently shared so we can improve understanding of all analysis aspects – including the data, algorithms, and code – to enable reuse and reproduction. Through the import of semantic workflow metadata into the scientific knowledge graphs, we aim to show how domain scientists will be able to more easily discover and retrieve relevant, meaningful workflows based on similarity due to workflow semantics "in the graph." We believe this work will show that semantic workflows are a core technology for improving scientific reproducibility and rigor in science data analysis. Our poster will include examples from our work analyzing and representing brain development and exposure science.

Acknowledgements. Thanks to T. McPhillips of UIUC and B. Ludäscher of UC-Davis for help with YesWorkflow, D. Garijo and V. Ratnakar of USC ISI for help with WINGS, and NSF Grant No. 1331023.

References

1. NIH Grants: Funding: Rigor and Reproducibility. https://grants.nih.gov/reproducibility/index.htm
2. Repetitive flaws: Strict guidelines to improve the reproducibility of experiments are a welcome move, Nature Editorial. http://www.nature.com/news/repetitive-flaws-1.19192
3. Challenges In Irreproducible Research: Nature News & Comment Special. http://www.nature.com/news/reproducibility-1.17552
4. Bowers, S., Ludäscher, B.: Actor-oriented design of scientific workflows. In: Conceptual Modeling ER 2005: Proceedings of the 24th International Conference on Conceptual Modeling, Klagenfurt, Austria, October 2005
5. Oinn, T., et al.: Taverna: a tool for the composition and enactment of bioinformatics workflows. Bioinformatics **20**(17), 3045–3054 (2004)
6. Gil, Y., et al.: Wings: intelligent workflow-based design of computational experiments. IEEE Intell. Syst. **26**(1), 62–72 (2011)
7. Davidson, S.B., Freire, J., J.: Provenance and scientific workflows: challenges and opportunities. In: Proceedings of the 2008 ACM SIGMOD International Conference on Management of Data, pp. 1345–1350. ACM Press, New York (2008)
8. Murta, L., Braganholo, V., Chirigati, F., Koop, D., Freire, J.: noWorkflow: capturing and analyzing provenance of scripts. In: Ludaescher, B., Plale, B. (eds.) IPAW 2014. LNCS, vol. 8628, pp. 71–83. Springer, Heidelberg (2015)
9. McPhillips, T., et al.: YesWorkflow: a user-oriented, language-independent tool for recovering workflow information from scripts. Int. J. Digit. curation **10**, 298–313 (2015)
10. McPhillips, T., et al.: Retrospective provenance without a runtime provenance recorder. In: USENIX Workshop on Theory and Practice of Provenance (2015)
11. DataONE Scientific Workflows, Provenance Working Group: ProvONE: a PROV extension data model for scientific workflow provenance. W3C unofficial draft, 27 March 2014. http://vcvcomputing.com/provone/provone.html
12. Lim, C., Lu, S., Chebotko, A., Fotouhi, F.: Prospective and retrospective provenance collection in scientific workflow environments. In: 2010 IEEE International Conference on Services Computing (2010)

Reconstructing Human-Generated Provenance Through Similarity-Based Clustering

Tom De Nies[✉], Erik Mannens, and Rik Van de Walle

Ghent University – iMinds – Data Science Lab, Ghent, Belgium
{tom.denies,erik.mannens,rik.vandewalle}@ugent.be

Abstract. In this paper, we revisit our method for reconstructing the primary sources of documents, which make up an important part of their provenance. Our method is based on the assumption that if two documents are semantically similar, there is a high chance that they also share a common source. We previously evaluated this assumption on an excerpt from a news archive, achieving 68.2 % precision and 73 % recall when reconstructing the primary sources of all articles. However, since we could not release this dataset to the public, it made our results hard to compare to others. In this work, we extend the flexibility of our method by adding a new parameter, and re-evaluate it on the human-generated dataset created for the 2014 Provenance Reconstruction Challenge. The extended method achieves up to 86 % precision and 59 % recall, and is now directly comparable to any approach that uses the same dataset.

1 Introduction

Even with the recommendation of the PROV model by W3C in 2013, there is still a plethora of data on the Web that lacks associated provenance. Research that works towards reconstructing this provenance is still very new in the community, and datasets suitable for evaluation are rare. Thus, together with VU Amsterdam, we initiated the 2014 Provenance Reconstruction Challenge[1]. The aim of this challenge was to help spur research into the reconstruction of provenance by providing a common task and datasets for experimentation. In this paper, we present our own evaluation results on this dataset.

2 The Dataset

Challenge participants received an open data set and the corresponding provenance graphs (in W3C PROV format). They could then work with the data trying to reconstruct the provenance graphs from the open data set. The data consists of two distinct sets: one machine-collected, and one human-generated. This way, we are able to evaluate the reconstruction accuracy for provenance that was automatically collected based on observations, and provenance that

---

[1] http://www.data2semantics.org/prov-reconstruction-challenge/.

© Springer International Publishing Switzerland 2016
M. Mattoso and B. Glavic (Eds.): IPAW 2016, LNCS 9672, pp. 191–194, 2016.
DOI: 10.1007/978-3-319-40593-3_19

was generated based on information provided by humans, which could not be captured automatically.

The machine-collected dataset can be downloaded at: http://git2prov.org/reconstruction/machine-generated-dev.zip, and the human-generated set at: http://git2prov.org/reconstruction/human-generated-dev.zip.

The ground truth (*groundtruth.ttl*) for the machine-generated dataset was generated from a number of Github repositories using the Git2PROV tool [3]. As raw data, it includes every version of each file that was ever present in the repository (including deleted files). However, the filenames are randomized, to simulate a scenario where all provenance was lost. Due to these randomized filenames, the timing metadata associated with the files may differ from the original. The correct timings can be found in the ground truth provenance. The main goal here is to reconstruct the derivation graph of the original files, serialized as PROV-O. Evaluations should report at a minimum the precision/recall of the detected PROV relations (`prov:wasDerivedFrom`, `prov:wasGeneratedBy`, etc.).

The ground truth for the human-generated dataset was created using the sources mentioned in news articles from *WikiNews*. The link between news articles and their sources is modeled using the `prov:hadPrimarySource` relation. The raw data consists of the entire HTML of the WikiNews articles, without the sources, and a list of URIs (*human_sources.txt*). In other words, the goal of this task is to match the source URIs from this list to the correct WikiNews article. Approaches may use any information embedded in the files or external information, save from the ground truth or WikiNews, for obvious reasons. Evaluations should report at a minimum the results of precision/recall of the `prov:hadPrimarySource` relations.

3   Our Approach

We applied our method as described in [2], applying the assumption *"if a set of documents is highly similar, there is a high chance they also share a common source"*. This method clusters all documents in the dataset using a lower bound on similarity, expressed as the threshold T_s. Then, for each cluster, the oldest document is selected, and asserted as the (indirect) primary source of all others in that cluster. Note that clusters can overlap, so multiple primary sources can be asserted for one document. The level of uncertainty is annotated using the similarity measured between the two documents to help end-users make a decision on which assertion to trust, if there is a conflict. As parameters, we used the **cosine similarity with TF-IDF weighting, 10 different the similarity thresholds** T_s, and **no cluster-size threshold** (so no re-clustering). Additionally, the following considerations were made during the implementation:

– For a number of articles which do not include a date, the original WikiNews articles were consulted, and the date reported there was used. In certain cases, this is the date of access by the writers of the article. Because a number of sources provide a datetime, while others only provide the day of publishing, *only the day of publishing* was used for all articles.

– We re-formatted the dataset to be usable with our software. To do this, the text and date had to be extracted from each HTML document, without advertisements, images, videos, etc. To obtain results that reflect the performance of our approach, not influenced by automatic text extraction methods, we performed this extraction manually, thereby assuming an *'ideal' text extractor*.

4   Evaluation

We evaluated our approach only on the human-generated dataset, for which it was primarily designed, and which is harder to capture in an automatic way. The results are shown in Table 1. At first glance, our method only achieved a rather disappointing maximum precision of 27 % and recall of 16 %. However, these results can be explained by looking deeper into how the human-generated dataset was constructed, and how our method tries to reconstruct it.

Table 1. Results of our method as described in [2] on the human-generated dataset

T_s	0.1	0.2	0.3	0.4	0.5	0.6	0.7	0.8	0.9	1.0
Precision	0.30	0.14	0.20	0.21	**0.27**	0.25	0	0	0	0
Recall	0.12	0.13	**0.16**	0.15	0.12	0.066	0	0	0	0

In our method as described in [2], we assume the *oldest document* in a cluster to be the (indirect) source of *multiple documents* – i.e., all others in the cluster. However, the ground truth dataset was constructed in exactly the opposite way: the *newest document* is derived from *multiple sources*. This means that with a very minor adjustment to our method, we might be able to achieve much better results. Therefore, we extended our method for this benchmark, by including a **new parameter** that allows the algorithm to select the *newest document* in every cluster instead of the oldest, and making all other documents in the cluster primary sources of the former. When we ran our reconstruction algorithm with this parameter enabled, it confirmed our suspicions, and we achieved much better results, as shown in Table 2. Now, our method achieves 86 % precision and 59 % recall with $T_s = 0.4$.

Table 2. Results of our slightly adjusted method on the human-generated dataset

T_s	0.1	0.2	0.3	0.4	0.5	0.6	0.7	0.8	0.9	1.0
Precision	0.52	0.54	0.70	**0.86**	0.77	0.69	0.2	0	0	0
Recall	0.26	0.51	0.57	**0.59**	0.33	0.18	0.016	0	0	0

5   Comparison to Related Work and Conclusion

While a number of domain-specific techniques used to reconstruct provenance exist, these techniques all predate the PROV standard and do not offer a comparable evaluation. For example, Zhao et al. [7] predict missing provenance based on semantic associations in the domain of reservoir engineering. Zhang et al. [6] exploit the logging capabilities of existing relational database management systems to retrieve lost source provenance traces. The work of [4,5] focuses on tracing news and quotes (referred to as *memes*) on the Web over time.

More recently, Aierken et al. [1] presented their multi-funneling approach to provenance reconstruction. They apply three techniques: one based on *IR techniques and the Vector Space Model (VSM)* similar to our approach, one based on the *machine learning and topic modeling*, and one based on *dynamic programming and matching the longest common subsequence*. They report a precision and recall of 77 % and 47 % for human-generated provenance, and 78 % and 68 % for machine-generated provenance, respectively. However, since their method relies heavily on training data, they used the human-generated challenge dataset as a training set for their method, and created a new WikiNews dataset using the same procedure for their evaluation. This means that while at first glance, our reported results seem to outperform theirs, they are not entirely comparable. However, their results together with ours – and the results we measured on our news dataset in [2] (68.2 % precision and 73 % recall) – can at least be interpreted as an indication of the level of accuracy that is achievable with the current state of the art in this field. While not perfect, these methods can certainly help a human-user reconstruct lost provenance, as opposed to doing it all manually.

References

1. Aierken, A., Davis, D.B., Zhang, Q., Gupta, K., Wong, A., Asuncion, H.U.: A multi-level funneling approach to data provenance reconstruction. In: IEEE 10th International Conference on e-Science, vol. 2, pp. 71–74. IEEE (2014)
2. De Nies, T., Coppens, S., Van Deursen, D., Mannens, E., Van de Walle, R.: Automatic discovery of high-level provenance using semantic similarity. In: Groth, P., Frew, J. (eds.) IPAW 2012. LNCS, vol. 7525, pp. 97–110. Springer, Heidelberg (2012)
3. De Nies, T., Magliacane, S., Verborgh, R., Coppens, S., Groth, P., Mannens, E., Van de Walle, R.: Git2PROV: exposing version control system content as W3C PROV. In: ISWC Posters & Demos, pp. 125–128 (2013)
4. Leskovec, J., Backstrom, L., Kleinberg, J.: Meme-tracking and the dynamics of the news cycle. In: Proceedings of the 15th ACM SIGKDD International Conference on Knowledge Discovery and Data Mining, pp. 497–506. ACM (2009)
5. Simmons, M.P., Adamic, L.A., Adar, E.: Memes online: extracted, subtracted, injected, and recollected. In: ICWSM 2011, pp. 17–21 (2011)
6. Zhang, J., Jagadish, H.V.: Lost source provenance. In: 13th International Conference on Extending Database Technology, pp. 311–322. ACM (2010)
7. Zhao, J., Gomadam, K., Prasanna, V.: Predicting missing provenance using semantic associations in reservoir engineering. In: Fifth IEEE International Conference on Semantic Computing (ICSC), pp. 141–148. IEEE (2011)

Social Media Data in Research: Provenance Challenges

David Corsar[✉], Milan Markovic, and Peter Edwards

Computing Science, University of Aberdeen, Aberdeen, UK
{dcorsar,milan.markovic,p.edwards}@abdn.ac.uk

Abstract. In this paper we argue that understanding the provenance of social media datasets and their analysis is critical to addressing challenges faced by the social science research community in terms of the reliability and reproducibility of research utilising such data. Based on analysis of existing projects that use social media data, we present a number of research questions for the provenance community, which if addressed would help increase the transparency of the research process, aid reproducibility, and facilitate data reuse in the social sciences.

Keywords: Provenance · Social media · Research process

1 Introduction

The social science research community faces challenges associated with the reliability, statistical validity, and generalizability of data obtained from social media [Tuf13], which may raise questions about the validity of research based on such data and hinder data reuse [fECoD13]. Provenance has previously been used to support audit, verification, and reproducibility in a number of domains [Mor11, CFLV12]; as such, we argue that documenting the provenance of social media data and its subsequent analysis could help address the challenges faced by the social sciences - by increasing the transparency of the research process, and supporting assessment of the analytical methods used.

2 Case Study - *Tweeting Transport*

To investigate this application of provenance we have analysed a number of projects that utilised social media data; one of these will now be described in order to provide context for the research questions in Sect. 3. The *Tweeting Transport* project [CYG+15] explored how Twitter[1] is used to provide transport information during major events, focusing on the 2014 Commonwealth Games[2].

The work described here was funded by a grant from the United Kingdom's Economic and Social Research Council Social Media - Developing Understanding, Infrastructure & Engagement (ES/M001628/1).

[1] http://www.twitter.com.

[2] http://www.glasgow2014.com.

M. Mattoso and B. Glavic (Eds.): IPAW 2016, LNCS 9672, pp. 195–198, 2016.
DOI: 10.1007/978-3-319-40593-3_20

Figure 1 provides a PROV [MGC+15] representation of the *Tweeting Transport* project. A dataset of tweets relating to transport disruption during the 2014 Games was created using TMI[3], a tool developed to monitor Twitter, and to store and export Tweets to CSV files for analysis. TMI was configured to capture tweets containing at least one of 331 keywords or hashtags, as well as tweets authored by eight different user accounts. These criteria were based on a review of travel information published via the official Games website[4] and a review of the wider transport disruption literature. Data were collected one week before the event, during the Games, and for one week afterwards (July/August 2014).

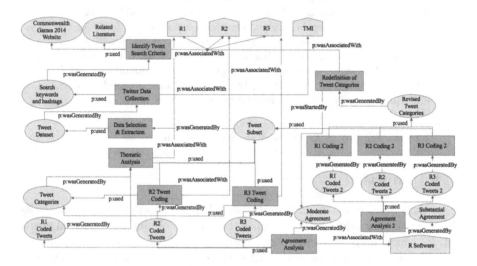

Fig. 1. PROV representation of the *Tweeting Transport* project.

Three types of analysis were subsequently performed to understand the kinds of travel information provided, and the Twitter users who disseminated this content. Here we summarise the first of these, which focused on Retweets and replies in response to Tweets sent by the official travel information Twitter account, @GamesTravel2014. The analysis involved thematic coding of each tweet by one researcher (R1 in Fig. 1), which categorised each tweet based on its content. These categories were used by two additional researchers (R2 and R3 in Fig. 1) to code the same data, which resulted in moderate agreement between the coders (as computed by the Fleiss Kappa implementation of the R tool[5]). Following discussions between the researchers, the categories were redefined, and the dataset recoded, resulting in substantial agreement. Seven types of travel information that were shared via Twitter were identified.

---

[3] https://github.com/SocialJourneys/TMI.

[4] http://www.glasgow2014.com/your-games/travel-and-transport.

[5] https://www.r-project.org/.

3   Research Questions

The approach to data collection and analysis described above is typical of such projects; [BT14] presents a taxonomy of social media providers, data types, and access mechanisms; data cleaning, tagging, and storing activities; and techniques and tools commonly used with such data. Documenting these various aspects of social media analytics forms the basis of our research questions.

RQ1 - What characteristics of social media data should be captured to facilitate transparency, and reproducibility of such research?

We argue that it is necessary to capture aspects of *why, how, where* and *when* [CCT09] data provenance. *Why* characteristics capture both why the dataset was created, and why each datum was included; *how* characteristics define how the data were acquired, for example, via the Twitter Stream API[6] and/or tools such as TMI; *where* characteristics define the source of the data, for example Facebook[7] or a third party service such as the Gnip[8] enterprise platform; and *when* defines both the temporal coverage of the data, and when collection took place. These are necessary to allow others to understand the data (including restrictions on reuse due to license conditions), and to understand how to reproduce the dataset if necessary.

RQ2 - How can existing provenance models be employed to record analysis of social media data?

The analysis (and associated stages, such as data preparation) can be viewed as a set of activities that use, generate, and exchange information. The *Tweeting Transport* project also illustrates why it will be necessary to capture the different agents that were involved in these activities (as three researchers conducted the Tweet coding activity independently). This is consistent with the *process flow* view of provenance [MGC+15], which PROV is capable of capturing. While models, such as PROV-SAID[9] extend PROV with the ability to capture information diffusion within social media platforms, further extensions are required to capture different types of analysis, such as thematic coding and recursive abstraction.

RQ3 - What information should the provenance record contain to facilitate transparency and reproducibility of research that utilises social media data?

This question considers the appropriate level(s) of granularity required. For example, is it necessary for the provenance record of the *Tweeting Transport* project to contain all of the information regarding the revision of the initial Tweet categories (as in Fig. 1), or does a description of the revised categories and coded Tweets provide sufficient detail to allow others to reproduce the research?

RQ4 - How can the provenance of social media analysis be captured?

One obvious approach here would be construction of a software tool, able to guide a researcher through creation of a description of their data and analytical

---

[6] https://dev.twitter.com/streaming/overview.

[7] https://www.facebook.com.

[8] https://gnip.com/.

[9] http://semweb.mmlab.be/ns/prov-said/.

processes. However, previous experience in the *ourSpaces* Virtual Research Environment [EPE+12] indicates that the descriptions obtained in this way are likely to be limited, as few users will provide details beyond the minimum required when describing, for example, a dataset. As such, we argue that it will be necessary to develop automated solutions that attempt to infer or reconstruct (parts of) the provenance record by, for example, examining data files generated by popular qualitative data analysis tools such as NVivo[10].

4   Future Work

As part of our investigation of these research questions, we are currently developing the model extensions necessary to enable capture of the provenance of research that uses social media data. Following this, we plan to develop a software tool that supports creation of provenance expressed using the new model; the tool will be evaluated by application to our case study projects. We are also developing a set of guidelines that will support research data archives to obtain the appropriate information from those conducting research using social media data, to provide others with greater understanding of the research undertaken, knowledge of how to verify, repeat and/or reproduce the research, and to facilitate greater data reuse.

References

[BT14]   Batrinca, B., Treleaven, P.C.: Social media analytics: a survey of techniques, tools and platforms. AI & Soc. **30**(1), 89–116 (2014)

[CCT09] Cheney, J., Chiticariu, L., Tan, W.-C.: Provenance in databases: why, how, and where. Found. Trends Databases **1**(4), 379–474 (2009)

[CFLV12] Cheney, J., Finkelstein, A., Ludascher, B., Vansummeren, S.: Principles of provenance. Dagstuhl Rep. **2**(2), 84–113 (2012)

[CYG+15] Cottrill, C., Yeboah, G., Gault, P., Nelson, J.D., Anable, J., Budd, T.: Tweeting transport: examining the use of twitter in transport events. In: Proceedings of the 47th Annual UTSG Conference (2015)

[EPE+12] Edwards, P., Pignotti, E., Eckhardt, A., Ponnamperuma, K., Mellish, C., Bouttaz, T.: ourSpaces – design and deployment of a semantic virtual research environment. In: Cudré-Mauroux, P., et al. (eds.) ISWC 2012, Part II. LNCS, vol. 7650, pp. 50–65. Springer, Heidelberg (2012)

[fECoD13] Organisation for Economic Co-operation and Development: New data for understanding the human condition. Technical report, February 2013

[MGC+15] Moreau, L., Groth, P., Cheney, J., Lebo, T., Miles, S.: The rationale of PROV. Web Semant. Sci. Serv. Agents World Wide Web **35**(Part 4), 235–257 (2015)

[Mor11] Moreau, L.: Provenance-based reproducibility in the semantic web. Web Semant. Sci. Serv. Agents World Wide Web **9**(2), 202–221 (2011)

[Tuf13] Tufekci, Z.: Big data: Pitfalls, methods and concepts for an emergent field. Technical report, March 2013

---

[10] http://www.qsrinternational.com/.

Fine-Grained Provenance Collection over Scripts Through Program Slicing

João Felipe Pimentel[1(✉)], Juliana Freire[2], Leonardo Murta[1],
and Vanessa Braganholo[1]

[1] Universidade Federal Fluminense, Niterói, Brazil
{jpimentel,leomurta,vanessa}@ic.uff.br
[2] New York University, New York, USA
juliana.freire@nyu.edu

Abstract. Collecting provenance from scripts is often useful for scientists to explain and reproduce their scientific experiments. However, most existing automatic approaches capture provenance at coarse-grain, for example, the trace of user-defined functions. These approaches lack information of variable dependencies. Without this information, users may struggle to identify which functions really influenced the results, leading to the creation of false-positive provenance links. To address this problem, we propose an approach that uses dynamic program slicing for gathering provenance of Python scripts. By capturing dependencies among variables, it is possible to expose execution paths inside functions and, consequently, to create a provenance graph that accurately represents the function activations and the results they affect.

1 Introduction

Scientists may use scripts to perform intensive computational tasks such as data analyses and explorations [2]. The results achieved by these tasks need to be explained and/or reproduced, and provenance is a key concept in this direction. However, collecting provenance of scripts is challenging [5].

Some automatic approaches capture provenance at the function level [2, 5, 9]. Approaches that consider functions as black-box constructs are able to gather the function activation (i.e., call) order, arguments, returned values, and information regarding file access, e.g., functions that opened files for read or write together with the file content before and after the function execution. These approaches adopt the function activation order to infer the dependence among data, potentially leading to false-positive links. For instance, Fig. 1 shows an intentionally simple implementation of the happy numbers problem [8], where the code calls two functions, *process* and *show*, in sequence (lines 17 and 20), leading to the inference that the *show* result depends on the *process* result. In fact, this inference happens to be true in the case shown in Fig. 1, when *DRY_RUN* is False. However, the same inference would lead to a false-positive result should the global variable *DRY_RUN* be *True*. This occurs because *final* would be assigned to 7, which does not depend on the result of *process*. However, as the script calls *process* before *show*, function-based approaches [5, 9] would say that *show* depends on *process*.

© Springer International Publishing Switzerland 2016
M. Mattoso and B. Glavic (Eds.): IPAW 2016, LNCS 9672, pp. 199–203, 2016.
DOI: 10.1007/978-3-319-40593-3_21

```
 3| def process(number):
 4|     while number >= 10:
 5|         new_number, str_number = 0, str(number)
 6|         for char in str_number:
 7|             new_number += int(char) ** 2
 8|         number = new_number
 9|     return number
10|
11| def show(number):
12|     if number not in (1, 7):
13|         return "unhappy number"
14|     return "happy number"
...
17| final = process(n)
18| if DRY_RUN:
19|     final = 7
20| print(show(final))
```

Fig. 1. Function *show* depends on *process* if **DRY_RUN** is *False*

In contrast, RDataTracker [4] captures the occurrence of variable bindings along with function level provenance. However, it requires the user to provide annotations. This can be both time consuming and lead to inconsistencies as the code evolves.

The goal of this work is to provide a more precise identification of function activation sequences that actually affect the results, without requiring modifications on the script. To do so, we use *program slicing* [10]. We capture and analyze dependencies among variables during the script execution (a trial), and apply *dynamic program slicing* [1] to identify which dependencies actually exist among functions and files. This empowers scientists to explore factors that influenced the result with confidence.

Although doing dynamic program slicing over Python is not new [3], we differentiate ourselves by capturing variable values and other provenance data in addition to slices. For instance, when we have n = 10; final = process(n), Chen et al. [3] capture only that *final* depends on *n* and the position in memory of these variables to link them. However, since we aim to support scientists during analysis and allow them to debug and reason about different trials, we also capture the values of *final* as 1; *process(n)* as 1; and *n* as 10; as well as when they were accessed. Moreover, we integrate our analysis with a system that collects other types of provenance, such as file accesses, activations, and environment attributes, allowing scientists to perform SQL and Prolog queries integrating variable dependencies and other provenance data.

As a preliminary proof of concept, we implemented this approach in noWorkflow [5–7], an open-source system that transparently captures provenance from Python scripts at the function activation level.

2 Fine-Grained Provenance Collection

Ideally, capturing variable values and dependencies should be done at expressions and statements level. However, some programming languages, such as Python and Lua, do not support following the execution of all expressions efficiently. The most fine-grained level execution following offered by these languages is to define tracing and profiling functions to follow the execution line by line and call by call, respectively.

We define a Tracker as a function hook that combines tracing and profiling functions in order to follow the execution line by line and call by call. When we follow calls, the Tracker receives events during both the start and return of function calls. We use these events to identify variable scopes and to avoid mixing up variables with the same name on different scopes. We follow the execution line by line to capture dependencies and provenance. Most dependencies occur between existing variables in the code. However, to ease the collection and identify dependencies between calls, we also create virtual variables. For instance, in line 17 of Fig. 1, we create a variable *process* representing the call to *process*. This way, we can say that *final* depends on *process*. In addition, in line 19, we create an extra variable *final* that has no dependencies to the previous one. With this new variable *final*, we can isolate dependencies, and indicate that *show* does not depend on *process*, and capture both values for variables *final*: 1 and 7. Finally, we create virtual variables *return* in lines 9 and 14, representing the return of these functions. For the *return* in line 9, we capture the value 1, and for the return in line 14, we capture the value *happy number*.

In some situations, we do not capture the complete execution provenance. In order to tackle the challenge of capturing provenance in an overwhelming fine-grained level, we allow users to specify a depth for provenance collection. When the execution reaches a call beyond the specified depth, we make the function return to depend on all of its parameters, correctly representing a well-designed function but potentially leading to false positives when developers add unnecessary arguments to the function calls. Similarly, we perform the same approximation if we find an external function that the user did not define, such as *print* in line 20 of Fig. 1.

We capture four different types of dependencies: return, direct, conditional, and loop. A return dependency occurs on function returns. A direct dependency occurs on assignments and *for* loop iterations. A loop dependency occurs on augmented assignments within loops. Finally, a conditional dependency occurs when the script creates variables within *if* and *while* scopes. All these dependencies together represent the data derivation throughout the script, allowing us to precisely identify which data contributed to the production of which other data.

To exemplify these types of dependencies, we present Fig. 2 as the result of running now dataflow -m simulation --rank-line | dot -Tpng fif.png after running a trial with noWorkflow. In this figure, brightest nodes represent variables while darkest nodes represent function calls for which we do not have definitions. The labels on these nodes show line number and variable name. We represent function calls for which we have definitions (process and show) as clusters. With this figure, it is easy to observe that *show* does not depend on *process*.

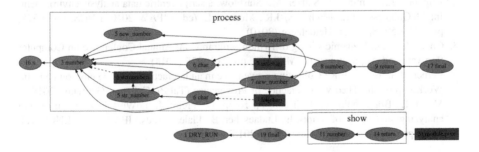

Fig. 2. Dependency graph

By comparing Figs. 1 and 2, we can observe that (i) "process" call (presented as a white rectangle) has a **return dependency** to "9 return", which is an artificial variable; (ii) "8 number" has a **direct dependency** to "7 new_number", because *new_number* appears on the left side of *number* assignment.; (iii) "7 new_number" has a **loop dependency** to "6 char", since the number of augmented assignments in the loop influences the final result of *new_number*; and (iv) "5 new_number" has a **conditional dependency** to "3 number", because the while condition uses *number*.

3   Conclusion and Future Work

In this work, we present an approach to enhance the provenance capture from scripts using dynamic program slicing in a transparent and automatic way. We implemented the approach on top of noWorkflow, which supports performing SQL queries, Prolog queries, and exporting dependency graphs for visualizations. noWorkflow is available as an open source software in https://github.com/gems-uff/noworkflow.

Our approach has some limitations. First, it currently does not support tracking dependencies on complex data structures and syntactic constructions such as lists, objects, exceptions, and generators. Second, because of the first limitation, it does not handle dependencies for file access, which are managed by file handle objects in Python. Third, it currently supports only Python scripts that do not combine multiple statements into a single line and do not split statements into multiple lines. Finally, its visualization may not be well suited for huge dependency graphs.

As future work, we plan on using Python AST *transform* to deal with the afore-mentioned limitations. In addition, we plan to explore visualization summarizations and other types of analyses and comparison techniques for the collected provenance. Finally, the collected provenance opens many future work opportunities, such as the visualization of the script evolution over time, debugging, identifying failures on scripts, mining recurrent execution patterns, and analysis of slow functions.

References

1. Agrawal, H., Horgan, J.R.: Dynamic program slicing. In: Conference on Programming Language Design and Implementation, pp. 246–256. ACM, New York, NY, USA (1990)
2. Angelino, E., Yamins, D., Seltzer, M.: StarFlow: a script-centric data analysis environment. In: McGuinness, D.L., Michaelis, J.R., Moreau, L. (eds.) IPAW 2010. LNCS, vol. 6378, pp. 236–250. Springer, Heidelberg (2010)
3. Chen, Z., et al.: Dynamic slicing of Python programs. In: Annual Conference on Computer Software and Applications (COMPSAC), pp. 219–228 (2014)
4. Lerner, B.S., Boose, E.R.: Collecting provenance in an interactive scripting environment. In: Workshop on the Theory and Practice of Provenance (TaPP), Cologne, Germany (2014)
5. Murta, L., Braganholo, V., Chirigati, F., Koop, D., Freire, J.: noWorkflow: capturing and analyzing provenance of scripts. In: Ludaescher, B., Plale, B. (eds.) IPAW 2014. LNCS, vol. 8628, pp. 71–83. Springer, Heidelberg (2015)

6. Pimentel, J.F., et al.: Tracking and analyzing the evolution of provenance from scripts. In: Mattoso, M., Glavic, B. (eds.) IPAW 2016. LNCS, vol. 9672, pp. 16–28. Springer, Heidelberg (2016)
7. Pimentel, J.F.N., et al.: Collecting and analyzing provenance on interactive notebooks: when IPython meets noWorkflow. In: Workshop on the Theory and Practice of Provenance (TaPP), Edinburgh, Scotland (2015)
8. Porges, A.: A set of eight numbers. Am. Math. Mon. **52**(7), 379–382 (1945)
9. Tariq, D. et al.: Towards automated collection of application-level data provenance. In: Workshop on the Theory and Practice of Provenance (TaPP), Boston, MA, USA (2012)
10. Weiser, M.: Program slicing. In: International Conference on Software Engineering (ICSE), pp. 439–449. IEEE Press, Piscataway, NJ, USA (1981)

Prov2ONE: An Algorithm for Automatically Constructing ProvONE Provenance Graphs

Ajinkya Prabhune[1](✉), Aaron Zweig[1], Rainer Stotzka[1],
Michael Gertz[2], and Juergen Hesser[3]

[1] Institute for Data Processing and Electronics, Karslruhe Institute of Technology,
Karlsruhe, Germany
{ajinkya.prabhune,aaron.zweig,rainer.stotzka}@kit.edu
[2] Institute of Computer Science, Heidelberg University, Heidelberg, Germany
gertz@informatik.uni-heidelberg.de
[3] Department of Radiation Oncology, Heidelberg University, Heidelberg, Germany
juergen.hesser@medma.uni-heidelberg.de

Abstract. Provenance traces history within workflows and enables researchers to validate and compare their results. Currently, modelling provenance in ProvONE is an arduous task and lacks an automated approach. This paper introduces a novel algorithm, called Prov2ONE that automatically generates the ProvONE prospective provenance for scientific workflows defined in BPEL4WS. The same prospective ProvONE graph is updated with the relevant retrospective provenance, preventing provenance to be captured in various non-standard provenance models and thus enabling research communities to share, compare and analyze workflows and its associated provenance. Finally, using the Prov2ONE algorithm, a ProvONE provenance graph for the nanoscopy workflow is generated.

1 Introduction

In the last decade, research communities have adopted workflow management systems (WfMS) for orchestrating their complex scientific workflows. Nanoscopy is a novel imaging technique in biological and medical research that aims to reduce the resolution gap between conventional light microscopy and electron microscopy [1]. In a nanoscopy workflow, the raw image datasets acquired by high-resolution microscopes are processed in multiple stages to produce final results. Nanoscopy Open Reference Data Repository (NORDR) [2] is provisioned to the researchers to store, process and access their data. For executing the nanoscopy workflows a WfMS[1] is integrated with NORDR. A critical aspect associated with the NORDR is the management of provenance information.

The paper addresses three main requirements of managing provenance in NORDR: (i) enable automated modelling of both prospective as well as retrospective provenance in a single provenance model; (ii) design an extensible provenance management component for NORDR; (iii) provision a dedicated provenance

---

[1] We use the Apache ODE workflow engine, site: http://ode.apache.org/.

© Springer International Publishing Switzerland 2016
M. Mattoso and B. Glavic (Eds.): IPAW 2016, LNCS 9672, pp. 204–208, 2016.
DOI: 10.1007/978-3-319-40593-3_22

storage system with efficient query processing. To fulfill the first requirement, the paper presents the Prov2ONE algorithm that generates a ProvONE [3] provenance graph for BPEL4WS[2] workflows. The algorithm is based on ProvONE due to the limitations of the Open Provenance Model (OPM) [5] and PROV [6] to model only the retrospective provenance [4]. The second requirement is met by presenting the provenance management architecture for NORDR and finally, for efficient storage and retrieval of provenance information, the ProvONE graphs are stored in a graph database (ArangoDB[3]).

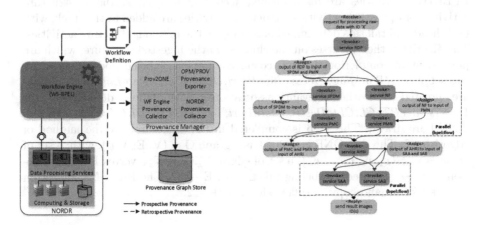

Fig. 1. Provenance management in NORDR

Fig. 2. Nanoscopy workflow defined in BPEL4WS

2 Provenance Management Architecture

The Fig. 1 briefly describes the various components of NORDR system that are essential for either modelling, collecting or storing the provenance information for a scientific workflow.

Workflow (WF) Engine: The WF engine is responsible for interpreting the workflow definition and invoking the necessary data processing services.

NORDR: The NORDR is a multi-layered architecture with many modules that primarily offers the various data processing and data storage service.

Provenance Manager: The provenance manager is responsible for handling all the provenance information generated before, during and after the execution of each scientific workflow. The Provenance Manager comprises four modules: (i) The Prov2ONE module holds the implementation of the Prov2ONE algorithm. (ii) NORDR Provenance Collector module collects the retrospective

---

[2] http://docs.oasis-open.org/wsbpel/2.0/OS/wsbpel-v2.0-OS.html.

[3] https://www.arangodb.com/.

provenance information from the NORDR. (iii) WF Engine Provenance Collector module collects the retrospective provenance information from the WF engine. (iv) OPM/PROV Provenance Exporter module enables interoperability between the ProvONE and OPM/PROV standard.

3   Prov2ONE Algorithm

The Prov2ONE algorithm comprises two components. In the first component, BPEL4WS activities are distinguished according to their status as structure activities or operation activities. Structure activities are added to the stack, with their head and tail sets determined according to the previous structure activities. The algorithm then recurses on the children of the ingested structure, which are popped upon completion. In the second component, labeled nodes defined by the set $\Sigma = (Workflow, Process, InputPort, OutputPort, DataLink, SeqCtrlLink)$ are created and the relevant associations, with labels defined by set $\Omega = (sourcePToCL, CLtoDestP, hasInPort, hasOutPort, DLToInPort, outPort\text{-}ToDL)$ are drawn. This step is completed in the GenerateProvOne method of Algorithm 2. The ProvONE is defined as a graph $G = (V, E, \lambda, \psi)$, with: a set of vertices $V = \{v_1, v_2, v_3, ..., v_n\}$, a set of edges $E \subseteq V \times V$, a vertex labeling function $\lambda: V \to \Sigma$, an edge labeling function $\psi: E \to \Omega$. The ProvONE algorithm is tested for a nanoscopy workflow shown in Fig. 2.

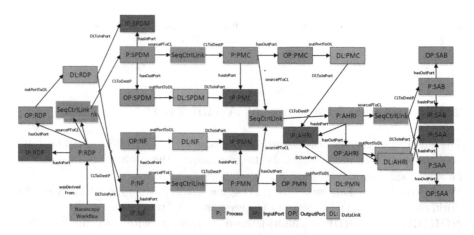

Fig. 3. ProvONE graph of nanoscopy workflow (Color figure online)

Algorithm 1. Prov2ONE Algorithm

1: List A := {$sequence, process, while, scope$}
2: List B := {$flow, pick, switch$}
3: List P := {$invoke, receive, assign, reply, \emptyset$}
4: List D := $\emptyset$, Stack S := {$[process, \{R\}, \{R\}]$}
5: C = {$c_1, c_2, c_3, ..., c_n$} is vector of BPEL children
6: **function** PROV2ONE(C)
7:     **for** c_i in C **do**
8:         **if** $c_i.operation \in P$ **then**
9:             GenerateProvOne(c_i)
10:        **end if**
11:        **if** $c_i.operation \in A \cup B$ **then**
12:            $top = POP(S)$
13:            **if** $top[0] \in A$ **then**
14:                $head = top[2]$
15:                **if** $top[1] == top[2]$ **then**
16:                    $top[1] = \emptyset$
17:                **end if**
18:                $top[2] = \emptyset$
19:            **else**
20:                $head = top[1], top[1] = \emptyset$
21:            **end if**
22:            **if** $c_i.operation \in A$ **then**
23:                $tail = COPY(head)$
24:            **else**
25:                $tail = \emptyset$
26:            **end if**
27:            PUSH(S, top)
28:            PUSH(S, [$c_i.operation, head, tail$])
29:            Prov2ONE($c_i.children$)
30:            $end = POP(S), top = POP(S)$
31:            **if** $top[1] = \emptyset$ **then**
32:                $top[1] = end[1]$
33:            **end if**
34:            **if** $top[0] \in A$ **then**
35:                $top[2] = end[2]$
36:            **else**
37:                $top[2] = top[2] \cup end[2]$
38:            **end if**
39:            PUSH(S, top)
40:        **end if**
41:    **end for**
42: **end function**

Algorithm 2. GenerateProvOne Method

1: **function** GENERATEPROVONE(c_i)
2:     $in = c_i.input, out = c_i.output$
3:     $\lambda(c_i) = Process$
4:     ADD(V, c_i)
5:     $top = POP(S)$
6:     **if** $top[0] \in A$ **then**
7:         ADD(V, s)
8:         $\lambda(s) = SeqCtrlLink$
9:         $\psi(E) = sourcePToCL$
10:        CONNECT($top[2]$, s, E)
11:        $\psi(E) = CLtoDestP$
12:        CONNECT(s, c_i, E)
13:        $top[2] = \{c_i\}$
14:    **else**
15:        ADD(V, s)
16:        $\lambda(s) = SeqCtrlLink$
17:        $\psi(E) = sourcePToCL$
18:        CONNECT($top[1]$, s, E)
19:        $\psi(E) = CLtoDestP$
20:        CONNECT(s, c_i, E)
21:        $top[2] = top[2] \cup \{c_i\}$
22:    **end if**
23:    PUSH(S, top)
24:    **if** $in \neq \emptyset$ **then**
25:        $\lambda(in) = InputPort$
26:        $\psi(E) = hasInPort$
27:        ADD(E, c_i, in)
28:        **if** $in \in D$ **then**
29:            dl = GET(D, out)
30:            $\psi(E) = DLToInPort$
31:            ADD(E, dl, in)
32:        **end if**
33:    **end if**
34:    **if** $out \neq \emptyset$ **then**
35:        $\psi(E) = hasOutPort$
36:        $\lambda(out) = OutputPort$
37:        ADD(E, c_i, out)
38:        $\lambda(dl) = DataLink$
39:        $\psi(E) = outPortToDL$
40:        ADD(E, out, dl), ADD(D, dl)
41:    **end if**
42: **end function**
43: **function** CONNECT(N, c_i, E)
44:     **for** $n \in N$ **do**
45:         ADD(E, n, c_i)
46:     **end for**
47: **end function**

4   Conclusion and Future Work

This paper presented a novel algorithm, called Prov2ONE, that generates the ProvONE prospective provenance graph for an arbitrary BPEL4WS workflow. Figure 3 shows the ProvONE graph generated by the Prov2ONE algorithm for the nanoscopy workflow. During the execution of the workflow, the retrospective ProvONE, i.e. *ProcessExec*, *Data* and *User* is linked to the ProvONE prospective graph with associations *wasAssociatedWith*, *wasGeneratedBy*, *used*, *was-DerivedFrom* and *dataOnLink*. The services for collecting and appending the retrospective provenance to the prospective ProvONE graph are implemented in the Provenance Manager component. By modelling both the prospective and retrospective provenance for a scientific workflow in the ProvONE, the redundant task of collecting, storing and maintaining provenance in various systems is entirely avoided. The architecture of the NORDR system is shown in Fig. 1, and for enabling efficient storage and querying of the provenance information, a graph database is used. Currently, we are implementing the OPM/PROV exporter module based on formal semantic mapping between ProvONE and OPM/PROV.

References

1. Cremer, C.: Optics far beyond the diffraction limit. In: Träger, F. (ed.) Handbook of Lasers and Optics, pp. 1359–1397. Springer, Heidelberg (2012)
2. Prabhune, A., et al.: An optimized generic client service API for managing large datasets within a data repository. In: IEEE BigDataService, pp. 44–51. IEEE (2015)
3. Cuevas-Vicenttín, V., et al.: ProvONE: A Prov Extension Data Model for Scientific Workflow Provenance (2015). http://purl.org/provone
4. Freire, J., Koop, D., Santos, E., Silva, C.T.: Provenance for computational tasks: a survey. Comput. Sci. Eng. **10**(3), 11–21 (2008)
5. Moreau, L.: The specification, open provenance model core (v1. 1). Future Gener. Comput. Syst. **27**(6), 743–756 (2011)
6. Moreau, L., Missier, P., et al. (eds.): PROV-DM: The PROV Data Model. W3C Recommendation (2013). http://www.w3.org/TR/prov-dm/

Implementing Unified Why- and Why-Not Provenance Through Games

Seokki Lee[1(✉)], Sven Köhler[2], Bertram Ludäscher[3], and Boris Glavic[1]

[1] Illinois Institute of Technology, Chicago, USA
slee195@hawk.iit.edu, bglavic@iit.edu
[2] University of California, Davis, Davis, USA
svkoehler@ucdavis.edu
[3] University of Illinois at Urbana-Champaign, Champaign, USA
ludaesch@illinois.edu

Abstract. Using provenance to explain *why* a query returns a result or why a result is *missing* has been studied extensively. However, the two types of questions have been approached independently of each other. We present an efficient technique for answering both types of questions for Datalog queries based on a game-theoretic model of provenance called *provenance games*. Our approach compiles provenance requests into Datalog and translates the resulting query into SQL to execute it on a relational database backend. We apply several novel optimizations to limit the computation to provenance relevant to a given user question.

1 Introduction

Explaining the existence and absence of query results through *provenance* respective *missing answer* techniques can help users to, e.g., debug and understand their data and queries. Recently, the two techniques have been unified [3] in a single framework based on a game-theoretic notion of provenance for queries with negation, particularly, for non-recursive Datalog¬.[1] The provenance game for a query Q and database instance I explains for each existing and missing query result how the rules of the query succeeded (respective failed) to derive it and why the derivation succeeded (respective failed), i.e., which tuples present or absent in the database instance caused rule derivations to succeed (respective fail). Typically, a user would not be interested in explanations for all answers and non-answers, but rather would like to understand why a particular tuple is (not) in the result. Given such a user question $Q(t)$, our approach computes a subgraph of the full game that answers precisely the user question. While provenance games provide a solid underlying theoretical foundation, these games are not necessarily the most user-friendly representation of provenance, i.e., they require some background in game theory to be interpreted correctly. Our system

---

[1] Intuitively, asking why a tuple t is absent from Q is equivalent to explaining why t is present in $\neg Q$. Thus, a provenance model with support for negation in queries enables *why* and *why-not* questions to be treated uniformly.

© Springer International Publishing Switzerland 2016
M. Mattoso and B. Glavic (Eds.): IPAW 2016, LNCS 9672, pp. 209–213, 2016.
DOI: 10.1007/978-3-319-40593-3_23

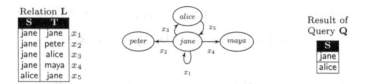

Fig. 1. Example database

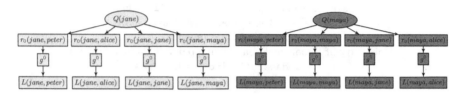

Fig. 2. Provenance explaining why Q(jane) and why-not Q(maya).

also supports several simpler forms of provenance that can be derived from a provenance game by graph transformations, e.g., we support graphs that encode provenance polynomials [2] for positive queries. Importantly, the core of our technique is independent of how provenance is represented eventually and, thus, new types of provenance representations can be added easily. The conventional method [3] for computing provenance games is not suited well for computing the part of the provenance game explaining a single answer or non-answer $Q(t)$, because it has to instantiate the full game which is prohibitively expensive, even for small instances. For example, for a database with 1000 values and a query with a single rule using 5 variables, the full game will contain more than 10^{15} nodes. Our approach computes the provenance bottom-up and only instantiates parts of the game if they may be relevant to answer the user question.

Example 1. *Consider relation* L *in Fig. 1, which stores links between personal webpages. For example, the tuple* (jane,peter) *denotes that Jane's webpage contains a link to Peter's webpage. A webpage may contain links to other parts of the page (a self-loop). Consider a query Q expressed in Datalog that returns webpages that have outgoing links:* $r_0 : Q(X) :- L(X,Y)$. *Given such a query, a user may be interested in understanding why or why-not a webpage occurs in the result of query Q. Figure 2 shows the simplified provenance graphs produced by our approach for several why- and why-not questions. For instance, tuple* (jane) *is in the result (denoted by the green background), because there is a link from her webpage to Alice's (tuple x_3) which causes rule derivation r_0(jane, alice) to succeed. Tuple* (maya) *is not in the result, because none of the four possible links connecting her webpage to any of the other webpages in the database exists. Thus all possible derivations of Q(maya) using rule r_0 have failed.*

2   Efficiently Generating Provenance Games

The input to our approach for computing provenance games is a Datalog program and either a *why* or *why-not* question, i.e., why is tuple t in the result respective missing from the result. Furthermore, the user can select whether one of the simplified provenance representations should be returned. Based on these inputs, we construct a new Datalog program that computes the edge relation of the provenance game graph for t as detailed in the following.

(1) Unify program with provenance request. We first unify the program with the question $Q(t)$ by propagating the constants in t to replace variables throughout the program in order to limit the computation to relevant parts of the game. For example, to explain why $Q(\text{jane})$ (on the left in Fig. 2), we only have to consider rule bindings where $X = \text{jane}$.

(2) Annotated rules. We then determine for which nodes in the graph we can infer their success/failure state based on the user question. For instance, we only need to consider successful instantiations of rule r_0 to explain why $Q(\text{jane})$. We store this information as annotations on rules and goals in the Datalog program.

(3) Capture rule derivations. Based on the annotated and unified game created in the previous steps, we generate rules capturing variable bindings for successful and failed rule instantiations (the annotations enable us to determine whether we can focus on successful or failed instantiations only) in order to construct the subgraph of a provenance game corresponding to a rule derivation. We call these rules *firing rules*.

Successful derivations. Reconsider question why $Q(\text{jane})$ from Example 1. The firing rule capturing successful bindings of r_0, the only rule of query Q, is derived from r_0 by adding Y (the only existential variable in r_0) to the head, renaming the head predicate as $F_{r_0,T}$, and replacing each goal with its firing version. Firing rules are created after the unification with the user question. Thus, for the example question, we would start from $r_0 : Q(\text{jane}, Y) :- L(\text{jane}, Y)$. Positive firing rules for edb predicates simply copy the predicate.

$$F_{r_0,T}(\text{jane}, Y) :- F_{L,T}(\text{jane}, Y) \qquad\qquad F_{L,T}(\text{jane}, Y) :- L(\text{jane}, Y)$$

Failed derivations. To construct a provenance graph fragment corresponding to a missing tuple, we find failed derivations with this tuple in the head and ensure that no successful derivations of the tuple exist (otherwise we may capture the irrelevant failed derivations of existing tuples). Furthermore, we need to determine which goals failed for each failed rule instantiation because only failed goals will be connected to the failed rule instantiations in the provenance game. For the why-not question $Q(\text{maya})$ shown in Fig. 2 (on the right side), we are only interested in failed instantiations of rule r_0 with $X = \text{maya}$. The generated firing rules are shown in Fig. 3. A negative firing rule (capturing failed derivations) is constructed by replacing every goal in the body with its F/T firing version. An F/T firing rule captures both existing and missing tuples and uses an additional boolean variable (V_1 in Fig. 3) in the head to record whether a tuple is existing

$$F_{Q,F}(\text{maya}) :- \neg\, F_{Q,T}(\text{maya})$$
$$F_{Q,T}(\text{maya}) :- F_{r_0,T}(\text{maya}, Y)$$
$$F_{r_0,F}(\text{maya}, Y, V_1) :- F_{Q,F}(\text{maya}),$$
$$F_{L,F/T}(\text{maya}, Y, V_1)$$
$$F_{r_0,T}(\text{maya}, Y) :- F_{L,F/T}(\text{maya}, Y, true)$$
$$F_{L,F/T}(\text{maya}, Y, true) :- L(\text{maya}, Y)$$
$$F_{L,F/T}(\text{maya}, Y, false) :- \text{adom}(Y), \neg L(\text{maya}, Y)$$

Fig. 3. Firing rules for failed derivations

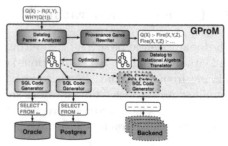

Fig. 4. GProM Implementation

or missing. We also add a firing rule for the negated head atom to the body to only capture bindings for missing tuples. Since query Q (in the Example 1) has only one goal, we simply capture whether this goal is won or lost for each rule instantiation using boolean variable V_1. As mentioned above, we use a F/T firing rule for relation L to determine whether a tuple exists in L.

(4) Filter out false positives. To be in the result of one of the firing rules obtained in the previous step is a necessary, but not sufficient condition for the provenance graph fragment corresponding to this rule binding to be connected to the user question. To guarantee that only relevant fragments are returned, we need to check for each fragment whether it is actually connected. We introduce additional rules that check connectivity one hop at a time.

(5) Compute edge relation. We compute the edge relation of the provenance game based on the rule binding information that the firing rules have captured. In addition to full game provenance, we support simplified provenance representations including the ones shown in Fig. 2.

Implementation. The generated Datalog program constructs and solves the provenance game simultaneously in a bottom-up manner. We have implemented this algorithm in our provenance middleware called GProM [1] that executes provenance requests using a database backend. The process of computing a provenance game for a user request is shown in Fig. 4. Our system also visualizes the resulting graph using Graphviz (http://www.graphviz.org/).

3   Conclusions

We present an efficient approach for explaining answers and non-answers to Datalog queries using provenance games. Our approach limits the computation to parts of the provenance relevant to a user question by constructing the game bottom-up and pruning unrelated parts from the computation.

References

1. Arab, B., Gawlick, D., Radhakrishnan, V., Guo, H., Glavic, B.: A generic provenance middleware for database queries, updates, and transactions. In: Tapp (2014)
2. Green, T., Karvounarakis, G., Tannen, V.: Provenance semirings. In: PODS. pp. 31–40 (2007)
3. Köhler, S., Ludäscher, B., Zinn, D.: First-order provenance games. In: Tannen, V., Wong, L., Libkin, L., Fan, W., Tan, W.-C., Fourman, M. (eds.) Buneman Festschrift 2013. LNCS, vol. 8000, pp. 382–399. Springer, Heidelberg (2013)

SisGExp: Rethinking Long-Tail Agronomic Experiments

Sergio Manuel Serra da Cruz[✉]
and José Antonio Pires do Nascimento

UFRRJ – Universidade Federal Rural do Rio de Janeiro, Seropédica, RJ, Brazil
serra@ufrrj.br, joseantonio.pires@embrapa.br

Abstract. Reproducibility is a major feature of Science. Even agronomic research of exemplary quality may have irreproducible empirical findings because of random or systematic error. This work presents SisGExp, a provenance-based approach that aid researchers to manage, share, and enact the computational scientific workflows that encapsulate legacy R scripts. SisGExp transparently captures provenance of R scripts and endows experiments reproducibility. SisGExp is non-intrusive, does not require users to change their working way, it wrap agronomic experiments as a scientific workflow system.

Keywords: Provenance · R scripts · Workflows · Precision agriculture

1 Introduction

In today's world, the demand for more food and green energy is skyrocketing. The current method for developing innovations in agronomy is based almost entirely on conventional, time- and labor-intensive experimental methods in which new varieties and management practices are evaluated using on-the-ground and field-scale experiments that may last for years. Despite ongoing agricultural model improvements, many are direct descendants of research investments made three–four decades ago, and many of the major advances in data management of the past decade have not been fully exploited [1].

The association of Agronomy with eScience through the use of sensors, satellites imagery, drones, modern experimental apparatuses, data streaming and *in silico* simulations are demanding new approaches to ensure reproducibility of agronomic experiments regarding the management of experiments' data.

Even agronomic research of exemplary quality, the complete reproduction of several on-the-ground experiments may be not always feasible. Thus, to make researches transparent and rigorous, with a minimum standard attainable for that to assess the real value of their scientific claims, the use of provenance metadata must be considered since the early stages of its experimental design until its statistical calculations, final executions, and publications. Our approach aims to allow researchers to manage, share, and enact the statistical workflows that encapsulate legacy R scripts [1, 2].

The key motivation for our research is to bring an approach to assist scientists to expand the reproducibility of their experiments. We are intentionally seeking to low

© Springer International Publishing Switzerland 2016
M. Mattoso and B. Glavic (Eds.): IPAW 2016, LNCS 9672, pp. 214–217, 2016.
DOI: 10.1007/978-3-319-40593-3_24

technological barriers while providing the capability of using of consolidated tools to encapsulate R scripts as statistical workflows and making the inputs and outputs and its provenance metadata useful and publicly accessible not only to the researcher team but also to third-party. In this paper, we present the SisGExp e-Science platform that enriches the management of agronomic experiments supported by RFlow [2] architecture that wraps R scripts. It mitigates limitations of statistical systems about the transparent and non-intrusive collection of prospective and retrospective provenance.

2 SisGExp Overview

Nowadays, agronomic experiments are based on on-the-ground experiments and also statistical scripts. Usually, these scripts are hard-coded by Statistics researchers to less skilled ones. These scripts act as statistical workflows using a textual language described by languages like R, Perl, Python. The scripts are not easier to used, shared and maintained by the inexperienced user. There are few mechanisms to collect provenance of statistical scripts without changing its source code [3, 4].

The rationale behind SisGExp is depicted as follows. As a first phase (data acquisition and planning), the researcher connects his account into SisGExp. Thus, he defines the computational steps of the experimental design of the agronomic experiment (parcels/variables/cultivars/randomizations/replications); picking legacy R scripts from libraries; inserting raw experimental data; registering structured annotations. During this phase, all prospective provenance related to the registered user/experiment, inputs, annotations and other settings are caught by SisGExp and then stored in the provenance repository. The accurate track of prospective provenance of the agronomic experiment is important because enables downstream analysis errors to be traced back to the original data sources.

As a second phase (which is indeed an iteration cycle of executions, analytics, and reflections). The researcher configures the computational parameters; select input files and R scripts (to prepare and analyze the inputs); select and run meta-workflow (hosted on a remote server) that encapsulate the R script (such configuration is achieved by a concrete workflow which takes advantage of the existing provenance engines of the SWfMS). During this phase, retrospective provenance related to the (re)execution of the computational trials are caught by either the SisGExp or the provenance engine and then stored in the provenance repository represented by the PostgreSQL RDBMS. At this phase, the researcher may repeat the cycle of selecting pairs of R script/meta-workflows, executing and monitoring to produce novel output files, checking them to gain insights and discover faults, debugging and annotating. The execution of the meta-workflows allows the collection of retrospective provenance metadata related to encapsulated R scripts. Nowadays, R system does not offer provenance gathering facilities, and the ongoing efforts to enrich the collection of provenance for R system require modifications in the R script to receive semantic commentaries or function calls. As far we are concerned such approach present some drawbacks. For instance, scientists must deal with multiple versions of R scripts, they should have a deep understanding of R language to insert the commands in the proper position in the script. These approaches introduce technological barriers that many scientists are not interested in confronting.

As a third phase (validation and dissemination). The computational trials were finished, thus, the scientists (PI, reviewers, visitors) may visualize, browse, query and evaluate both the scientific results and the provenance metadata of all three phases of the agronomic experiments. The scientist has an integrated repository of data and provenance metadata that can be analyzed or shared through the SisGExp interface services. The four main components are: Experiments Management System (SisGExp), the statistical system (R System), the SWfMS (Kepler SWfMS), the provenance collector engine and a relational database management system (Fig. 1).

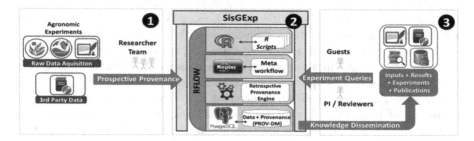

Fig. 1. Conceptual overview of SisGExp.

2.1   Meta-workflows

In this work, a statistical meta-workflow is a generic and reusable solution to encapsulate legacy R scripts. It acts as a wrapper that captures the script and all its statistical functions as a sequence of activities of a workflow, allowing its implementation in an SWfMS with all the benefits of built-in provenance.

The ExecScript is the concrete workflow developed in Kepler SWfMS (invoked remotely by SisGExp) that represents the concept of statistical meta-workflow. The workflow consists of several actors and file connectors, R specific actors and a composite sub-workflow actor and the SDF director that orchestrates the execution of the actors. Among the actors, we highlight the "Provenance Recorder" (PR) used to configure and collect the retrospective provenance during the execution of the workflow and stored it directly in the PostgreSQL database.

2.2   Data and Metadata Repository

The repository is the warehouse of experiments' data and provenance metadata. It provides accounts to registered users allowing them to store and upload experiments, audit and share results and provenance either privately or publicly in relational representation.

By default, files submitted to the repository are private and can only be accessed by owners. However, researchers can choose to share files and results with others in two ways: making a resource publicly available to any SisGExp guest visitor or sharing it with specific SisGExp's registered users. Except reader, all other roles, and the owner can append new annotations (prospective provenance) to a resource or dataset after it has been created. It is suitable for sharing provenance between a collaborating team of humans and/or applications.

The repository stores prospective and retrospective provenance metadata and also experiments' data. Prospective provenance is generated through the interaction of the researcher with SisGExp during the three phases of the experiment. The retrospective provenance is collected during the generation of the experiment's results; they are automatically captured by the SWfMS.

The provenance repository uses two schemas *public* and *expdata*. The *public* schema is linked with retrospective provenance collected by the Kepler System. The *expdata* schema is related with prospective provenance; it was planned and implemented to meet the demands of agronomic experiments. The schemes aim to register the life cycle of the agronomic experiments.

3   Conclusion

Good science requires documentation and reproducibility. We foresee an increasing use of computational models leading to virtual agronomic studies that can complement and substitute (to some degree) on-the-ground methods.

Our approach empowers researchers to reuse and encapsulate legacy R scripts. Compared to related works, the main advantages of SisGExp are: (i) it systematically captures two types of provenance (prospective and retrospective) of the statistical experiments. (ii) it does not require researchers to change their manner of working: scripts do not need to be modified. (iii) it enhances reproducibility of agronomic experiments, because the proposed schemes can register either experiments data and provenance of results that can be reused, shared or queried by peers. As part of future work, we intend to extend SisGExp to support other provenance systems generating prospective and retrospective for other scripting languages such as Python and Perl.

References

1. Driemeier, C.E., et al.: Data analysis workflow for experiments in sugarcane precision agriculture. In: IEEE 10th International Conference on e-Science, vol. 1, pp. 163–168 (2014). http://doi.org/10.1109/eScience.2014.10
2. Nascimento, J.A.P., Cruz, S.M.S.: Rflow: uma arquitetura para execução e coleta de proveniência de workflows estatísticos. X Simpósio Brasileiro de Informática na Agricultura, 12pp. (2015). (In Portuguese)
3. Gandrud, C.: Reproducible Research with R and R Studio, 2nd edn. Chapman and Hall/CRC, Boca Raton (2015)
4. McPhillips, T., et al.: YesWorkflow: a user-oriented, language-independent tool for recovering workflow information from scripts. Int. J. Digit. Curation 10(1), 298–313 (2015)

Towards Provenance Capturing
of Quantified Self Data

Andreas Schreiber[1(✉)] and Doreen Seider[2]

[1] German Aerospace Center (DLR), Cologne, Germany
`andreas.schreiber@dlr.de`
[2] Medando UG (haftungsbeschränkt), Cologne, Germany
`doreen.seider@medando.de`

Abstract. Quantified Self or self-tracking is a growing movement where people are tracking data about themselves. Tracking the provenance of Quantified Self data is hard because usually many different devices, apps, and services are involved. Nevertheless receiving insights how the data has been acquired, how it has been processed, and who has stored and accessed it is crucial for people. We present concepts for tracking provenance in typical Quantified Self workflows. We use a provenance model based on PROV and show its feasibility with an example.

Keywords: Provenance · Quantified self · Wearables · PROV

1 Introduction

Self-tracking with wearable devices, smartphone apps, or desktop applications became popular in recent years. Such a self-surveillance is called *Quantified Self* (QS) [3,8]. It is a movement that describes a community of people who record and analyse data about themselves for medical reasons, self-improvement, technological interests, or other reasons. People collect various types of data related to them, to get a better understanding of themselves.

We show how to practically capture provenance for QS workflows consisting of wearable devices, (mobile) applications, and services (Sect. 2). To capture provenance based on a QS provenance model [5,9], we give an overview about some practical methods for provenance capturing (Sect. 3) and show the feasibility with an example, where we capture provenance by an Android application and a Python script (Sect. 4).

2 A Typical Quantified Self Workflow

To better understand a typical QS workflow, we present a workflow for weight tracking (Fig. 1). The workflow starts with the user, who steps on a *Withings* online weight scale. The scale connects through WLAN to the Withings Cloud storage to update the weight data set. Withings notification server is executed

© Springer International Publishing Switzerland 2016
M. Mattoso and B. Glavic (Eds.): IPAW 2016, LNCS 9672, pp. 218–221, 2016.
DOI: 10.1007/978-3-319-40593-3_25

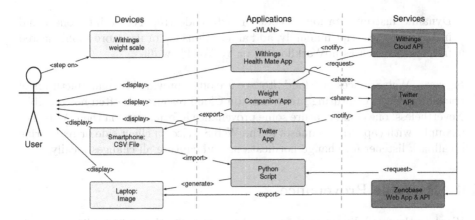

Fig. 1. Example QS workflow for weight tracking.

after the update to notify subscribed applications. The Android application *WeightCompanion*[1] gets updates for new weight data. Users can visualize and edit data or export data sets to CSV files. For example, the user can copy the CSV file to a laptop and import and process it with self-written Python scripts. The user could also use a third-party service to collect and analyze the data.

3   Capture Methods for Provenance

For "real-world" QS workflows, the following techniques are available for capturing provenance:

Wearable Devices and Other Sensors. Sensors, as wearables or traditional medical sensors are usually very closed embedded systems. Adding functionality is not designated by their manufacturers; it would require changing their firmware. Adding functionality for capturing provenance would only be possible for devices with programming interfaces (e.g., *Microsoft Band* or various smart watches).

Applications and Scripts. Smartphone, desktop, or web-based applications usually need very different, specific, techniques for capturing provenance. Depending on their architecture and availability, changing the applications code itself or adding functionality via an API are the most desirable techniques. If both are not possible or wanted, some other techniques are:

- Wrapping the application and capture information from files, or databases that the application creates or uses.
- Grabbing information from the communication infrastructure (e.g., via messaging infrastructures such as MQTT, ZeroMQ, or Enterprise Service Buses [1]).

---

[1] http://play.google.com/store/apps/details?id=de.medando.weightcompanion.

– Dynamic instrumentation of code or byte code [10]. For scripts, one could instrument the script manually, add annotations [2], or use more sophisticated frameworks such as noWorkflow [7] or YesWorkflow [6].

Services. Web Services or Cloud Storage are often provided by manufacturers of tracking devices. Capturing provenance on Cloud resources is often not possible. Nevertheless, one could capture some provenance information via their APIs. For example, with capturing requests to the Web Service on client side or registering a callback listener for change notifications and capture all changes locally.

4   Example Provenance

We show the feasibility of some approaches with a practical "slice of life" example from the weight tracking workflow: First the weight data is exported from an Android application to a CSV file, then this CSV file is imported and visualized by a Python script.

We added provenance capturing to the WeightCompanion. The application generates provenance documents using the Java library *ProvToolbox*[2], which we ported to Android. The Python script imports a CSV file and visualizes the weights data. The CSV file is imported into a *pandas DataFrame* object. Then the data is visualized using *matplotlib*. Provenance is captured using a Python library[3] for PROV-DM. Both examples send the PROV document to the *ProvS-*

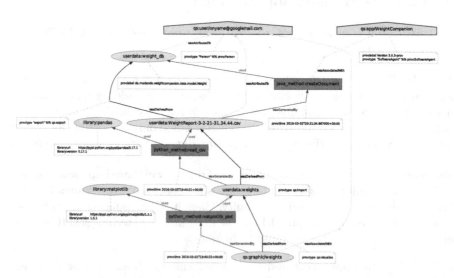

Fig. 2. Merged provenance of a graph of weight measurements (https://provenance. ecs.soton.ac.uk/store/documents/113794/)

[2] http://lucmoreau.github.io/ProvToolbox/.
[3] https://github.com/trungdong/prov.

tore [4] directly. We merged the individual PROV documents using ProvToolbox (Fig. 2).

5   Conclusions and Future Work

We presented techniques for capturing provenance of QS workflows. Future work will focus on refining the QS provenance model and on providing documentation for developers of QS applications and services. Technically, we plan to provide provenance templates to help more flexible and maintainable recording of provenance.

References

1. Allen, M.D., Chapman, A., Blaustein, B., Seligman, L.: Capturing provenance in the wild. In: McGuinness, D.L., Michaelis, J.R., Moreau, L. (eds.) IPAW 2010. LNCS, vol. 6378, pp. 98–101. Springer, Heidelberg (2010)
2. Bachmann, A., Bergmeyer, H., Schreiber, A.: Evaluation of aspect-oriented frameworks in python for extending a project with provenance documentation features. Python Pap. **6**(3), 3 (2011)
3. Hoy, M.B.: Personal activity trackers and the quantified self. Med. Ref. Serv. Q **35**(1), 94–100 (2016)
4. Huynh, T.D., Moreau, L.: ProvStore: a public provenance repository. In: Ludaescher, B., Plale, B. (eds.) IPAW 2014. LNCS, vol. 8628, pp. 275–277. Springer, Heidelberg (2015)
5. Janisch, B.: Developing an abstract Quantified Self Provenance model. Master project, University of Applied Sciences Bonn-Rhein-Sieg (2015). http://elib.dlr.de/100752/
6. McPhillips, T., et al.: Yesworkflow: a user-oriented, language-independent tool for recovering workflow information from scripts. Int. J. Digit. Curation **10**(1), 298–313 (2015)
7. Murta, L., Braganholo, V., Chirigati, F., Koop, D., Freire, J.: noWorkflow: capturing and analyzing provenance of scripts. In: Ludaescher, B., Plale, B. (eds.) IPAW 2014. LNCS, vol. 8628, pp. 71–83. Springer, Heidelberg (2015)
8. Picard, R., Wolf, G.: Sensor informatics and quantified self. IEEE J. Biomed. Health Inf. **19**(5), 1531 (2015)
9. Schreiber, A.: A provenance model for quantified self data. In: Antona, M., Stephanidis, C. (eds.) UAHCI 2016, Part I. LNCS, vol. 9737. Springer, Switzerland (2016)
10. Stamatogiannakis, M., Groth, P., Bos, H.: Looking inside the black-box: capturing data provenance using dynamic instrumentation. In: Ludaescher, B., Plale, B. (eds.) IPAW 2014. LNCS, vol. 8628, pp. 155–167. Springer, Heidelberg (2015)

A Review of Guidelines and Models
for Representation of Provenance Information
from Neuroscience Experiments

Margarita Ruiz-Olazar[1(✉)], Evandro S. Rocha[1],
Sueli S. Rabaça[1], Carlos Eduardo Ribas[1], Amanda S. Nascimento[1,3],
and Kelly R. Braghetto[1,2]

[1] Research, Innovation and Dissemination Center for Neuromathematics,
São Paulo, Brazil
`{mrolazar,erocha,suelisr,ribas,kellyrb}@ime.usp.br`
[2] Department of Computer Science, Institute of Mathematics and Statistics,
University of São Paulo, São Paulo, Brazil
[3] Department of Computer Science - Exact Sciences and Biological Institute,
Federal University of Ouro Preto, Ouro Preto, Minas Gerais, Brazil
`anascimento@iceb.ufop.br`

Abstract. To manage raw data from Neuroscience experiments we have
to cope with the heterogeneity of data formats and the complexity of
additional metadata, such as its provenance information, that need to
be collected and stored. Although some progress has already been made
toward the elaboration of a common description for Neuroscience experimental data, to the best of our knowledge, there is still no widely adopted
standard model to describe this kind of data. In order to foster neuro-
cientists to find and to use a structured and comprehensive model with
a robust tracking of data provenance, we present a brief evaluation of
guidelines and models for representation of raw data from Neuroscience
experiments, focusing on how they support provenance tracking.

Keywords: Neuroscience · Experimental data · Electrophysiology ·
Neuroimaging · Provenance information

1 Introduction

There are different kinds of experiments in Neuroscience, such as behavioral,
cognitive, electrophysiological (Ephy) and neuroimaging (NI). The last two
always involve the collection of data in digital format, e.g. electroencephalogram
(EEG), event related potential (ERP) and functional magnetic resonance imaging (fMRI). Each experiment involves the generation and manipulation of large
quantities of both raw and processed data. To enhancing reproducibility of Neuroscience studies, researchers need to know the precise acquisition parameters

This work was produced at FAPESP Research, Innovation and Dissemination Center
for Neuromathematics (grant 2013/07699-0, S. Paulo Research Foundation).

M. Mattoso and B. Glavic (Eds.): IPAW 2016, LNCS 9672, pp. 222–225, 2016.
DOI: 10.1007/978-3-319-40593-3_26

and the experimental conditions on how the raw data was acquired. These kind of information, generally called *provenance information*, are metadata which is used to record the experimental protocol (a specific preparation for realization of the experiment by scientists), the purpose of the experiment and details about its data results, as well as formal annotations and notes made by scientists.

In Neuroscience, the provenance information of raw data are too often lost or when digitized end up becoming text files or spread-sheets without a standardized structure. A unified data model for handling metadata is still an open research problem. The problem is compounded when the volume of collected data begins to grow. Unlike the progress in workflow-based systems, which provide consistent mechanisms to manage the provenance of derived data generated through workflows, the availability of open data models and free software tools to support raw data routine collection is limited. Thus, the creation of standardized models and formats for representing and storing raw data and its provenance information is not a trivial task and depends on collaborative efforts from the Neuroscience community.

Against this background, the presented work should be understood as a contribution to the necessary discussion about the importance of storing provenance information of experimental raw data in a structured and comprehensible way. With this motivation, we present a brief bibliographical review and comparison of the guidelines and models most widely used by neuroscientists in the representation and storage of experimental data. From our analysis, we have identified the types of provenance information supported by these directives. The formal specification of many of them is still a work in progress.

2   List of Guidelines and Data Models

In this research we considered fundamental provenance information based on the seven W's (Who, What, Where, Why, When, Which, (W) how) [1]. In Neuroscience domain, examples of provenance information of experimental raw data are: the scientists responsible for the experiment and collection of data, the description of the subject study groups (who); the details about the recording protocol or behavioral data collection, (e.g. the material used to record behavioral data, the types of data collection performed) (what); the details of the task or experimental protocol used in the collection of raw data (how); the start/end date-time for data collection (when); the purpose of the experiment (why); the information about the experimental conditions to which the groups of subjects are submitted, such as behavioral and stimulus conditions (which); the information about the laboratory where data was collected (where) and even publications or other results that have arisen from the study of the collected data.

Due to the great variability in experimental protocols and heterogeneity of collected data formats, Neuroscience experimental raw data and its provenance information require specific and innovative ways of representation and storage. Several recent works have already addressed the problem, proposing Minimum Information (MI) guidelines and new data models. MI guidelines are checklists

Table 1. Minimum information guidelines for Neuroscience experiments.

Guidelines	Data focus	Provenance information
MINI [2]	Ephy	Study subject (who); recording protocol (what); experiment context* (when/why/where) task/protocol (how); behavioral and stimulus conditions (which)
MINEMO [3]	ERP/EEG	Study subjects (who); Research Lab and publication information (where); experiment context* (why/when); experiment condition (which); experiment task (how); behavioral data collection (what)
fMRI [4]	NI	Human subject (who); experimental design (how); image properties and data acquisition (what)

*Experiment context includes general information about of the experiment (e.g. name, local, purpose, start and end date-time and other descriptions).

which define the minimum information a researcher needs to report when publishing the results of an experiment. Table 1 lists the three MI guidelines created for Ephy and NI experiments and details the provenance information they cover.

The guidelines generally include information that is considered important for data analysis and for understanding the performed experiment. However, they are neither complete data representation models nor data storage models.

Table 2 shows data models for representing and storing Neuroscience experimental data. The most adopted schema to organize and to share data and metadata is HDF5 (*Hierarchical Data Format*). HDF5 is a compact and binary schema to store numerical data, such as EEG, to which it is possible to associate metadata in a flexible way. However, its hierarchical structure, similar to files

Table 2. Data Format of provenance information supported by data models

Data Model	Data focus	Provenance data format
[a]NDF	Ephy	Based on MINI; the metadata is registered in a structured format, using an entry form. XML files or files with (unstructured) text data can also be added. Provenance information is not mandatory
[b]NWB	Ephy	Metadata is described in a flexible way using XML or unstructured text files. Data and metadata files are grouped and organized in a HDF5 structure
[c]odML	Ephy	Metadata format is defined by user and is stored using an extended key-value pairs structure
[d]NIX	Ephy	Based on odML, it allows storing additional information in textual content files grouped under a specific schema based on HDF5
[e]NIDM	NI	It uses OWL and PROV-DM structure. (under development)
[f]XCEDE	NI	Data and metadata are stored using hierarchical XML based format
[g]DICOM	NI	Data and metadata are embedded in a image file header and can never be separated. It is a closed standard

[a]http://www.carmen.org.uk/
[b]https://crcns.org/NWB/
[c]http://www.g-node.org/projects/odml
[d]https://github.com/G-Node/nix/wiki
[e]http://nidm.nidash.org/
[f]https://github.com/incf-nidash/XCEDE
[g]http://medical.nema.org/dicom/

and directories from traditional file systems, hampers the representation of more complex relationships among data (as is the case of data from experiments with several groups of participants).

The provenance information in models showed in Table 2 are not mandatory. The models allow storing metadata in a free format defined by user. XML and files with (unstructured) textual content are the most used file formats. The NI domain, with NIDM, is already achieving a consensus on data representation. NIDM, still under development, is based on standard ontologies and models, such as PROV-DM, to register provenance information. PROV-DM provides a set of classes, properties, and restrictions that can be used to represent and interchange provenance information generated in different systems and under different contexts. It can also be specialized to create new classes and properties to better model provenance information for different applications and domains.

3   Concluding Remarks

As shown in this review, there is a distinct lack of standardized models to store metadata for Neuroscience experimental raw data. Therefore, the reproducibility – a core scientific principle – of experiments and the reuse of data in other contexts may be seriously compromised. We believe that overcoming these issues require a coordinated effort from the neuroinformatics community. While there is not yet any standard data model, computational tools are the main support resource for neuroscientists interested to track provenance information of their experimental raw data. To contribute in this scenario, we are involved in the development of a free, open-source software tool – the *Neuroscience Experiments Systems* (NES). One of the purposes of NES is to assist in the management of Ephy and NI raw data while providing provenance recording and interoperability by using several proposals from the scientific community for data and metadata representation. NES is an initiative of the *Research, Innovation and Dissemination Center for Neuromathematics* (NeuroMat), hosted at University of São Paulo. NES source code and documentation is available at https://github.com/neuromat/nes.

References

1. Goble, C.: Position statement: musings on provenance, workflow and (semantic web) annotations for bioinformatics. In: Workshop on Data Derivation and Provenance, Chicago, vol. 3 (2002)
2. Gibson, F., et al.: Minimum Information about a Neuroscience Investigation (MINI): Electrophysiology. In: Nat, Precedings (2008)
3. Frishkoff, G., et al.: Minimal Information for Neural Electromagnetic Ontologies (MINEMO): a standards-compliant method for analysis and integration of event-related potentials (ERP) data. Stan. genomic Sci. 5(2), 211–223 (2011)
4. Poldrack, R., et al.: Guidelines for reporting an fMRI study. Neuroimage 40(2), 409–414 (2008)

Tracking and Establishing Provenance of Earth Science Datasets: A NASA-Based Example

Hampapuram K. Ramapriyan[1(✉)], Justin C. Goldstein[2,3],
Hook Hua[4,5], and Robert E. Wolfe[3,6]

[1] Science Systems and Applications, Inc., Lanham, MD, USA
Hampapuram.Ramapriyan@ssaihq.com
[2] ICF International, Fairfax, VA, USA
jgoldstein@usgcrp.gov
[3] US Global Change Research Program, Washington, D.C., USA
robert.e.wolfe@nasa.gov
[4] California Institute of Technology, Pasadena, CA, USA
hook.hua@jpl.nasa.gov
[5] NASA Jet Propulsion Laboratory, Pasadena, CA, USA
[6] NASA Goddard Space Flight Center, Greenbelt, MD, USA

Abstract. Information quality is of paramount importance to science. Accurate, scientifically vetted and statistically meaningful and, ideally, reproducible information engenders scientific trust and research opportunities. Therefore, so-called Highly Influential Scientific Assessments (HISA) such as the U.S. Third National Climate Assessment (NCA3) undergo a very rigorous process to ensure transparency and credibility. As an activity to support the transparency of such reports, the U.S. Global Change Research Program has developed the Global Change Information System (GCIS). Specifically related to the transparency of NCA3, a recent activity was carried out to trace the provenance as completely as possible for all figures in the NCA3 report that predominantly used NASA data. This paper discusses lessons learned from this activity that traces the provenance of NASA figures in a major HISA-class pdf report.

Keywords: Information systems · Data provenance · Information quality · HISA reports · Climate Assessment · Lessons learned

1 Introduction

Accurate, scientifically vetted and statistically meaningful and, ideally, reproducible scientific information engenders scientific trust and research opportunities. To support the transparency of reports such as the Highly Influential Scientific Assessment (HISA) that is the U.S. Third National Climate Assessment [1], the U.S. Global Change Research Program (USGCRP) has developed the Global Change Information System (GCIS). The GCIS is a web-based resource that facilitates tracing of connections among various entities of which a report is comprised, such as key messages and findings, figures, images used in the figures, data used to generate the images, etc. to foster comprehension of the mechanisms that led to the various conclusions in a report. It is available online at: http://data.globalchange.gov.

© Springer International Publishing Switzerland 2016
M. Mattoso and B. Glavic (Eds.): IPAW 2016, LNCS 9672, pp. 226–229, 2016.
DOI: 10.1007/978-3-319-40593-3_27

This paper presents the lessons learned from a NASA-funded activity to ensure that the NCA3 figure inputs derived from NASA data and their connections to findings and key messages were as complete as possible.

2 GCIS

The GCIS is an open-source, web-based resource for traceable, sound global change data, information, and products. GCIS contains sufficient metadata and links to the sources of data, information and products, guiding users to global change products selected by the 13 USGCRP member agencies. It serves as a key access point to assessments, reports and tools produced by USGCRP [2–5]. The World Wide Web Consortium (W3C) definition of provenance underlies that of GCIS.

The GCIS data model used to structure global change information represents entities such as reports, chapters, figures, bibliographic entries, organizations and people, and uses widely-adopted relationships, including provenance, among such entities. Each item referenced in the GCIS has a unique, persistent identifier takes the form of a Uniform Resource Identifier (URI), but may include other common identifiers such as Universally Unique Identifiers (UUIDs), and Digital Object Identifiers (DOIs).

The W3C Provenance Working Group has defined an interoperable specification (PROV) for the representation of provenance information. The standard is very general, intended to support the breadth of any domain through built in points of extensibility. Generally this provenance can be expressed as {entities (inputs and outputs), agents and activities}. To codify the provenance of GCIS information we are leveraging Provenance for Earth Science (PROV-ES) extension of WC3 PROV that is being developed by the NASA Earth Science Data Systems Working Group (ESDSWG).

We have leveraged the GCIS Application Program Interfaces (API) to extract GCIS content to ingest into a PROV-ES search service for faceted search and provenance exploration. NCA3 content such as figures, persons, and activities are extracted from GCIS as JSON documents. Using scripts, key GCIS concepts and their attributes are mapped onto W3C PROV types. Extensions to baseline PROV concepts are added as additional qualified named attributes. The mapping enables us to map GCIS-specific information into standard and interoperable W3C PROV. For example, a *gcis:Figure* is mapped onto a W3C PROV *prov:Entity*, but with additional attributes.

The GCIS discovery service includes a provenance faceted search capability enabling users to facet navigate GCIS resources in the context of provenance. More specifically, it enables users to "drill-down" by applying a sequential set of selection criteria across different facets (values) of the GCIS content.

3 NCA3 Figures Using NASA Data

NASA data from satellites, instruments and/or models have been used in 20 of the NCA3 figures. One such figure: Fig. 16.3 "Flooding and Hurricane Irene", supports the NCA3 Key Message: "Infrastructure will be increasingly compromised by climate-related hazards, including sea level rise, coastal flooding, and intense precipitation events." It shows an image of Hurricane Irene over the northeastern U.S. acquired from NASA's MODIS instrument on-board the Aqua satellite. The caption was a starting point for gathering more detailed metadata. The figure can be found at http://nca2014.globalchange.gov/report/regions/northeast/graphics/flooding-and-hurricane-irene.

4 Provenance Tracing and Lessons Learned

4.1 Provenance Tracing

The provenance of each of the 20 figures was manually analysed to trace back to the contributing sources (images, data, and analysis methods) to the best extent possible. The results were documented in the form of "activities" used for generating the figures. An activity is defined by a clearly identified set of inputs and outputs, and a method of generating the outputs from the inputs. A majority of the figures require performance of more than one activity. One or more inputs and/or activities may be needed to generate the figure. The method may be as simple as adapting a figure from an article or it could be more complicated and include a detail description of the activity. Where more than one activity is involved in the trace back, activity n is used for generating inputs needed for activity $n - 1$. Specification of a complete set of activities for a given figure constitutes its provenance trace.

4.2 Lessons Learned

The key lessons learned from this effort are summarized below. These lessons are similar to the ones reported in [6] regarding experience with collecting metadata for the NCA3 report. They also report that some of the lessons learned have been applied to improve the metadata collection process in the more recent health assessment report planned for release in 2016.

- It is difficult to trace back to derive provenance after reports are completed and delivered. This is because generally, the authors contributing to influential reports are very busy individuals who have spent a considerable amount of time in their research and who have applied significant effort into gathering materials and writing their sections or chapters. If in this process they have not maintained complete documentation to assist in tracing back to derive provenance, then it will involve either more work for the authors or an independent effort to investigate provenance.
- Attempts to follow up with authors on provenance could be misinterpreted as questioning their research.
- To avoid these issues, it is useful to provide the authors with detailed instructions and templates before they start writing their sections or chapters in influential reports. Generally, it is useful to provide readers with information in the form of inputs, outputs and methods (descriptive and/or mathematical) for each dataset used, images or figures generated, and key messages.
- Even with instructions and templates provided to the authors, during the generation of a report it is beneficial for an independent team to check for completeness of

traceability from a non-expert reader's point of view. If the independent team is involved starting with the early drafts of the report, the traceability check can be accomplished with minimal impact on the report publication schedule.

- Due to the very nature of a HISA, all underlying information should be held in a long-lived repository and be easily accessible to users for at least as long as the reports are deemed to be of interest to the community.

Acknowledgements. The authors would like to thank the other members of the Provenance Team - Steve Aulenbach, Brian Duggan, Gerald Manipon, Dexter Tan, Curt Tilmes, Brian Wilson and Stephan Zednik. Goldstein's work at the USGCRP National Coordination Office (NCO) was supported by an NSF contract with UCAR and a subsequent NASA contract with ICF International. Hua's work was supported by a NASA contract with the Jet Propulsion Laboratory, California Institute of Technology, Pasadena, CA. Ramapriyan's work was supported by a NASA contract with Science Systems and Applications, Inc. Wolfe's work was performed as a NASA employee on detail to USGCRP.

References

1. Melillo, J.M., Richmond, T.C., Yohe, G.W. (eds.): Climate Change Impacts in the United States: The Third National Climate Assessment. U.S. Global Change Research Program, 841pp. (2014). doi:10.7930/J0Z31WJ2
2. Tilmes, C., Fox, P., Ma, X., McGuinness, D.L., Privette, A.P., Smith, A., Waple, A., Zednik, S., Zheng, J.G.: Provenance representation for the national climate assessment in the global change information system. IEEE Trans. Geosci. Remote Sens. **51**(11), 5160–5168 (2013). doi:10.1109/TGRS.2013.2262179
3. Tilmes, C., Privette, A.P., Chen, J., Ramachandran, R., Bugbee, K.M., Wolfe, R.E.: Linking from observations to data to actionable science in the climate data initiative. In: 2015 IEEE International Geoscience and Remote Sensing Symposium (IGARSS), pp. 1354–1357, July 2015. doi:10.1109/IGARSS.2015.7326027
4. Waple, A.M., Champion, S.M., Kunkel, K.E., Tilmes, C.: Innovations in information management and access for assessments. Clim. Change Spec. Issue Nat. Clim. Assess. Innov. Sci. Engagem. 1–15 (2016). doi:10.1007/s10584-015-1588-7. (Jacobs, K. Moser, S., Buizer, J. (eds.))
5. Wolfe, R.E., Duggan, B., Aulenbach, S.M., Goldstein, J.C., Tilmes, C., Buddenberg, A.: Providing provenance to instruments through the US global change information system. In: 2015 IEEE International Geoscience and Remote Sensing Symposium (IGARSS), pp. 143–145. doi:10.1109/IGARSS.2015.7325719
6. Champion, S.M., Kunkel, K.E.: Data management and the national climate assessment: a data quality solution. In: American Geophysical Union, Fall Meeting, San Francisco, December 2015. (Presentation charts by personal communication. https://goo.gl/aSG4GM)

DataONE: A Data Federation with Provenance Support

Yang Cao[1($\boxtimes$)], Christopher Jones[2], Víctor Cuevas-Vicenttín[3],
Matthew B. Jones[2], Bertram Ludäscher[1], Timothy McPhillips[1],
Paolo Missier[4], Christopher Schwalm[5], Peter Slaughter[2],
Dave Vieglais[6], Lauren Walker[2], and Yaxing Wei[7]

[1] University of Illinois, Urbana-Champaign, Illinois, USA
sycao5@gmail.com
[2] National Center for Ecological Analysis and Synthesis, UCSB, Santa Barbara, USA
[3] Universidad Popular Autónoma del Estado de Puebla, Puebla, Mexico
[4] School of Computing Science, Newcastle University, Newcastle upon Tyne, UK
[5] Woods Hole Research Center, Falmouth, MA, USA
[6] University of Kansas, Lawrence, USA
[7] Environmental Sciences Division, ORNL, Oak Ridge, TN, USA

Abstract. DataONE is a federated data network focusing on earth and environmental science data. We present the provenance and search features of DataONE by means of an example involving three earth scientists who interact through a DataONE Member Node. DataONE provenance systems enable reproducible research and facilitate proper attribution of scientific results transitively across generations of derived data products.

1 Introduction

Scientific workflow provenance is valuable in computational science. Provenance can help scientists better understand and share their work with others while maintaining attribution. We refer to two types of provenance: *prospective* and *retrospective* provenance, where the former refers to a specification of a data transformation process or *workflow* [5], and the latter refers to the derivations that account for the actual outcomes of an execution of the process.

DataONE (Data Observation Network for Earth) is a federated data network for open, persistent, robust, and secure access to well-described and easily discovered Earth observational data [3]. DataONE's primary goals include support for: data discovery, access, integration, and synthesis; education, training, and building community; and data sharing. The DataONE infrastructure consists of three principal components:

Member Nodes (MN) represent existing or new data repositories that support the DataONE Member Node API; *Coordinating Nodes* (CN) serve the coordination and discovery needs of the network; and the *Investigator Toolkit* which contains tools that enable programmatic interaction with DataONE infrastructure through a REST service API exposed by the CNs and MNs.

M. Mattoso and B. Glavic (Eds.): IPAW 2016, LNCS 9672, pp. 230–234, 2016.
DOI: 10.1007/978-3-319-40593-3_28

DataONE Search is a web-based application that lets users seamlessly and efficiently discover publicly accessible data packages within the DataONE federated network of Member Node repositories. It allows users to search across space (geographical region), time, and using a set of keywords. Users sign in to DataONE Search using ORCID credentials, Google accounts, or institutional accounts. DataONE enables new user features like provenance-based browsing as part of its search facility. In the next section, we will present new DataONE provenance tools and the visualization of provenance with DataONE Search [3].

2 Provenance Feature Description

We present two features related to provenance: *Run Manager*, an API for capturing retrospective provenance from R [14] and MATLAB [7] script runs; and *YesWorkflow* [9], a script annotation and provenance querying tool, designed to help users better understand the structure and intent of a script, and to expose and query its provenance.

We introduce the provenance and search features of DataONE by means of an example involving three Earth scientist personas who interact through a DataONE Member Node: In Fig. 1, Alice has developed a script for producing C_3/C_4 carbon soil maps [15]. She uses the YesWorkflow (YW) tool to mark-up the script and expose the underlying workflow view (i.e., prospective provenance) that is inherent in her soil mapping code as shown in Fig. 2.

By using the *Run Manager* to run her script, Alice not only obtains the expected results, but she also captures their provenance, compliant with DataONE's ProvONE data model. ProvONE [2] is an extension of the W3C PROV-O [12] standard for representing provenance, and includes specializations for representing both retrospective provenance about the runtime execution and

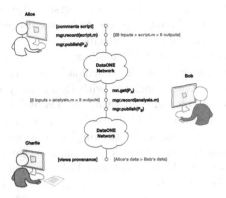

Fig. 1. Provenance Use Case: (1) Alice runs script.m with the DataONE Run Manager to create data package P_A, which she publishes to the DataONE network; (2) Bob later finds and downloads Alice's data, uses it in his analysis.m, creating and then publishing package P_B; (3) Charlie searches DataONE, finds Bob's P_B, and recognizes its dependence on Alice's P_A.

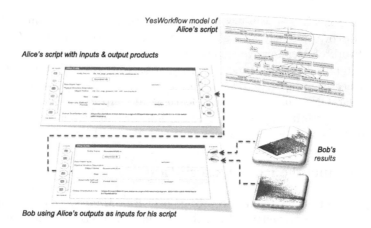

YesWorkflow model of Alice's script

Alice's script with inputs & output products

Bob's results

Bob using Alice's outputs as inputs for his script

Fig. 2. Charlie's view on the DataONE demo site: (1) A YesWorkflow model for Alice's soil processing script; (2) Data lineage from Bob's results back through his script inputs to Alice's data package; (3) Two visualizations produced by Bob's water use efficiency analysis script.

prospective provenance about the structure and flow of the analytical script or workflow. At the end of the experimentation phase, Alice is ready to publish her results to a DataONE Member Node. To do so, she uses the DataONE MATLAB tool to automatically generate a DataONE-compliant data package in OAI-ORE format, including the ProvONE provenance document, the script itself, and its YW-generated workflow view.

Bob's interaction with DataONE begins with a user interface search, i.e., using the keyword "grass", he discovers Alice's data package, amongst others. He decides to use three NetCDF output data files which are part of her package, as input to his Grassland Water Use Efficiency Analysis script [6]. Having identified the data of interest in the Member Node, Bob uses its public identifier *id* to retrieve it and use it in his own code. Specifically, the MemberNode.get(session, id) call, available from the MATLAB toolbox, not only retrieves Alice's data package, but it also ensures that the download event is recorded as part of a new provenance document, associated with Bob's analysis. If Bob manually downloaded Alice's data (i.e., without using the DataONE tool), then the link between the data packages would likely be broken, leading to a disconnect in provenance and requiring additional "stitching" operations [11].

Instead, by retaining the same identifier throughout, the tool implicitly establishes a connection between Alice's work and Bob's, namely by adding a provenance statement of the form (*Bob's_execution*, prov:used, *Alice's_data_id*). Bob then proceeds to operate on the data using the DataONE MATLAB toolbox just as Alice did, eventually publishing a new data package with his own results and their provenance. At this point, the two provenance documents are physically disjoint, as they reside in different data packages, but they are logically connected, namely through the prov:used statement mentioned above. As they are both indexed by the CN upon publication of the data package, this logical connection emerges automatically when a third party, say Charlie, explores one of the two data packages:

Charlie discovers Bob's data packages on DataONE and is able to navigate back to the data that Bob used, i.e., Alice's data package depicted in Fig. 2 [8, 10]. When he searches the DataONE network using the same keyword "grass" from the web search interface, two data packages are displayed as shown in Fig. 2. One data package was created by Alice [16], the other was created by Bob [13].

Crucially, the provenance of the two datasets is now manifested visually along with their logical connection, as shown in the DataONE Search web UI [4] (Fig. 2) and is available to Charlie. Specifically, Charlie can not only visualize the two data packages (Alice's is at the top and Bob's at the bottom), but he is also aware of the derivation of Alice's data through Bob's script.

Provenance details for any input or output in the provenance graph can be viewed by clicking on the icons shown in the figure. DataONE Search also provides human language descriptions of how data are used or generated via the script and models, and provides navigation to ancestors and descendants in the data derivation chain. In this example, Charlie quickly learns that Alice's script takes twenty-five input files [15] and produces six outputs, shown on the left and right side of Alice's data package, respectively. The bottom three outputs in Alice's data package are the NetCDF data files that represent three different world map grids of percentage of grass types (C_3 grass fraction, C_4 grass fraction, and total grass fraction) [15]. In addition, a model graph is displayed at the intermediate layer that was generated by the YesWorkflow tool declaring step by step how data are used and derived in the script [9]. Similarly, the provenance information is associated with Bob's data package in Fig. 2 [1, 6, 13].

3   Conclusions

As outlined above, we have described new and unique provenance capabilities in the large, scientific data federation network DataONE. The search feature was released to the public in late 2015; the R and MATLAB provenance tools in early 2016.

References

1. Cao, Y., Jones, C., Cuevas-Vicenttín, V., Jones, M.B., Ludäscher, B., McPhillips, T., Missier, P., Schwalm, C., Slaughter, P., Vieglais, D., Walker, L., Wei, Y.: DataONE: A Data Federation with Provenance Support, Demo-Paper (long version) (2016). https://github.com/DataONEorg/provweek2016-demo/blob/master/dataone-demo-latex-version/dataone-prov-demo-long.pdf
2. Cuevas-Vicenttín, V., et al.: ProvONE: A PROV Extension Data Model for Scientific Workflow Provenance (2015). https://purl.dataone.org/provone-v1-dev
3. Data Observation Network for Earth (DataONE). www.dataone.org, search.dataone.org

4. DataONE Search Demo Site. https://search-sandbox-2.test.dataone.org
5. Freire, J., Koop, D., Santos, E., Silva, C.T.: Provenance for computational tasks: a survey. Comput. Sci. Eng. **10**(3), 11–21 (2008)
6. Huntzinger, D., Schwalm, C., Wei, Y., Cook, R., Michalak, A., Schaefer, K., Jacobson, A., Arain, M., Ciais, P., Fisher, J., Hayes, D., Huang, M., Huang, S., Ito, A., Jain, A., Lei, H., Lu, C., Maignan, F., Mao, J., Parazoo, N., Peng, C., Peng, S., Poulter, B., Ricciuto, D., Tian, H., Shi, X., Wang, W., Zeng, N., Zhao, F., Zhu, Q.: NACP MsTMIP: Global 0.5-deg Terrestrial Biosphere Model Outputs (version 1) in Standard Format. http://dx.doi.org/10.3334/ORNLDAAC/1225
7. Jones, C., Cao, Y., Slaughter, P., Jones, M.B.: MATLAB DataONE Toolbox (2016). https://github.com/DataONEorg/matlab-dataone
8. Katz, D.S., Smith, A.M.: Implementing Transitive Credit with JSON-LD. CoRR abs/1407.5117 (2014). http://arxiv.org/abs/1407.5117
9. McPhillips, T., Song, T., Kolisnik, T., Aulenbach, S., Belhajjame, K., Bocinsky, K., Cao, Y., Chirigati, F., Dey, S., Freire, J., Huntzinger, D., Jones, C., Koop, D., Missier, P., Schildhauer, M., Schwalm, C., Wei, Y., Cheney, J., Bieda, M., Ludäscher, B.: YesWorkflow: a user-oriented, language-independent tool for recovering workflow information from scripts. Int. J. Digit. Curation **10**, 298–313 (2015). http://www.ijdc.net/index.php/ijdc/article/view/10.1.298
10. Missier, P.: Data trajectories: tracking reuse of published data for transitive credit attribution. In: Proceedings of the 11th International Data Curation Conference, DCC (2016). http://homepages.cs.ncl.ac.uk/paolo.missier/doc/DT.pdf
11. Missier, P., Ludäscher, B., Bowers, S., Anand, M.K., Altintas, I., Dey, S., Sarkar, A., Shrestha, B., Goble, C.: Linking multiple workflow provenance traces for interoperable collaborative science. In: 5th Workshop on Workflows in Support of Large-Scale Science (WORKS) (2010). http://www.dataone.org/sites/all/documents/DataTol.pdf
12. W3C PROV-O: The PROV Ontology. https://www.w3.org/TR/prov-o/
13. Schwalm, C.: Data-Package of "Bob" (2016). https://goo.gl/rYOZyh, https://search-sandbox-2.test.dataone.org/#view/metadata_07277c1f-b2c2-467c-8aa2-792863524a21.xml
14. Slaughter, P., Jones, M.B., Jones, C.: recordr: provenance tracking for R (2016). https://github.com/NCEAS/recordr
15. Wei, Y., Liu, S., Huntzinger, D., Michalak, A., Viovy, N., Post, W., Schwalm, C., Schaefer, K., Jacobson, A., Lu, C., Tian, H., Ricciuto, D., Cook, R., Mao, J., Shi, X.: NACP MsTMIP: Global and North American Driver Data for Multi-Model Intercomparison (2014). http://dx.doi.org/10.3334/ORNLDAAC/1220
16. Wei, Y.: Data-Package of "Alice" (2016). https://goo.gl/BsHSuK, https://search-sandbox-2.test.dataone.org/#view/metadata_e859d2dd-c5e6-4ec6-892f-1b00bb6f8f65.xml

Erratum to: Trade-Offs in Automatic Provenance Capture

Manolis Stamatogiannakis[1]([✉]), Hasanat Kazmi[2], Hashim Sharif[2],
Remco Vermeulen[1], Ashish Gehani[2], Herbert Bos[1], and Paul Groth[3]

[1] Computer Science Institute, Vrije Universiteit Amsterdam, Amsterdam,
The Netherlands
{manolis.stamatogiannakis,r.vermeulen,h.j.bos}@vu.nl
[2] SRI International, Menlo Park, USA
{hasanat.kazmi,hashim.sharif,ashish.gehani}@sri.com
[3] Elsevier Labs, Amsterdam, The Netherlands
p.groth@elsevier.com

Erratum to:
Chapter 3: M. Mattoso and B. Glavic (Eds.)
Provenance and Annotation of Data and Processes
DOI: 10.1007/978-3-319-40593-3_3

The text that was missing is:

Acknowledgments. This material is based upon work supported by the National Science Foundation under Grant IIS-1116414. Any opinions, findings, and conclusions or recommendations expressed in this material are those of the authors and do not necessarily reflect the views of the National Science Foundation.

The updated original online version for this chapter can be found at 10.1007/978-3-319-40593-3_3

© Springer International Publishing Switzerland 2016
M. Mattoso and B. Glavic (Eds.): IPAW 2016, LNCS 9672, p. E1, 2016.
DOI: 10.1007/978-3-319-40593-3_29

Author Index

Printed in the United States
By Bookmasters